JOHN DURY

Advocate of Christian Reunion

J. MINTON BATTEN

PROFESSOR OF CHURCH HISTORY · SCARRITT COLLEGE

THE UNIVERSITY OF CHICAGO PRESS

CHICAGO · ILLINOIS

THE UNIVERSITY OF CHICAGO PRESS · CHICAGO
Agent: THE CAMBRIDGE UNIVERSITY PRESS · LONDON

PREFACE

THE reunion of the churches is a subject of vital interest in our age. It will probably become increasingly important as Christians face the challenging problems of world reconstruction in the years that follow the second World War. The magnitude of the tasks involved may compel Christians to think anew in terms of establishing closer bonds of fellowship, co-operation, and unity. This volume presents a study of the reunion activities of John Dury, whose efforts furnish materials for a unique chapter in the history of Christian irenics. The writer is under lasting obligations to Professor John T. McNeill, who opened the way to the study of the mass of Dury materials and furnished kindly guidance through years of research in the history of seventeenth-century irenics. My wife, Lina Cofer Batten, has given invaluable aid both in the collection of materials and in the preparation of the manuscript for publication.

J. M. B.

TABLE OF CONTENTS

CHAPTER I

THE CHURCHES IN AN AGE OF DISCORD

RICHARD BAXTER correctly described the seventeenth century as a "contentious, dividing Age."[1] Divisive tendencies had been strong in the preceding century; but in the period of the Reformation the Protestant leaders had generally maintained that there was one universal Church. Their protests against the accumulated abuses of medieval Roman Catholicism and the counter-charges issued by a revived Roman Catholicism produced the cleavage of Western Christendom and broke the formal unity of the Church. The separatists from Rome experienced a new freedom from Roman obedience. This new freedom prepared the way for a revival of the long-neglected concept of catholicity expressed in universal free communion. Despite inevitable differences of opinion emerging in the storm and stress of the times, the Protestant leaders desired the visible unity of the Church and were in accord in their expressions of longing for the establishment and recognition of a Catholic Protestantism.[2]

But tendencies which the reformers failed to curb soon produced a succession of divisions. The separatists from Rome showed a marked tendency to form separate communions, which, at first, followed territorial and national lines. Owing to political, personal, nationalistic, and theological differences, the lines of demarcation by which Christendom was being divided steadily became more clearly defined. These lines of cleavage were also present within the Roman Catholic Church, despite the continuation of formal unity.[3] In the second half of the sixteenth century the rise of rigid types of Protestant scholasticism intensified the strife over confessional differences and the Wars of Religion increased the hatreds of the age.

These characteristic developments of the sixteenth century appeared with new force in the church life of the seventeenth century. Centrifugal tendencies dominated the age. The Gallican movement and the rise of Jansenism indicate the presence of these divisive

[1] *Universal Concord* (1660), title-page.

[2] John T. McNeill, *Unitive Protestantism* (New York, 1930), pp. 133–254.

[3] David Schaff, *Our Fathers' Faith and Ours*, pp. 215–18.

trends within the Roman Catholic Church. The strife between Protestants and Roman Catholics became more bitter at the opening of
the century, as the full weight of the new strength gained by Roman Catholicism during the Counter Reformation began to manifest
itself in varied efforts designed to limit the sphere of Protestant influence. This struggle between Protestants and Roman Catholics increased in bitterness as the Thirty Years' War drew out its long and
weary course. The establishment of the territorial system and the
difficulties arising out of the application of the principle *cuius regio
eius religio* constantly threatened the stability of the settlement of
religious affairs in Germany.[4]

Discord was also rife among Protestants as the seventeenth century opened. In Germany the relations between the Lutheran and
Reformed Churches became more unfriendly as the Reformed
Church made steady inroads into Lutheran territory.[5] The struggle
of the Reformed Church for recognition similar to that which had
been granted to Lutherans by the Treaty of Augsburg occasioned a
mass of polemical literature, which contained personal attacks of a
type that inevitably provoked further discord.[6] A long series of controversies among the Lutherans of Germany—such as the Antinomi-
an, Osiandrian, Crypto-Calvinistic, Majoristic, and Syncretistic disputes—had divided the Lutheran theologians. Efforts to promote
peace between contending factions by the adoption of the Formula
of Concord merely served to produce new types of divergent opinions
and to encourage the development of Lutheran scholasticism.[7] In
Germany and elsewhere the Erastian policies of temporal rulers also
aroused discord and strife among the Christians of principalities and
nations.

The Calvinists, especially those of the Netherlands, were divided
over the issues raised by the vigorous protest of Arminius and his associates against the rigid type of Calvinistic scholasticism which was
developing at the time. Numerous divisive tendencies of far-reaching
importance appeared in the British Isles. Strife between Anglicans

---

[4] K. D. Macmillan, *Protestantism in Germany*, pp. 88–123; Karl Müller, *Kirchengeschichte*,
II, Part II, 256–69; and Werner Elert, *Morphologie des Luthertums*, I, 313 ff.

[5] Müller, *op. cit.*, pp. 93 ff., 580 ff.

[6] Hans Leube, *Kalvinismus und Luthertum im Zeitalter der Orthodoxie* (Leipzig, 1928), I,
39–49.

[7] See the concise summary of the divisive tendencies among Lutherans as given by Karl
Heussi, *Kompendium der Kirchengeschichte*, pp. 296–300; cf. also Müller, *op. cit.*, pp. 80 ff.,
609 ff.

and Scottish Presbyterians was inevitable after the crown of England passed into the possession of the Stuarts, who were determined to mold the Church of Scotland after the model of the Church of England. Within the Church of England there was increasing discord between Puritan and strict Anglican groups. Vigorous controversies arose between the Established Church and the Free Churches. During the course of the seventeenth century the tense situation in England was further complicated by the strife of contending champions of Presbyterianism and Independency.

The course of events in the early years of the seventeenth century added to the confusion of the churches. Adherents of rival confessions sought to master their opponents by absorption or conquest. National and dynastic rivalries, mingled with dissension over religious issues, plunged Europe into the holocaust of the Thirty Years' War. Similarly, differences of opinion regarding ecclesiastical affairs and the clash of rival theories of political policy culminated in civil war in England. Thus the appeal to arms intensified the hatreds of the age. Protestant scholasticism provoked new quarrels over confessional differences and served to make theological controversy the dominant interest of most of the leaders of the churches.[8] Incessant controversy over matters of doctrine, polity, and worship and the consequent emergence of new religious denominations are the characteristic features of the church history of the seventeenth century. The dominant tendencies of the age indicated a definite drift toward the destruction of the unity of spirit and purpose among Christians as well as of the corporate unity of the churches.

But amid all the strife of parties there were efforts to heal the divisions of Christendom. Irenic leaders protested against the prevailing controversial trends and advocated various types of union projects, such as the union of groups of Protestants, the union of all Protestants, and the union of Protestants and Roman Catholics.[9] In

---

[8] On Protestant scholasticism in the seventeenth century see the useful summary by A. C. McGiffert, *Protestant Thought before Kant*, pp. 141–54; and the more detailed study by Otto Ritschl, *Dogmengeschichte des Protestantismus*, Vol. IV.

[9] Accounts of the varied reunion attempts of the sixteenth and seventeenth centuries are presented by M. Tabaraud, *De la réunion des communions chrétiennes* (Paris, 1808); C. W. Hering, *Geschichte der kirchlichen Unionsversuche seit der Reformation bis auf unsere Zeit* (2 vols.; Leipzig, 1836, 1838); C. G. Neudecker, *Die Hauptversuche zur Pacification der evangel.-protest. Kirche Deutschlands* (Leipzig, 1846); D. Schenkel, *Der Unionsberuf des evangelischen Protestantismus* (Heidelberg, 1855); F. Brandes, *Geschichte der evangelischen Union in Preussen*, Vol. I (Gotha, 1872); C. Sepp, *Polemische en irenische Theologie* (Leyden, 1881); H. Leube, *op. cit.*, Vol. I; G. J. Slosser, *Christian Unity: Its History and Challenge* (New York, 1929); and John T. McNeill, *op. cit.*

the period of the Reformation many statesmen and theologians sought to adjust the quarrels between Protestants and Roman Catholics and labored to secure reunion by varied methods, such as personal conferences, political pressure, and force of arms. Repeated attempts were also made to settle the differences between the Lutheran and the Reformed branches of Protestantism. Men in the first ranks of Protestant leadership—including Melancthon, Bucer, Bullinger, Calvin, Beza, and Cranmer—devoted careful thought and diligent activity to the preparation of plans designed to heal the divisions among Protestant groups. Measures proposed by these leaders have been given serious consideration in many subsequent reunion negotiations. They may yet play a prominent part in the coming Catholicism of the future.

Numerous advocates championed the revival of the principle of conciliarism as a means for establishing bonds of unity among the churches. Thus Calvin urged the call of a general council for the reunion of Christendom and advocated the formation of a reformed, conciliar church of Europe.[10] Cranmer sought, with the hearty approval of Calvin, to secure the preparation of a reformed consensus by a conference of Protestant leaders as the initial step toward union.[11] In this connection he projected a plan for a pan-Protestant council which would serve as the Protestant counterpart of the Council of Trent and define the faith and order of a new Catholicism which should be based on the gospel instead of on the papal system.[12]

After the failure of these proposals, irenic advocates made repeated attempts to soothe the rancor of interconfessional strife by directing attention to the fact that the differences which divided the Protestant Churches did not involve beliefs which were essential to salvation and by stressing the fact that the articles of faith on which they could agree were more numerous and important than those in which they differed.[13] Likewise, efforts were made to adjust differences between parties and schools of thought within the various churches, as in the

---

[10] John T. McNeill, "Calvin's Efforts toward the Consolidation of Protestantism," *Journal of Religion*, VIII (1928), 411–33.

[11] John T. McNeill, "Cranmer's Project for a Reformed Consensus," *ibid.*, pp. 539–65.

[12] J. V. Bartlet and A. J. Carlyle, *Christianity in History*, p. 505.

[13] In 1581 Jean François Sallvard (or Salvard), working in collaboration with Beza and others, prepared and published at Geneva a work entitled *Harmonia confessionum fidei, orthodoxarum et reformatarum ecclesiarum* (see *Bulletin de la Société de l'histoire du protestantisme français*, XXXVI [1887], 387 ff., 443 ff., 498 ff., 623 ff.). This *Harmonia* was approved by the National Synod of Vitré in 1583. It was translated into English and published at Cambridge in 1586. A new edition was published at London in 1643 under the title, *Harmony*

case of the adoption of the Formula of Concord by a number of Lutheran princes and theologians.[14] Practical attempts were also made to unite adherents of the differing Protestant confessions within a nation, such as the drafting of the Consensus of Sendomir (1570) by the Lutherans, Reformed Churches, and Bohemian Brethren of Poland.[15]

This interest in peace and unity was not completely forgotten amid the discord prevailing among the churches during the seventeenth century, as may be indicated by a list of the distinguished irenic leaders who lived in that century. Such a list would recall the names of Andreae, Pareus, William Forbes, John Forbes of Corse, Davenant, Comenius, Calixtus, Hugo Grotius, Ussher, Owen, Baxter, Burroughs, Stillingfleet, Molanus, Leibnitz, Bossuet, and Spener.[16] Repeatedly during the course of the century rulers and statesmen, including Gustavus Adolphus, Oxenstierna, Ladislav IV of Poland, Hugo Grotius, Cromwell, Frederick William of Brandenburg, and William VI of Hesse-Cassel, co-operated with irenic theologians in efforts to promote the settlement of the discord which prevailed in the churches. In every decade of the seventeenth century there were significant negotiations which were designed to promote Christian communion, settle the peace of the churches, and advance the cause of Christian reunion. Likewise in each decade of the century one or more books on the problem of the reunion of the churches appeared—books which deserve a lasting place in the literature of Christian irenics and furnish many suggestions which could be of service in present-day efforts to secure co-operation and unity among the churches.[17]

---

of the Confessions of Faith of the Christian and Reformed Churches (see Philip Schaff, The Harmony of the Reformed Confessions, pp. 15, 16; cf. also C. A. Briggs, Theological Symbolics, p. 209).

[14] Leube, op. cit., I, 1–39.

[15] The Consensus of Sendomir exercised far-reaching influence on reunion efforts in Germany during the seventeenth century. An account of the preparation of the Consensus of Sendomir and its influence on later reunion efforts is presented by D. E. Jablonski, Historia Consensus Sendomiriensis (Berlin, 1731).

[16] Scholarly monographs on the reunion activities of some of these irenic leaders have been prepared: Hans Friedrich, Georg Calixtus der Unionsmann des 17. Jahrhunderts (Anklam, 1891); Matthew Spinka, "The Irenic Program and Activity of John Amos Comenius" (typed Ph.D. diss., University of Chicago, 1923) and John Amos Comenius, That Incomparable Moravian (Chicago, 1943); and G. J. Jordan, The Reunion of the Churches: A Study of G. W. Leibnitz and His Great Attempt (London, 1927).

[17] Among the more important irenic works of the seventeenth century, the following should be noted: John Valentine Andreae, Fama fraternitatis (circulating in manuscript by 1610;

The following pages will indicate that John Dury occupied a unique position among these irenic leaders. Certainly the range of his irenic efforts was broader than that of any other leader who attempted to heal the divisions of Christendom in the seventeenth century. In fact, he is the only irenic leader of the period who presented overtures of peace in an effort to settle each of the major types of ecclesiastical controversy which disturbed the peace of the churches, viz., the alignment of Roman Catholics against Protestants; of Lutherans against Calvinists; of the Lutherans who accepted the Formula of Concord against the Lutherans who rejected it; of Calvinists against Arminians; of Anglicans against Scottish Presbyterians; of Puritans against strict Anglicans; of Anglicans against Separatists; and of English Presbyterians against English Independents. For fifty-two years, with unwearied zeal, he devoted his life to what he called the establishment of "ecclesiastical pacification" between these groups.

In the long course of his activity Dury sought to make use of the irenic methods, programs, and literature which had been originated by his predecessors and contemporaries. He also developed and advocated many new proposals designed to advance the peace of the churches. Some of the plans which he drafted and the negotiations which he conducted distinctly foreshadowed types of irenic effort which are being used in effective ways in the present-day movement toward Christian reunion. He labored to unify the efforts of contemporary irenic leaders and to apply the combined force of their influence throughout the borders of Christendom. With keen insight into contemporary history, he attempted to advance his cause by making skilful use of successive changes in international politics, con-

---

published, 1614); David Pareus, *Irenicum de unione et synodo evangelicorum concilianda* (1614); William Forbes, *Considerationes modestae et pacificae controversiarum de justificatione, purgatorio, invocatione sanctorum, Christo mediatore et Eucharistia* (published posthumously at London, 1658; at Helmstadt, 1704); John Forbes, *Irenicum amatoribus veritatis et pacis in Ecclesia Scoticana* (1629); John Davenant, *An Exhortation to Brotherly Communion Betwixt the Protestant Churches* (1641); Hugo Grotius, *Via ad pacem ecclesiasticam* (1642), *Votum pro pace ecclesiastica* (1642); John Amos Comenius, *De dissidentium in rebus fidei Christianorum reconciliatione hypomnemata quaedam amici ad amicum* (1643), *Christianismus reconciliabilis reconciliatore Christo* (1646); George Calixtus, *Judicium de controversiis theologicis quae inter Lutheranos et Reformatos agitantur, et de mutua partium fraternitate atque tolerantiae propter consensum in fundamentis* (1650); John Matthiae, *Ramus olivae septentrionalis* (1656); Richard Baxter, *Universal Concord* (1660); Edward Stillingfleet, *Irenicum: A Weapon Salve for the Churches Wounds* (1661); John Owen, *Union among Protestants* (1680); and Gerhard Molanus, *Regula circa Christianorum omnium ecclesiasticam* (1691). Additional writings of similar character and of equal importance will be cited in the following account of Dury's reunion negotiations.

temporary developments in the field of political theory, and new currents in the stream of Christian thought.

Dury's union activities necessitated almost constant travel through the Protestant countries of Europe. No churchman of the seventeenth century had better opportunities to observe the condition of the churches. At times he traveled as a semiofficial representative of civil governments, and his letters and pamphlets furnish a hitherto un-worked mine of information regarding both the history of the relationships between the churches and the history of European diplomacy. It was his habit to make careful records of all his conferences and negotiations with leaders of church and state. There were few important contemporaries in the Protestant countries of Europe whom Dury did not seek to approach in an effort to win their support for one or more of his many reunion schemes. Rulers, churchmen, statesmen, and leaders in the fields of science and literature pass in review in his writings, and their views on the subject of the reunion of the churches are presented in detail. We have records of his negotiations with rulers and statesmen such as Charles I; Charles II; Oliver Cromwell; Gustavus Adolphus; Oxenstierna, the Swedish Chancellor; William Penn; Sir Thomas Roe, the English diplomat and Privy Councillor; Hugo Grotius, the founder of international law; the Stadtholder Frederick Henry of Orange; Elizabeth, Queen of Bohemia; Christian IV, King of Denmark; the Landgrave William VI of Hesse-Cassel; and Frederick William, the Great Elector. Likewise we have records of his negotiations with the leading churchmen of his age, including James Ussher, Primate of Ireland; Archbishops Abbot, Laud, and Juxon; the English Bishops, Davenant, Hall, Morton, and Bedell; the Puritan divines, White of Dorchester, Joseph Mede, and Richard Sibbes; the Independent leaders, Burroughs and Thomas Goodwin; the New England divines, Norwood and Davenport; the Scottish Covenanter, Alexander Henderson; John Forbes and the other Aberdeen Doctors; Comenius, the leader of the Unitas Fratrum; John Matthiae, the outstanding irenic leader among the Swedish clergy; and the German divines, John Valentine Andreae, George Calixtus, John Bergius, and Philip Jacob Spener, the founder of the Pietist movement. Dury was also in contact with leaders in the fields of science, philosophy, and literature, such as Descartes; Milton; Samuel Hartlib; Henry Oldenburg, the first secretary of the Royal Society; John Pell, the mathematician; and Robert Boyle, the chemist.

We have the records and, in many cases, the text of the memorials and communications advocating the cause of Christian reunion which Dury addressed to such bodies as the English House of Commons; the Convocation of the Church of England; the Congregational clergy of New England; the synod of the Swedish clergy; the synods of the Reformed Church in Holland; the Convention of the Protestant Estates in Germany; the city councils of the Free Cities of Germany; the civil and ecclesiastical assemblies of the Swiss cantons; the General Assembly of the Huguenot Churches of France; the General Assembly of the Church of Scotland; and those addressed to the universities and academies in Sweden, Scotland, England, France, Holland, and Germany. Over ninety of Dury's papers, memorials, pamphlets, and books have been printed.[18] There is convincing evidence that unpublished papers relating to his reunion negotiations may be found in the archives of many of the Protestant countries of Europe. Hundreds of Dury's letters are calendared in the *Calendar of State Papers* of the Public Record Office and in the *Reports* of the Historical Manuscripts Commission. These sources, together with the numerous references to Dury's negotiations in the writings of his contemporaries, furnish abundant material for the biography of Dury and afford ample evidence of the unique place which he occupied among the irenic leaders of the seventeenth century.

The literature of church history abounds in scattered references to Dury. Special phases of his work have provided fruitful fields for research during two centuries. Despite this recurring interest in the man and his work, no detailed biography dealing with all phases of his activities has appeared. Two theses, which treat limited periods of his work on the Continent, were written by German students during the first half of the eighteenth century.[19] In the nineteenth century various phases of Dury's efforts were discussed in a number of scholarly magazine articles.[20] In 1905 an unsatisfactory analysis and

---

[18] See the "Trial List of the Printed Writings of John Dury" as given on pp. 213–22.

[19] G. H. Arnold, *Historia Joannis Duraei* (Wittenberg, 1716), a dissertation prepared under the supervision of J. C. Coler; and C. J. Benzelius, *Dissertatio de Johanne Duraeo pacificatore celeberrimo maxime de actis eius Suecanis* (Helmstadt, 1744), a dissertation prepared under the supervision of J. L. Mosheim.

[20] The more important of these magazine articles are as follows: Frederick H. Brandes, "John Dury and His Work for Germany," *Catholic Presbyterian Review* (Edinburgh), VIII (1882), 91–102; S. Hubler, "Unionsbestrebungen des John Durie," *Berner Beiträge zur Geschichte der schweizerischen Reformationskirchen* (Bern, 1884), pp. 276–328; C. A. Briggs, "The Work of John Durie on Behalf of Christian Union in the Seventeenth Century," *Presbyterian Review* (New York), VIII (1887), 297–309; H. Tollin, "Johann Duraeus," *Geschichts-Blätter für Stadt und Land Magdeburg* (Magdeburg), XXXII (1897), 227–85, XXXIII (1898), 27–81; and Theodor

evaluation of his writings in the interest of educational reform was published.[21] A detailed monograph on Dury's mission as Cromwell's messenger to the churches on the Continent was prepared by Karl Brauer in 1907.[22] In 1932 Gunnar Westin presented an excellent study of Dury's negotiations during the years 1628–34, with special reference to his relationships to leaders of church and state in Sweden.[23] With the exception of the last three publications mentioned above, all recent accounts of Dury's activities have been limited to brief statements in church and secular histories and to biographical sketches which, in every case, indicate that their authors have failed to make full use of the more important collections of source materials which are available in the letters, memorials, pamphlets, and books of Dury.

Dury's efforts were, in most cases, unsuccessful. Although he often helped to soothe the bitter partisan hatreds of his day, each of his major reunion proposals was rejected. The "contentious, dividing Age" in which he lived was unwilling to accept the peace proposals of this genial Scotsman. It is not strange that his zealous efforts to promote a great cause failed to produce immediate results. His pleas for peace, co-operation, and unity among the churches ran counter both to the spirit of his age and to that of the centuries which followed. But Christians of the twentieth century manifest an increasing interest in the cause to which Dury consecrated his life. The progressive destruction of civilization by two world conflicts within a single generation is prompting many to think of the church as the one institution with a message that can curb the evils of the present and guide society toward a more hopeful future. Realizing that the church cannot meet the needs of our day unless it learns the lessons of peace, co-operation, and unity, advocates of Christian reunion are beginning anew to plead the cause to which Dury gave his life. Union advocates today may profit by the study of the program and activities of this irenic leader, who zealously devoted his time and talent to the task of persuading men of the seventeenth century to promote the communion of the saints and to establish the reunion of the churches.

Klahr, "Johannes Duraeus: Sein Leben und seine Schriften über Erziehungslehre," *Monatshefte der Comenius Gesellschaft* (Berlin and Münster), VI (1897), 65–76, 191–203.

[21] H. J. Scougal, *Die pädagogischen Schriften John Durys: ein Beitrag zur Geschichte der englischen Pädagogik* (Jena, 1905).

[22] *Die Unionstätigkeit John Duries unter dem Protektorat Cromwells* (Marburg, 1907).

[23] *Negotiations about Church Unity, 1628–1634* (Uppsala, 1932).

CHAPTER II

DURY'S PREPARATION FOR IRENIC ACTIVITY

JOHN DURY'S forefathers figure prominently in Scottish history as ministers of a militant type who helped to establish the Reformation in Scotland and championed the preservation of Presbyterianism when its existence was threatened by royal interference. His grandfather, John Dury (1537–1600), was for a time a conventual brother in the monastery at Dunfermline.[1] His monastic superiors charged him with heresy, and he was imprisoned by order of his cousin, George Dury, Abbot of Dunfermline. Later he was sentenced to be shot, but another was executed in his place. Having escaped this fate, he was sentenced to life-imprisonment but gained his liberty through the intervention of the Earl of Arran. Dury then married Marion, daughter of Sir John Majoribanks, Provost of Edinburgh. Six children—three sons and three daughters—were born of this union. Each of the three sons later received ordination in the Church of Scotland and each of the three daughters married ministers.[2]

John Dury championed the cause of the Reformation from 1560 onward. In 1563 he became an exhorter, and seven years later he was settled as the Presbyterian minister at Leith. As an ardent friend and devoted follower of John Knox, he took a leading part in the struggles of those stirring times. In August, 1573, he became minister of St. Giles, Edinburgh. His athletic bearing, attractive personality, and earnest championship of the new order served to make him popular with his parishioners. After 1575 he was associated with Andrew Melville and Walter Balcanquhal in their efforts to thwart the movement to secure an effective restoration of prelacy in Scotland. He was noted for his preaching against the court and for his denunciation of prevailing abuses.[3]

[1] On the career of John Dury see D. Calderwood, *History of the Kirk of Scotland*, III, 637 and *passim*; J. Spottiswoode, *History of the Church of Scotland*, II, 290 and *passim*; *Dictionary of National Biography*, *s.v.* "John Durie"; and H. Scot, *Fasti Ecclesiae Scoticanae*, I, 52, 164; V, 409, 410.

[2] Christian, the oldest daughter, married George Gledstanes, the Archbishop of St. Andrews; Elizabeth, the second daughter, married James Melville, the nephew of Andrew Melville.

[3] A news-dispatch summary of one of Dury's forceful sermons is cited by the Historical Manuscripts Commission, *Report IV*, Part I, p. 667.

Because of his vigorous criticism of the Duke of Lennox, Dury was banished from Edinburgh and prohibited from exercising his rights as a minister. He was allowed to return after the Raid of Ruthven in 1582. Upon his return he was met at Leith by his parishioners, who marched with him into Edinburgh, where they paraded on High Street, singing the One Hundred and Twenty-fourth Psalm in four parts, thus showing both their loyalty to their minister and their skill in psalmody.[4] But still there was no peace for this stormy petrel of the Scottish Church. In 1583, James VI banished him from Edinburgh to Montrose because he had dared to speak well of the Raid of Ruthven,[5] but two years later he was allowed to return and continue his ministry in peace. In 1590, James VI granted him a pension of £140 because of "the grait chargis and expenses maid by him mony zeirs [years] in advancing the publict effayres of the kirk and the greit houshold and famelie of barnis quhairwith he is burdynit."[6]

Robert Dury, second son of the John Dury mentioned above and the father of John Dury the advocate of Christian reunion, was born in the year 1555.[7] He was educated at St. Mary's College, St. Andrews. Upon completion of his course at the university, he traveled for some time on the Continent, where he visited Rochelle and other noted centers of the Huguenot movement. After his return to Scotland he was engaged in teaching until the year 1588, when he became the minister at Abercrombie in Fife. In 1590 he became Andrew Melville's assistant at Anstruther. He served as minister at Anstruther from 1592 to 1605. As a close friend and associate of Andrew Melville, he soon assumed a position of leadership in the councils of the party advocating church autonomy.

He was deeply concerned about the obligations of the Protestant Churches in the field of Christian missions. This interest in the missionary imperative was to be shared later by his son, who often

---

[4] H. Scot (op. cit., I, 52) cites a contemporary account of this incident as follows: "At the Nether Bow they took up the 124th Psalm, 'Now Israel may say, and that truly,' and sang it in such a pleasant tune, in all four parts, these being well known to the people, who came up the street bareheaded and singing, till they entered the kirk. This had such a sound and majesty as affected themselves and the huge multitude of beholders . . . . with admiration and amazement. The Duke [Lennox] himself was a witness, and tare his beard for anger, being more affrayed at this sight than anything he had ever seen since he came to Scotland."

[5] P. Hume Brown, History of Scotland, II, 194.

[6] Dictionary of National Biography, s.v. "John Durie."

[7] On the career of Robert Dury see T. McCrie, Life of Andrew Melville, I, 328; II, 119, 122, 308 and passim; William Steven, History of the Scottish Church at Rotterdam, pp. 312, 315 and passim; Dictionary of National Biography, s.v. "Robert Dury"; and Scot, op. cit., V, 177, 182.

sought to persuade the churches to forget their differences in order that they might make a concerted attempt at world evangelization. Robert Dury was intrusted with the duty of supervising missionary activity in the Scottish Isles. In 1598 he visited the Isle of Lewis in an effort to promote a plan for civilizing and Christianizing the natives. He succeeded in establishing ten parish churches among them. He later inaugurated similar missionary activity in the Orkney and Shetland Islands and also in the Highlands, where an interest in Protestant opinions was beginning to manifest itself.

Robert Dury was one of the chief supporters of Andrew Melville in his efforts to resist the attempts of James VI to introduce the Anglican type of episcopacy into Scotland. The strife between James VI and the leaders of the party advocating church autonomy approached a crisis in 1605, when the Scottish Privy Council, acting under orders from the king, prohibited the meeting of the General Assembly. Defying this order and repudiating the jurisdiction of the king over the General Assembly, Dury, Melville, and four other leaders summoned the Assembly to meet at Aberdeen. James VI then decided to prosecute those who were responsible for the call of the Assembly by charging them with high treason.[8] Dury was arrested and spent several months in prison at Blackness Castle. After a trial before the Privy Council at Linlithgow (January 10, 1606), he was found guilty of treason and banished from Scotland. Accompanied by his family, he went to Bordeaux and thence to Holland—a country which furnished a welcome refuge to the oppressed of many lands at this time.

Dury finally settled at Leyden. From 1609 until his death in 1616 he served as the first pastor of the Presbyterian congregation of English and Scottish refugees in that city.[9] From 1611 to 1616 his congregation was accustomed to worship in the same house in which John Robinson conducted public worship for the Pilgrim group.[10] Throughout the later period of his life Dury preserved his friendship with Melville, who had also been exiled from Scotland and was then engaged in teaching in the theological academy at Sedan. Thomas McCrie states that Melville "felt most attached to Dury and his letters to him are written in a most confidential strain, mingled with a kind hearted and familiar pleasantry."[11]

---

[8] Brown, *op. cit.*, II, 243 ff. [9] Steven, *op. cit.*, pp. 312, 315.

[10] See H. M. Dexter, *Congregationalism of the Last Three Hundred Years as Seen in Its Literature*, p. 387 n.

[11] *Op. cit.*, II, 308. The text of a number of letters from the Dury-Melville correspondence is given by McCrie in Appendix X of this work.

John Dury, the fourth son of Robert Dury and Elizabeth Ramsey, his wife, was born in Edinburgh in the year 1596. In childhood he had abundant opportunity to learn of the storm and stress of religious controversy and conflict. He was only four years of age at the time of the death of his grandfather; but it is probable that throughout his childhood years he heard oft repeated stories of the imprisonment, banishment, and other sufferings of that rugged champion of the Scottish Church.

Dury was ten years of age when his father was forced to leave Scotland in the midst of a severe Scottish winter. It is possible that, even in childhood, he began to develop an attitude of protest against the prevailing ecclesiastical strife, which had occasioned so much suffering within the circle of his own family. Perhaps, as a youth, he watched with interest the efforts of William Forbes and other men of pacific spirit to promote a peaceful settlement of church affairs in Scotland. It is certain that his experiences during the twenty years, 1606–26, gave him opportunities for education, travel, and personal contacts which were of a type well adapted to prepare him for his career as an advocate of Christian reunion.[12]

John Dury accompanied his father to the Continent in 1606. He received his first training in his own home and in the schools of Leyden. The environment at Leyden gave abundant opportunities for personal contact with representatives of varied types of religious polity and belief, such as the militant Presbyterianism of his father, the Congregationalist principles of Robinson and the Pilgrim group, and the numerous systems of theological opinion then current among the Dutch. As a cosmopolitan city and noted educational center, Leyden also furnished excellent facilities for the study of languages. That Dury made the best of these advantages is indicated by the ease with which he was later able to write books and conduct a vast correspondence in English, French, Latin, and German. He was especially proficient in his mastery of German.[13]

Following the established tradition of his family, Dury decided to

[12] E. Bloesch (*Geschichte der schweizerisch-reformierten Kirchen*, I, 442) stresses the fact that Dury's experiences and training as a youth were well adapted to give him breadth of vision and to prepare him for his career as an irenic leader.

[13] In the accounts of Dury's life numerous references are made to his marked ability as a linguist. Thus, A. à Wood (*Athenae Oxonienses*, I, 230) states that Dury "travelled in the various countries beyond the seas, especially thro' most parts of Germany, where he visited the chief recesses of the Muses, and by long continuance spoke the German Tongue so well and fluent, that many Englishmen after his return took him to be a German native."

prepare himself for the study of theology. He was admitted to the University of Leyden on August 3, 1611.[14] This university, founded in 1575, was then at the height of its prestige. It had become for Holland, says Lindsay, "what Wittenberg had been to Germany, Geneva to Switzerland, and Saumur to France."[15] A group of able teachers, including Junius, Scaliger, Drusius, James Arminius, Francis Gomarus, and Simon Episcopius, brought new fame to the university.[16] Dury regarded himself as deeply indebted to the faculty for the training which he received at Leyden. In later years he was especially appreciative of the kindly interest manifested by Leyden professors in his reunion negotiations.[17] Theological debate was popular in the university during Dury's student years. The controversy between Arminius and Gomarus and the publication of the *Remonstrance* in 1610 had provoked agitated discussions, which soon spread from classrooms to the pulpits and to domestic and political circles. Thus, as a student, Dury had ample opportunity to observe the deepening lines of demarcation between types of Protestant thought and the increasing bitterness of theological strife.

After several years of study at Leyden, Dury entered the French Huguenot Academy at Sedan. Here he was trained in theology by distinguished Huguenot teachers and by able instructors from many lands who taught in this school. The faculty at Sedan during Dury's residence included such men as Daniel Tilenus, Jacques Cappel, and a "Pleiades of distinguished Scotchmen," such as Principal Walter Donaldson, Andrew Melville, John Smith, and John Colville.[18] Andrew Melville, who had been released from imprisonment in the Tower of London at the request of Huguenot leaders, taught theology from 1611 to 1622 and carried on a vigorous propaganda in behalf of Calvinism in opposition to Tilenus, whom he charged with

[14] The record of his matriculation is quoted by A. Eekhof, *De theologische faculteit te Leiden in de 17de Eeuw*, p. 356.

[15] T. M. Lindsay, *A History of the Reformation in Lands beyond Germany*, p. 264.

[16] C. A. Briggs, *History of the Study of Theology*, II, 264.

[17] In a Memorial addressed to the Faculty of the University of Leyden, under date of May 31, 1661, Dury said: "Praeter respectum quem me debere profiteor Academiae vestrae, in qua educationem obtinui meam, et facultati vestrae, quae inter Protestantes velut primae magnitudinis stella eminet, reverendi admodum viri fratres, agnosco me vobis magnopere obligatum, propter amicabilem et utilissimam consiliorum vestrorum in negotio pacis ecclesiasticae promovendo communicationem, quam antehac mihi praestitistis." For the full text of this Memorial see Eekhof, *op. cit.*, pp. 355–57.

[18] Briggs, *op. cit.*, II, 264; cf. Henry Cowan, *The Influence of the Scottish Church in Christendom*, p. 253.

Arminianism.[19] He took a special interest in directing the training of Dury. "Besides the civilities which he showed to all students," says McCrie, "Melville paid particular attention to such of his countrymen as came to the University of Leyden. Among these was John Dury, afterward well known for the persevering exertions which he made to accomplish a union between the Lutheran and Reformed Churches."[20] A letter from Melville to Robert Dury, written in 1616, indicates his high regard for the young student and contains the following statement: "Receave fra this bearer, your sonne John, his oration with thanks, and great hope he shall be a good instrument after our departing."[21] In September, 1616, Dury attracted attention by winning a prize of £15 for a Latin oration, which he delivered before the Synod of Amsterdam.[22]

It is probable that Dury again studied in Holland at Leyden and Amsterdam after the completion of his course at Sedan.[23] For three years, 1621–23, he served as tutor of the son of Barthelemy Panhuysen, a wealthy Dutch merchant.[24] This work provided opportunity for further travel and study in France, where he became acquainted with Moses Amyraut and other distinguished leaders among the French Huguenots. A. à Wood, in his *Athenae Oxonienses* under date of 1624, states that "John Dury, a Scotchman, became a sojourner in the University in the month of July of this year, for the sake of the public library, but how long he continued there, I cannot tell."[25] Although it is probable that Dury was in residence at Oxford for only a few months, he had opportunity to gain valuable information regarding conditions within the Anglican Church which was to be of service to him in his later reunion negotiations.

After thus receiving a most varied training in the schools and after enjoying unusual opportunities for travel and personal contacts with men of differing types of theological opinion, Dury was now prepared to take up the work of the ministry. In the year 1624 he was called to serve as minister of a small congregation of English and Scottish

---

[19] On Melville's career at Sedan see McCrie, *op. cit.*, Vol. II, chaps. i, ix, x.

[20] *Ibid.*, II, 303.

[21] *Ibid.*, p. 529.

[22] H. Tollin, "Johann Duraeus," *Geschichts-Blätter für Stadt und Land Magdeburg*, XXXII (1897), 230.

[23] *Ibid.*; cf. Ruth Grannis, Introduction to Dury's *Reformed-Librarie Keeper*, p. 18.

[24] T. A. Fischer, *The Scots in Germany*, p. 175.   [25] I, 230.

Presbyterians who were connected with the factory of the English
Company of Merchant Adventurers at Elbing in West Prussia. He
received Presbyterian ordination in Holland, probably at Dort, and
began his ministry at Elbing in the latter part of the year 1624.[26]
Here Dury came into contact with factors which served to give an altogether new direction to his career.

Elbing had been under the protection of Poland since 1484, but in
the year 1626, during the course of the war between Sweden and Poland, Gustavus Adolphus occupied the city as the first step in an effort to gain a footing in West Prussia, preparatory to intervention in
the Thirty Years' War.[27] The quiet Prussian town thus began to
play an important part in the military and political history of the
times. Moreover, there were unusual currents in the intellectual and
ecclesiastical life of the city and surrounding districts which were of
far-reaching significance. John Amos Comenius began his residence
in the near-by Polish border city of Lissa in the year 1628. Here he
founded a famous gymnasium, began to draft his great program of
educational reform, and persuaded Protestants of many faiths to
dwell together in unity and in peaceful observance of the terms of
the Consensus of Sendomir.[28]

A new interest in Christian mysticism was aroused in this area by
the widespread circulation of the writings of John Arndt, Valentin
Weigle, and Jacob Boehme. These writers, influenced to a large degree by the German Mystics and by various medieval and Renaissance currents of Neo-Platonic mysticism, sought to revive the ideas
of the sixteenth-century leaders of the type of Paracelsus. With
varying points of emphasis they stressed the duty of searching for
truth by means of listening to the voice of God speaking to the individual soul and by the study of God's handiwork in the world of nature. Their writings prompted an increasing interest in personal
piety in contrast to the prevailing stress on assent to creeds, and they

---

[26] Tollin, *op. cit.*, XXXII, 231. Shortly afterward, Dury began to have doubts about the
validity of his ordination because of some unspecified irregularities in connection with it. In
The Unchanged Peacemaker (1650), pp. 8, 11, he said: "In the year 1626 I had acquainted Dr.
Hall, then Bishop of Exeter, with my scruple of conscience about Ordination, and the doubts
which I had of the lawfulness of it, as to me from the Church wherein I had gotten it. . . . . It is
false that I ever renounced my Ordination received from a forraign Church; but . . . . lost (for
reasons needless to be particularized) the comfort and assurance of the lawfulness of it."

[27] W. F. Reddaway, "The Vasa in Sweden and Poland," *Cambridge Modern History*, IV,
185, 186.

[28] J. Kvačala, *J. A. Comenius*, pp. 11 ff.; Spinka, *John Amos Comenius, That Incomparable
Moravian*, pp. 44 ff.

also helped to encourage new activity in the field of scientific investigation.[29]

John Valentine Andreae did his great lifework at Calw, a city located near Elbing. In him all these varied interests and currents of thought found a sane and influential champion. He co-operated with Comenius in the preparation of plans for educational reform encouraged Bible study; emphasized the need of practical piety as of utmost importance to the churches in the age of orthodoxy; stressed the advisability of founding international academies for the promotion of scientific research; and advocated the establishment of peace and unity among the churches.[30] Within the city of Elbing a young merchant of encyclopedic mind, Samuel Hartlib, kept in contact with all these currents of thought and became the advocate of each of these causes.[31] Dury had formed a friendship with Hartlib as early as the year 1627.[32] Their friendship would inevitably bring Dury into close contact with this revival of interest in educational reform, improved methods of Bible study, practical piety, scientific research, and union effort. It is certain that Dury was vitally interested in each of these projected fields for reforming activity when he began his first major attempt at "ecclesiastical pacification."[33]

The Swedish occupation of Elbing was followed by the inauguration of a new system of civil administration in the city and surrounding districts. Gustavus Adolphus appointed Dr. Caspar Godemann, a Swedish Privy Councillor, as President of the Court of Appeals in

[29] See Margaret L. Bailey, *Milton and Jacob Boehme*, pp. 1–30.

[30] An excellent discussion of these interests of Andreae is presented by Felix Emil Held, *Christianopolis: An Ideal State of the Seventeenth Century*, pp. 1–126.

[31] On the life of Hartlib during his residence at Elbing see F. Althaus, "Samuel Hartlib, ein deutsch-englisches Charakterbild," *Historisches Taschenbuch* (1884), pp. 193 ff.; and G. H. Turnbull, *Samuel Hartlib, with Special Regard to His Relations with J. A. Comenius*, pp. 4 ff.

[32] Althaus (*op. cit.*, p. 197) expresses doubt as to the establishment of the Dury-Hartlib friendship while Dury was in Elbing. D. Masson (*Life of Milton*, III, 195) is of the opinion that this friendship dates from Dury's residence at Elbing. This doubt and uncertainty were obviously due to lack of familiarity with Dury's writings. Hartlib, writing in 1650 in his Preface to Dury's *Unchanged Peacemaker* (p. iii), said: "I am called upon . . . . to testifie my knowledge concerning a most dear and precious friend, which in Conscience, I think myself every way bound to do, seeing I have been acquainted with him [Dury] these 23 years, and with all his public Proceedings so intimately, that to be a Co-agent with him therein according to my ability, was one of my principal studies."

[33] This is clearly evidenced in Dury's *The purpose and Platform of My Journey into Germany* (1630). For the full text of this paper see J. Kvačala, *Korrespondence Jana Amosa Komenského* pp. 6 ff.

this new administration.[34] Godemann and his associate, Councillor
Mylius, were interested in church affairs and were deeply concerned
over the perils which Protestantism was facing because of the successive defeats sustained by the armies of the Protestant states in the
early period of the Thirty Years' War. Godemann was convinced
that Protestantism was doomed unless some form of union could be
established which would enable Protestants to offer a united front in
resistance to the advancing forces of Roman Catholicism. He had
observed with interest the groups of Polish refugees who belonged to
the Lutheran, Reformed, and Bohemian Brethren Churches. He
found that they were able to adjust their differences and live in harmony under the terms of the Consensus of Sendomir.[35] As early as
the year 1626 he began to advocate the union of the Lutheran and
Reformed branches of Protestantism on a similar basis.[36] To promote
such a union he drew up and circulated a memorial concerning the
Lord's Supper. In this paper he attempted to prove that the differences between the Lutheran and the Reformed Churches in their
teaching about this sacrament were not of sufficient importance to
justify their refusal to co-operate against their common foe.

There can be no doubt that political interests were partly responsible for this layman's interest in the cause of Christian reunion.[37] It
is probable that Godemann was acting under orders from Gustavus
Adolphus when he began his efforts at Elbing to advocate the union
of Protestants.[38] Since 1614 the Swedish king had been interested in
the preparation of plans for a great Evangelical Alliance which would
serve as a counterweight against the Roman Catholic Reaction.[39]
Dynastic necessity as well as personal conviction made him the champion of Protestantism.[40] He had pushed the Russians so far from the

[34] C. W. Hering, *Geschichte der kirchlichen Unionsversuche seit der Reformation bis auf unsere Zeit*, II, 89 ff.

[35] Hans Leube, *Kalvinismus und Luthertum im Zeitalter der Orthodoxie*, I, 192 ff.

[36] Tollin, *op. cit.*, XXXIII, 28 ff.

[37] Frederick H. Brandes, "John Dury and His Work for Germany," *Catholic Presbyterian Review*, VIII (1882), 25. Both Caspar Godemann and his father, Jacob Godemann, were inter-
ested in securing the co-operation of the Lutheran and Reformed Churches. Gunnar Westin
(*Negotiations about Church Unity, 1628–1634* [Uppsala, 1932], p. 77 n.) states that Jacob
Godemann started Dury on his long career as an advocate of Christian reunion. However,
Dury repeatedly states that he was influenced chiefly by Caspar Godemann.

[38] See Tollin, *op. cit.*, XXXIII, 28 ff.

[39] John Wordsworth, *The National Church of Sweden*, pp. 289, 290.

[40] See the excellent discussion of conditions in the Swedish Church during the reign of
Gustavus Adolphus by Westin, *op. cit.*, pp. 42–59; cf. Georg Mentz, *Deutsche Geschichte im
Zeitalter der Reformation, der Gegenreformation und des Dreissigjährigen Krieges*, pp. 395 ff.

Baltic that they would now find it difficult "to jump over the little stream"; he had defeated Poland and gained possession of a number of Prussian ports. With the "dominion of the Baltic" thus secure in the East, he was now free to turn his attention to German affairs. The cry of the Protestants for help appealed strongly both to his personal sympathies and to his political ambitions. He regarded the establishment of peace among the Protestant churches as an essential step toward recovery from the losses which the Protestant movement had already sustained.

Dury first learned of Godemann's interest in Christian reunion through reading a presentation copy of the Councillor's pamphlet on the Lord's Supper. By the year 1628 he had met Godemann, and they soon became intimate friends.[41] This friendship influenced the whole of Dury's subsequent career. Godemann suggested that Dury should devote his life to the advocacy of Christian reunion. Dury was profoundly impressed by the challenge of the task. He thought that the very nature of the gospel as a message of peace and the "necessity of the times" pointed to the need of new efforts to settle the peace of the churches. He believed that he was divinely called to this work.[42] Before the close of the year 1628 he had resolved to devote his life to the advocacy of Christian reunion and took upon himself a "Vow of Perseverance in the Worke"—a vow which he often quoted and faithfully kept until his death fifty-two years later.[43]

Godemann assured Dury that Gustavus Adolphus, "his King and Master, would be glad to advance" the movement in the interest of the peace of the churches.[44] Dury was interested in the current rumors to the effect that the Swedish king would soon intervene in German affairs. He hoped that Gustavus Adolphus would prove to be

[41] Dury gives the best detailed account of his relations with Godemann in his *Consultationum irenicarum prodiorthosis*, pp. 118, 119. In the Introduction to his *Epistolary Discourse* (1644), Dury wrote: "Concerning myself, I do ingenuously confess that the mere love of peace and quietness, and the hope of doing good to the Church of God, did move me to embrace this endeavor when I was called thereunto in Prussia, by Dr. Godeman, a Chancellor of State to the late King of Sweden in the year 1628."

[42] In his *Memoriall concerning Peace Ecclesiasticall* (pp. 2, 3) Dury states that he regarded the situation as challenging him to present himself "unto God, and to all his servants, without partiality, as an humble solicitor of the counsels of Peace, for the public good of Protestant Churches, that therein the truth of his Gospel may bee confessed and made known unto the world. . . . . Let mee then bee looked upon as a publicke solicitor of peaceable counsels and thoughts, and as a provoker of godly men unto the affections of charitable duties; for this is the summe of that which I intend."

[43] For the text of this "Vow" see Newman Smyth, "John Dury: A Peacemaker among the Churches," *Constructive Quarterly*, IV, 407, 408.

[44] See Dury, *A Briefe Relation of That which hath been lately attempted to Procure Ecclesiastical Peace Amongst Protestants*, p. 1.

the leader who would unite all German Protestants. With this idea in mind he addressed a petition to the King when he visited Elbing in the year 1628. In this petition—Dury's first formal paper on Christian reunion—he appealed to the Swedish King to sponsor a movement to secure unity among Protestants, volunteered his services for the work, and argued for Swedish intervention in Germany in order that the Protestant cause might be saved from destruction.[45] He justified his boldness in making these requests by stating that a sense of divine guidance prompted him to approach the one man who was able to save Protestantism from utter ruin. He expressed the hope that Gustavus Adolphus, "as an angel of God, among the kings of this age," would consent to serve "as the Head of the Councellors of this peace, and be the Fountain, as it were, of all our Pacificall Deliberations, so that all things be related unto your Majesty, afore ought be done, and that after your approbation, every matter be put into execution." He asked for an audience in order that he might present his reunion proposals and stressed his willingness to serve as agent in the reunion negotiations. "For I wish nothing so much," he wrote, "as the approbation, or improbation of your Royall Judgement, concerning the reuniting of the Churches, rent in pieces, meerly by the factious ambition of some of the clergy."

Apparently Gustavus Adolphus made no direct answer to this petition, but Godemann, his representative, encouraged Dury to continue the work. It is probable that Dury also received some encouragement from the publication of the *Elbing Propositions* of 1629, in which Gustavus Adolphus announced his plans for a liberating expedition in behalf of the German Protestants. In the meantime Dury had begun systematic propaganda for reunion by seeking to persuade the Lutheran and Reformed clergy of Elbing and the surrounding cities to express themselves in favor of the union of the churches. In co-operation with Godemann, he conducted an extensive correspondence in an effort to establish more cordial relations between the Lutheran and Reformed ministers of Elbing, Danzig, and other cities of West Prussia.[46] The pastors of Danzig approved

---

[45] This petition was printed at London in 1641 under the title, *The Copy of A Petition, As it was tendered by Mr. Dury, to Gustavus, the Late King of Sweden, of glorious memory, when He was at Elbing in Prussia, in the yeer 1628.* The full text of the Petition is given by Westin, *op. cit.*, pp. 187–91.

[46] For the text of a letter addressed by Dury to the "Evangelical Ministers of Danzig," under date of May 31, 1629, see J. Kvačala, *Korrespondence Jana A. Komenského*, p. 5. It is of interest as one of the earliest extant letters of Dury. This letter indicates that there was close co-operation between Dury and Godemann in union propaganda at this time.

the inauguration of a new effort to establish peace between the contending churches. Dury also attempted to arouse interest in his cause by personal interviews with influential men. It is probable that he formed friendships with John Valentine Andreae and John Amos Comenius at this time.[47] Hartlib was deeply interested in Dury's program for union effort, and, on leaving Elbing for England in 1628, he promised to act as Dury's agent in advocating Christian reunion in England—a promise which he kept faithfully throughout the remainder of his eventful career.[48] Godemann introduced Dury to Axel Oxenstierna, then Governor General of West Prussia, and he seemed disposed to favor the irenic program.[49]

In the year 1629, Sir Thomas Roe, the distinguished English diplomat, visited Elbing while on a mission as ambassador of the King of England to seek a reconciliation between Sweden and Poland and to build up a Protestant alliance in opposition to the Hapsburgs.[50] Roe had for years interested himself in projects for the union of the churches, as is indicated by the fact that, while he was serving as the English ambassador at Constantinople, he had discussed with Cyril Lucar a scheme for co-operation between the Greek Orthodox and the Anglican Church.[51] Dury was introduced to Roe by Godemann.[52] When he had explained his plans, they were given cordial indorsement, and for the next ten years Roe was Dury's chief patron.[53] As an earnest Christian layman, Roe saw the advantages which the realization of Dury's plans would bring to Christendom. As a farsighted diplomat, he recognized the need of peace and union among Protestants in order to offset the gains of the Roman Catholic Reaction, to save Protestantism in Germany, and to accomplish the realization of his cherished hope for the restoration of the Palatinate to

---

[47] Kvačala, *J. A. Comenius*, pp. 26 ff.

[48] Dury, *Unchanged Peacemaker*, p. iii; cf. Masson, *op. cit.*, III, 195; Althaus, *op. cit.*, pp. 197 ff.

[49] Westin, *op. cit.*, pp. 81 ff.

[50] A. W. Ward, *Cambridge Modern History*, IV, 92. For a more detailed account of Roe's mission, together with official documents relating to his negotiations, see *The Camden Miscellany*, VII, 98 ff.

[51] Wordsworth, *op. cit.*, p. 292.

[52] W. C. Dowding, *German Theology during the Thirty Years' War*, p. 170.

[53] Most of Dury's biographers have limited their accounts of the connection between Dury and Roe chiefly to this meeting at Elbing, and they have overlooked the fact that Roe was Dury's most important supporter and adviser for a period of ten years. This oversight was due to the failure to utilize the wealth of material contained in the Dury-Roe correspondence in the *Calendar of State Papers*.

Frederick V, the brother-in-law of Charles I. As an Anglican he hoped that the English Church, supported by Charles I, would offer itself as a mediator between the Lutheran and Reformed Churches, just as he was acting at this time as a mediator between Sweden and Poland.

Roe discussed with Oxenstierna the political advantages which might be gained for the Protestant cause as a result of Dury's plan for the reconciliation of the churches and secured a promise from the Swedish statesman to the effect that he would use his influence as far as possible in winning the Lutherans to the support of the project.[54] Roe and Oxenstierna hoped that Dury's proposals would receive cordial support from both Gustavus Adolphus and Charles I. They thought that the work could be advanced most effectively under English auspices, as England had maintained a neutral position during the long period of theological and political strife in Germany.[55] They also agreed that an immediate effort should be made to enlist the support of leaders of church and state in England in behalf of Dury's project. War conditions had forced the closing of the English factory at Elbing in the year 1630. Roe advised Dury to give up his pastorate and devote all his time to reunion negotiations. He was especially interested in having Dury present his cause in England. Despite the protest of his parishioners, who were unwilling to lose the services of their pastor,[56] Dury resigned his post and went to England, where he spent months in propaganda effort. His arrival in England marks a new stage in his reunion activities. His work had now become international in its scope.

[54] Dury, *Consultationum irenicarum prodiorthosis*, p. 119.

[55] Dury, *Briefe Relation*, pp. 2, 3.

[56] In the *Unchanged Peacemaker*, p. 3, Dury wrote of his parting with his parishioners at Elbing as follows: "They did unwillingly dismiss me; but I thought myself bound in conscience for the prosecuting of a more universal work, which was to sollicit the Councels of peace amongst Protestants, to quit them, and cast myself upon Providence, in following that design."

CHAPTER III

FIRST MAJOR EFFORT AT "ECCLESIASTICAL PACIFICATION"

ON ARRIVAL in England in the year 1630, Dury soon discovered that conditions prevailed which would make it impossible for him to secure the united support of the ecclesiastical and civil authorities in behalf of his efforts to make peace between the Lutheran and Reformed Churches of Germany. The lines of cleavage between the religious parties in England were becoming more clearly defined with each passing month. The "Resolutions on Religion," presented by a committee of the House of Commons in the Parliament of 1629, had served to call attention to the dangers which threatened Protestantism at home and abroad.

The era of the personal government of Charles I had begun with the dissolution of this Parliament. The policy of William Laud in religious affairs was thenceforth cordially supported by the King and bitterly opposed by the Puritans and the Presbyterians. A large group of Moderates or Low Churchmen, who were neither Puritans nor Nonconformists, steadily opposed the innovations which the Laudian regime was introducing into the Anglican Church. Laud's efforts to enforce conformity through the use of the Courts of Star Chamber and High Commission served to increase the bitterness of feeling between the opposing factions. At the time of Dury's arrival this factional spirit had been intensified anew by the sensational trial and brutal punishment of Alexander Leighton, the author of *Sion's Plea against Prelacy*.

The factions within church and state were sharply divided in their views regarding England's obligations to German Protestantism. Charles I manifested a sympathetic interest in the fortunes of his sister, Elizabeth, who had married the unfortunate Frederick V. But his interest in German affairs was purely dynastic, and the tangled history of his foreign policy indicates that he was not deeply concerned over the welfare of German Protestantism. He was quite as willing to secure the restoration of the Palatinate to Frederick V by means of a fortunate bargain with the Hapsburgs as to attain the

same end by giving effective assistance to the German Protestants in
their struggle to stem the rising tide of the Roman Catholic Reaction. On the other hand, the Puritans wished Charles to intervene in
German affairs and use his utmost efforts both to secure the restoration of the Palatinate and to save German Protestantism as a whole.
Naturally the Puritans were dissatisfied in 1629, when Charles arranged a peace with France and Spain without provisions in favor of
the Continental Protestants, for whose benefit the wars against Spain
and France were supposed to have been fought.

Dury brought to England a number of letters commending his
plans for reunion effort which had been written by divines of Prussia
and also letters of recommendation from Roe which were addressed
to Charles I, Abbot, Laud, and a number of the Moderates among
the bishops.[1] He made his first attempt to secure support for his
plans at court. He hoped that he would thus be able to gain official
sanction for his plans and that he would be authorized by the English
Church and state to act as mediator between the Lutheran and Reformed Churches of Germany. He was, however, disappointed in his
expectations. Neither the King nor the representative leaders of the
Church of England were willing to grant him this official authorization.

In fact, Dury received a rather chilling reception at Whitehall.
Charles I referred his proposals to Abbot and Laud. After they had
heard Dury's plans they professed to be interested in the objectives
which he defined but indicated clearly that they were unwilling
to give official authorization for his proposed union negotiations.
They were willing to indorse such negotiations only as the efforts of
a private individual. They suggested that he should return to Germany and confer with Gustavus Adolphus regarding his plans and
then arrange such measures as might seem advisable to the Swedish
king and the Protestant princes of Germany. They also gave Dury
permission to write to the divines of Prussia and to Oxenstierna testi-
fying the readiness of the English clergy to co-operate in so good a
work.[2] They suggested that the German princes might prepare the
way for future advances in the promotion of peace among the
churches if they would prohibit railing disputes in the pulpits, forbid
the use of party names, discountenance debates about forms and

---

[1] Gunnar Westin, *Negotiations about Church Unity, 1628–1634* (Uppsala, 1932), pp. 97 ff.

[2] See the text of Dury's letters to Oxenstierna as presented in *ibid.*, pp. 198 ff.

ceremonies of public worship, and protect the legalized ceremonies of worship from all disturbance.[3]

After this failure to gain the desired official authorization, Dury spent several months in efforts to secure the support of individual leaders of the English Church. Roe had furnished him with a certificate which stated:

> John Dury was employed to effect a reconciliation between the Lutheran and other Reformed Churches, and that all persons well affected to that work might safely subscribe a declaration, to be left in his hands, that he had faithfully solicited this good cause, and that they would be willing to join with those of like affection beyond the seas.[4]

Making extensive use of this certificate, Dury was able to approach leaders of the various parties within the English Church. In these personal conferences he requested subscription to a document which he describes as a "testimonie subscribed by their hands to witnesse for them in private that they desired not onely for their owne parte to further so good and holie a purpose; but also entreated others to joyne with them in it."[5] His efforts to secure subscriptions to this paper did not meet with marked success. Only thirty-eight divines would sub-

---

[3] Dury's account of his interviews with Laud and Abbot is given in his *Briefe Relation*, pp. 3 ff. It is probable that these peace measures were suggested by Dury and merely sanctioned by Abbot and Laud. Abbot, a thoroughgoing Puritan, cordially approved Dury's proposals. However, Dury overestimated the significance of his support. The Archbishop was then in disfavor at court, and, since he had been suspended from the exercise of the rights of archepiscopate jurisdiction, no sanction which he could give to Dury's project would have been official in character. There is some question as to Laud's willingness to approve Dury's project at this time. As will be demonstrated later, Laud steadfastly refused to give any kind of official sanction to Dury's negotiations until Dury was ordained as a priest of the Anglican Church. William Orme, in his *Life of Baxter*, II, 224, states that "Laud heard him accordingly, professed to be friendly to his project and seemed to adopt some of his recommendations." Briggs ("The Work of John Durie in Behalf of Christian Union in the Seventeenth Century," *Presbyterian Review*, VIII, 297) says of Laud: "Doubtless this great man had at heart the reunion of Christendom which was a much grander scheme than Dury had in mind." Masson (*Life of Milton*, II, 368) is of the opinion that Laud regarded Dury's idea as "visionary nonsense." Dury, in his "Summarie Relation" (*Presbyterian Review*, VIII, 301), states that Laud had only given him permission "to go over into Germanie to trie by way of private negotiation howe farre in the worke of Ecclesiasticall Pacification matters might be ripened and broughte aboute to a settled correspondencie and consultation in that matter betwixt the Churches." Unquestionably, Dury overestimated the strength of the support which the Church of England was willing to give him. In his negotiations in Germany shortly after this he seems to have regarded himself as a representative of the Church of England. Brandes ("John Dury and His Work for Germany," *Catholic Presbyterian Review*, VIII [1882], 27) states that "it cannot be denied that he now deceived himself, as well as others, by imagining that this [a letter of recommendation signed by Abbot and a group of his friends] was an authoritative document given to him by the Church of England, and by calling himself accordingly a delegate of that church."

[4] *Calendar of State Papers, Domestic Series, 1631–1633*, p. 75.

[5] Dury, "Summarie Relation," p. 301.

scribe.[6] Besides the nominal support of Laud and the cordial support
of Abbot, Dury could secure indorsement from only three of the English bishops, viz., John Davenant of Salisbury,[7] Joseph Hall of Exeter, and William Bedell of Kilmore and Ardagh.[8]

Sir Thomas Roe, having completed his diplomatic mission to
Sweden, Poland, and Denmark, returned to England in the summer
of 1630. Capitalizing on the marked success of his negotiations on
the Continent, he immediately began persistent agitation both to secure English support for Gustavus Adolphus and to induce the authorities of the English Church to give full indorsement for Dury's
scheme looking toward English mediation between the Lutheran and
Reformed Churches. Roe was now in high favor with Oxenstierna
and Gustavus Adolphus, but he found himself thwarted by party
divisions in England.[9] The dominant High Church party, following
the leadership of Laud, rejected his new appeals in support of the proposed union effort, refusing co-operation on the ground that Dury
was a Presbyterian and that some Presbyterians had signed the paper indorsing his scheme.[10]

Dury remained optimistic despite these discouraging developments in England. News from the Continent prompted him to think
that the course of events there was more favorable for the success of
his plans. The French Huguenots were now displaying a friendly
attitude toward their Lutheran brethren, which was given public expression in the manifesto of the National Synod of the Churches of
France at Charenton, September, 1631.[11] In Germany there was a

---

[6] John Wordsworth, *The National Church of Sweden*, p. 292. E. L. T. Henke (*Georg Calixtus und seine Zeit*, I, 501) notes the fact that the clergymen who subscribed to the paper were
men of Presbyterian or Puritan sympathies. Among the subscribers were Richard Sibbes,
Daniel Featley, Stephen Marshall, John Davenport, John White, Henry Burton, Samuel
Ward, Philip Nye, and Thomas Goodwin.

[7] From 1630 to 1638 Davenant was one of the most ardent supporters of Dury's union
schemes. For an account of his views on Dury's proposals see Morris Fuller, *The Life, Letters,
and Writings of John Davenant*, pp. 419 ff.

[8] A. Clogie, chaplain to Bishop Bedell, stated that Bedell "was anxious for God, not only in
his own sphere, to propagate the truth, but also to work reconciliation amongst the reformed
churches abroad. In order whereunto he allowed Mr. Dury, that undertook that negotiation,
£20 *per annum*, which were duly received for him by Mr. Hartlib; who also printed some of his
letters, of the matter and manner of evangelical union, worthy to be read of all that are lovers
of truth and peace"; see E. S. Shuckburgh (ed.), *Two Biographies of William Bedell*, p. 145.

[9] See Westin, *op. cit.*, pp. 113 ff.; cf. Mrs. M. A. Everett Green, *Elizabeth, Queen of Bohemia*,
p. 280.

[10] Brandes, *op. cit.*, p. 26.

[11] Dury, in his *Briefe Relation*, pp. 51, 52, gives a translation of an extract from the acts of
this Synod, indicating the willingness of the Huguenots to permit intercommunion and co-
operation with the Lutherans.

steadily increasing interest in the adjustment of current disputes over church affairs. The Protestant cause had reached its lowest ebb in 1629, when the Edict of Restitution was issued. The drastic terms of this Edict caused many Protestants to think anew in terms of peace, co-operation, and unity. Genuinely concerned lest Protestantism should be utterly destroyed within the empire, the Lutheran and Reformed leaders arranged a colloquy for the discussion of their differences. It was decided that this colloquy should be held in connection with the meeting of the Convention of the Protestant Estates of the Empire at Leipzig in February and March, 1631.

At this Leipzig Convention the leaders of church and state in Germany attempted to adjust their differences and unite in an effort to prevent the execution of the Edict of Restitution. A conciliatory spirit pervaded the theological discussions at the Leipzig Colloquy.[12] In these discussions the Calvinists were represented by John Bergius, Theophilus Neuberger, and John Crocius. The Lutherans were represented by Matthias Hoë von Hoënegg, Polycarp Leyser, and Heinrich Höpffner. These theologians discussed all the articles of the Augsburg Confession and reached practical agreement on each of the doctrines in that Confession except three, viz., the Person of Christ, the Lord's Supper, and Predestination.[13]

Such agreement was remarkable in view of the fact that one of the participants, Hoë von Hoënegg, had distinguished himself as the most relentless champion of Lutheranism and was accustomed to maintain the thesis that "on ninety-nine points the Calvinists were in accord with the Arians and the Turks."[14] Immediately after the

[12] Dury presents numerous documents relating to the Leipzig Colloquy in his *Irenicorum tractatuum prodromus*, pp. 87–111. Among these documents he includes an account of the Colloquy which was written by Hoë von Hoënegg and signed by all the participants. On the Leipzig Colloquy see also C. W. Hering, *Geschichte der kirchlichen Unionsversuche seit der Reformation bis auf unsere Zeit* (2 vols.; Leipzig, 1836, 1838), I, 327–59; Frederick H. Brandes, *Geschichte der evangelischen Union in Preussen*, I, 102–11; and Hans Leube, *Kalvinismus und Luthertum im Zeitalter der Orthodoxie* (Leipzig, 1928), I, 123 ff. Tollin (*op. cit.*, XXXII, 234) represents Dury as present at the Leipzig Colloquy. The same error occurs in a number of accounts of Dury's activities.

[13] Bishop Joseph Hall (*Works*, XI, 493) states that the participants in the Colloquy "ran with wonderful frankness, harmony and dilligence, through every article, by turn, of the Confession of Augsburg. And having honestly balanced (as was right) the sentiments of either party, to the exclusion of all prejudice and predilection, they found at length that they all agreed unanimously in one and the same common truth, through all heads but three, of that Confession; and even on those three they did not differ so entirely, but what there seemed to be room still left for mutual arrangement." Cf. the recent discussion of the points of difference between Calvinism and Lutheranism by George Wünsch, *Evangelische Ethik des Politischen*, pp. 176 ff.

[14] J. H. Kurtz, *Church History*, III, 13.

close of the Colloquy, Godemann wrote Dury a letter in which he described the results of the discussions and informed him that the time was most advantageous for the opening of his negotiations in Germany.[15] John Bergius, court preacher of Brandenburg and one of the participants in the Leipzig Colloquy, also wrote to Dury, informing him that the situation was most favorable for the inauguration of his mission on the Continent.[16]

These letters prompted Dury to hasten preparations for his journey to the Continent. Before leaving England he drafted a carefully planned program for his negotiations. This program, entitled *The purpose and Platform of My Journey into Germany*, includes an interesting summary of the objectives which Dury had in mind at this time.[17] His immediate objective was the establishment of peace between the Lutheran and Reformed Churches of Germany; but it is evident that he was also seeking for methods and measures which would make possible the union of the Reformed Churches of Switzerland, Germany, Holland, and Scotland with the Lutheran and Anglican Churches. He lists a proposed itinerary through Prussia, Pomerania, Brandenburg, Saxony, Hesse, the Hanse Towns, Holland, and thence to England. Various types of union negotiations were to be used on this journey. In addition to these experiments in union activity, he planned to investigate rare books, new inventions, new educational methods, and new plans for the organization of learned societies, thus evidencing his intention to co-operate in promoting the interests which were being championed by the Comenius-Andreae-Hartlib group.

Dury left England for the Continent in July, 1631. His *Summarie Relation of that which John Durie hath Prosecuted in the Worke of Ecclesiasticall Pacification in Germanie since Ye Latter End of Julie 1631 till 26 September 1633* presents a detailed narrative of his first major effort at "ecclesiastical pacification." It faithfully reflects the unsettled conditions prevailing in Europe during one of the most trying periods of the Thirty Years' War and abounds in illustrations of Dury's feverish haste to get in touch with men who were in position

---

[15] Brandes, "John Dury and His Work for Germany," p. 26.

[16] Theodor Klahr, "Johannes Duraeus: Sein Leben und seine Schriften über Erziehungslehre," *Monatshefte der Comenius Gesellschaft* (Berlin and Münster), VI (1897), 63.

[17] For the complete text of this paper see Kvačala, *Korrespondence Jana A. Komenského*, pp. 6, 7.

to advance his cause.[18] He was confident that the success of his plan was assured if he could secure the effective support of Oxenstierna and Gustavus Adolphus. With this idea in mind, he passed through Holland and thence by way of Hamburg and Lübeck to Stettin, where he hoped to meet Oxenstierna and Gustavus as they passed southward in the triumphal progress of the victorious Swedish army.

On arrival at Stettin, Dury found that Gustavus had already passed through the city and that Oxenstierna had not yet arrived. He waited at Stettin until December 14 and then decided to press on to Würzburg, hoping to secure an audience with the King by means of Roe's letter of recommendation and the friendly offices of the English ambassador, James Spens.[19] In the *Summarie Relation* he describes the journey to Würzburg and the skilful management which enabled him to secure the coveted audience with the Swedish king. Dury relates the story of this interview as follows:

Presenting my letter I told him from whom it was and to what purpose it was written, he asked mee if I was hee of whome my Lord Spense had told him of and when hee understood that I was the man hee sayde he would be glad to heare the state of the business which I did prosecute. Two dayes after hee gave mee audience and haveing understood and approoved both the scope (which was to seeke concord by way of a familiar correspondency and deliberacon without all disputation of poynts controverted) and the meanes (which were private and publicke exhortations to prepare and dispose the mynds nowe somewhat alienated [to] obligatorie promises of mutuall undertakinge the worke to bind the consciences; aimable treaties and deliberacons to seeke and finde out the best meanes; and forraine intercession and mediations to take up and conclude the buisines whereof already a foundation was laid at Leipsicke in a conference holden ye same yeare in March betwixt the Lutheran and reformed divines), he promised to give mee Promotoriall letters to further this end and meanes towards all the Evangelicall States and princes of the Empire to testifie unto them his earnest desire to set forward so good a purpose and to entreate them to set aworke their ablest Divines to joyne with mee in it. These letters I did not crave then because I was not yet readie to make use of them, ... I haveinge resolved firste to visite the chiefe Divines of the reformed Churches to knowe their resolution before I would undergoe the worke in a way of a publicke reccomendacon.[20]

From this account it is evident that Dury's project received the hearty approval of Gustavus Adolphus. Here, says Briggs, "we see

[18] One manuscript of Dury's *Summarie Relation* was discovered by Charles A. Briggs and published by him in the *Presbyterian Review*, VIII, 301–9. A slightly variant text is quoted by Westin, *op. cit.*, pp. 264–76.

[19] Dury, *Briefe Relation*, p. 4. Dury, in his *Consultationum irenicarum prodiorthosis*, p. 120, indicates that letters from Abbot, Roe, and the English divines both enabled him to secure an audience with the King and provided the basis for the discussion of problems of church unity during the interview.

[20] *Presbyterian Review*, VIII, 301, 302.

Gustavus Adolphus as the great patron of this movement for peace among Protestants, if not its real initiator. It was a sad blow to Protestantism when he was slain on the battlefield of Lützen. No one was so well fitted to combine the forces of Protestantism as the heroic Swede."[21] It is evident that Dury's proposals fitted in perfectly with the King's own policies. He wished to deliver the Lutherans and Calvinists of Germany from the tyranny of their conquerors. But this deliverance could be accomplished more easily if peace and unity could be established among German Protestants. If unity among German Protestants and deliverance from imperial oppression could be accomplished under Swedish leadership, then Sweden's hegemony in Protestant Europe would be assured.

Hering, Brandes, and other writers who prepared accounts of Dury's interview with Gustavus Adolphus before the discovery of Dury's *Summarie Relation* were inclined to accept the view that the Swedish king did not approve the plans for union negotiations which Dury proposed in the interview at Würzburg.[22] Brandes emphasizes Dury's failure to receive letters of recommendation from the King as evidence of lack of interest or opposition on the part of Gustavus Adolphus. However, the *Summarie Relation* indicates clearly that such letters were offered and that Dury refused to receive them until he had made further advances in negotiations with the Reformed Churches.

The refusal to accept the "Promotoriall letters" offered by Gustavus Adolphus at Würzburg was most unfortunate. Gustavus died on the field of Lützen before Dury again had opportunity to secure his written indorsement of the union project. Brandes also bases his conclusion that Gustavus did not heartily indorse Dury's plans on the fact that Oxenstierna, after the death of the King, refused to take a position of leadership in promoting the scheme for establishing peace and unity among the churches. Such a conclusion is wholly unwarranted, because Oxenstierna was then acting under pressure of circumstances produced by an entirely different political and military situation. The documents which have been preserved indicate that Dury had the approval and cordial support of the King.[23] At the re-

---

[21] *Ibid.*, p. 298.

[22] Hering, *op. cit.*, II, 91, 92; Brandes, *Evangelischen Union in Preussen*, I, 277–79.

[23] Dury always insisted that Gustavus Adolphus was sincere in his promises of support. In a letter to Roe, dated January 28, 1633, he said: "The ground I have for believing that the King of Sweden would have united the Churches is his own promise to me at Würzburg, when he

quest of Gustavus Adolphus, the Swedish chaplains, Fabricius and Matthiae, held a number of conferences with Dury at Würzburg. Fabricius was unwilling to support the reunion movement, but Matthiae pledged active co-operation.[24] He had been interested in union projects for years, and the friendship which he formed with Dury during their stay at Würzburg lasted throughout the remainder of his life. He frequently urged the Swedish church authorities to support Dury and take an active part in the movement toward Christian reunion.[25]

In January, 1632, Dury began to center his efforts upon an attempt to interest leaders of the Reformed Churches of Germany in his union proposals. He had hoped to secure a conference of these leaders. Such a conference being impossible because of war conditions, he decided to seek personal interviews with as many influential leaders as possible. He spent months in a constant round of conferences with statesmen and churchmen of those sections of Germany in which the Reformed Church had gained strength. These interviews won the support of many prominent clergymen. John Bergius, the court preacher of Brandenburg, cordially indorsed his union plans. Likewise he received assurances of support from John Crocius and Theophilus Neuberger, the leading divines of Hesse; from Daniel Tossanus, court chaplain of the Elector Palatine; and from John Harbingun, the chief divine in the territories of the Duke of Isenberg. At Nuremberg, Dury met a number of the exiled preachers from the Upper Palatinate and reported that "they resolved to joyne in endeavors with mee and write their brethren in other places that some determinate course might be followed by common consent in the business."[26]

Similar conferences were held with groups of clergymen in Hanau, Hesse, the Palatinate, Deuxpont, and in the Wetterau.[27] But the clergy who promised support to Dury were not uniformly successful in their efforts to enlist the co-operation of their princes in the reunion movement. The Elector of Brandenburg and the Landgrave of Hesse were interested in Dury's plan, but they thought that it was

---

told me that he thought himself called of God and bound in his conscience to do it and offered to give me address to Sweden if I might further the work there and letters to the princes of Germany, which I should have got if he had lived. If you will hear more of this, ask of Sir Thomas Dislington, who was with him before his death and can give better assurance" (see *Calendar of State Papers, Domestic Series, 1625–1649*, p. 444).

[24] Hering, *op. cit.*, II, 92.   [25] Wordsworth, *op. cit.*, pp. 289 ff., 293 ff.

[26] "Summarie Relation," *Presbyterian Review*, VIII, 302, 303.

[27] Dury, *Briefe Relation*, p. 5.

necessary to advance with caution because of the complicated political situation. Some of the princes who ruled in small principalities
where the Reformed Churches had been established, including the
rulers of Isenberg and the Wetterau, were enthusiastic in their
support of the union movement. Strangely enough, Frederick V,
Elector Palatine and King of Bohemia, despite his many reverses, remained uncompromising in his attitude of opposition toward Lutheranism and steadfastly refused to tolerate the presence of Lutherans
in his ancestral dominions if they should be restored to him.[28]

In the midst of this busy round of interviews, Dury sought to
widen the scope of his union efforts by means of extensive correspondence with princes, statesmen, ecclesiastical leaders, assemblies
of clergymen, and the theological teachers in the universities. It was
his custom at this time to inclose in his letters copies of two tracts
which he had prepared. These tracts are important because of the
insight which they give into Dury's program for Christian reunion.[29]
They are also important because they exerted a direct influence upon
the union movement in Brandenburg in later times.[30] Furthermore,
these tracts give evidence of Dury's strong reaction against the Protestant scholasticism of the day and indicate his recognition of the
necessity of emphasis upon a more practical type of piety. Most of
the English writers on Dury have failed to note the fact that Dury,
in emphasizing the superiority of "practical divinity" over the prevailing dogmatism, was attempting to inaugurate a movement in
theological circles similar to that later developed by Spener and the
German Pietists.[31] Dury, like many of the Puritans in England and
Calixtus and his followers in Germany, attempted to exalt the practical and ethical elements in religion above the dogmatic emphases.[32]

[28] See S. R. Gardiner, *The Thirty Years' War*, p. 150; and Green, *op. cit.*, p. 292.

[29] For the text of the two tracts see *Unschuldige Nachrichten von alten und neuen theologischen Sachen* (1716), pp. 800–817, under the titles: *Generalis mediorum quaerendae ecclesiasticae pacis delineatio* and *De modo procedendi*. Summaries of the tracts are presented by Hering, *op. cit.*, II, 92 ff.; and Brandes, *Evangelischen Union in Preussen*, I, 279 ff.

[30] See Brandes, *Evangelischen Union in Preussen*, I, 280.

[31] *Ibid.* Brandes argues that the name of Dury should be given a prominent place in the list of the forerunners of the Pietist movement. Karl Brauer (*Unionstätigkeit John Duries unter dem Protektorat Cromwells* [Marburg, 1907], p. 1) criticizes A. Tholuck for overlooking this influential feature of Dury's work in his *Vorgeschichte des Rationalismus*, Vol. II: *Das kirchliche Leben des 17. Jahrhunderts* (Berlin, 1861).

[32] See C. A. Briggs, *General Introduction to the Study of Holy Scripture*, pp. 572–75. Briggs, in his *Theological Symbolics*, p. 22, also pays tribute to Dury as a peacemaker who "tried to rally the Christians of his time on what he called Practical Theology: that is, such doc-trines of Faith and Morals as were not scholastic, but of practical importance."

The first of the two tracts, issued under the title *Generalis mediorum quaerendae ecclesiasticae pacis delineatio*, is concerned with the causes of divisions among Christians and the means which might be employed in the healing of such divisions. Dury here develops the idea that the discord between the two evangelical parties in Germany was due to three principal causes: the differences in doctrinal views, the intemperate zeal for disputes, and the variations in outward forms and ceremonies used by the churches. Therefore, every effort should be made to secure agreement on essential doctrines, to cultivate the spirit of love in the hearts of Christians, and to secure uniformity in church ceremonies. These objectives can be obtained, he argues, through the work of mediators who should be chosen partly from theologians who are known to be men of pacific temperament; partly from statesmen who are genuinely interested in reconciling the contending churches; and partly from the representatives of foreign churches who are in position to act as disinterested parties.

As a practical means for promoting a spirit of unity among Christians, Dury suggests that men's minds must be turned from controversial matters to more useful interests, such as the investigation of the true meaning of the Scriptures, research directed toward the discovery of the opinions and practices of the early Christians, and the long-neglected study of practical theology. Here Dury maintains the thesis that the study of practical theology would serve as a wholesome restraint to the prevailing Protestant scholasticism. He suggests that professors, men chosen for their genuine piety and religious experience as well as their learning, should be given professorships in each of the universities in order that they might give courses in practical theology.[33] Likewise, attempts must be made to curb the controversial spirit within the churches by developing irenic attitudes among the pastors and people. Superintendents should see that ministers are not allowed to excite the minds of their hearers with disputes over scholastic questions. Quarrelsome discussions of dogmatic problems must give place to sermons designed to edify the hearers and implant love in their hearts. None should be admitted to the pastoral office without adequate proof of a vital religious experience. A work should be prepared which would embody the best ideas

[33] The suggestion that practical theology should be given a place in the theological discipline of the universities won gradual acceptance. By the end of the seventeenth century courses in practical theology had been introduced into a number of the universities, though varied terminology was used in reference to the new type of courses (see Otto Ritschl, "Literarhistorische Beobachtungen über die Nomenklatur der theologischen Disziplinen im 17. Jahrhundert," *Studien zur systematischen Theologie* [1918], pp. 78 ff.).

on the subject of practical divinity which are to be found in the more valuable English and German treatises in that field.

He also suggested that a special consistory should be constituted, with both laymen and clergymen as members and that powers should be given to this consistory to suppress all disturbers of the peace of the churches, to punish those who used schismatic and party names in an abusive manner, and to see that all candidates for pastoral office should pledge themselves to avoid party spirit. Clergymen who continued to criticize their brethren for nonconformity to doctrines and ceremonies of human origin should be removed from office after a third warning by the consistory. Books should be censored before publication in an effort to curb the controversial spirit. Young ministers, after completing their theological courses, should serve in the ministry under the supervision of more experienced clergymen until they had gained an experimental knowledge of the practical aspects of their duties. The work of every clergyman should be under strict supervision in order that all pulpit and parish work might be conducive to the establishment of peace among the churches and the promotion of personal piety among the members of the churches.

In the second tract, entitled *De modo procedendi*, Dury outlined the methods which he considered best adapted to the promotion of the cause of Christian reunion. Reunion efforts, he argues, must be conducted by skilful negotiators. These negotiators should be courageous and tactful men who are genuinely interested in the establishment of Christian concord. They must be chosen from the ranks of both clergy and laity, as their negotiations would inevitably deal with political as well as ecclesiastical interests. The negotiators must do their work through a gradated system of conferences in which they should seek out the causes of discord among Christians and attempt reconciliations between opposing factions. At first the negotiators should deal with local groups. The clergy of each district should be persuaded to indorse a union program. The clergy of the Lutheran Churches must be persuaded to arbitrate their own differences, and then they should be induced to adopt a conciliatory attitude toward the Reformed Churches.[34] A similar series of conferences must be in-

---

[34] Dury hoped that such a series of conferences among the Lutherans would establish a more cordial relationship between the separate Lutheran churches of the different principalities. He also hoped that the conference method might influence the Lutheran clergy to be less insistent upon the acceptance of the Formula of Concord. Brandes ("John Dury and His Work for Germany," p. 23) says that "Dury felt sure that the remedy for all the evils then suffered by the Church of the Reformation in Germany could only be found in the healing of that wound which had been inflicted by imposing the Concordia."

augurated in the Reformed Churches. Then negotiators from both the Lutheran and the Reformed Churches of Germany should hold a series of meetings such as the Leipzig Colloquy for the purpose of adjusting their differences and arranging for the establishment of a united German Protestantism. In all these negotiations persistent efforts must be made to enlist the interest and support of the clergy, the princes, and the masses of the people.

Finally, a General Assembly, composed of representatives of all the evangelical churches of Germany and the other Protestant countries, must be held. This Assembly should seek to settle upon a common creed, a formal statement of the essentials of practical piety which should be emphasized in Christian teaching, a common form of public worship, and a constitution for a new form of Christian organization which should embrace all Protestant Churches.[35] This General Assembly should use as the basis of its discussions the points of agreement which had been accepted in the preliminary negotiations between the representatives of local groups in the different churches. The whole of this extended series of conferences must be conducted in a conciliatory spirit and with a determined effort to avoid scholastic disputation. During the course of the negotiations none of the parties involved should be allowed to publish polemical treatises. In the General Assembly there should be two presidents, in order that

[35] Brandes (*ibid.*, p. 29) states that Dury had in view "a new form of government combining all Evangelical Churches in one great body, by extending Presbyterianism throughout the whole Church." He draws this conclusion from Dury's proposals for the use of a gradated system of representative assemblies in reunion negotiations. However, Dury was not insistent that the united church should be "Presbyterian" in polity. It was the purpose of Gustavus Adolphus to confederate the Protestant political powers into a single body, the Corpus Evangelicorum, but he did not intend that such a union should destroy the identity, autonomy, and individual peculiarities of the uniting states (see Gardiner, *op. cit.*, pp. 145, 148, 165). Dury wished to accomplish the same for the churches. He would allow variations in the national churches which formed constituent parts of the united church and employ the conciliar principle in the establishment and maintenance of bonds of union between the national churches. It is probable that Dury was as well informed regarding the variations in polity among the Protestant churches as was any man who lived in the seventeenth century. Throughout the whole of his career he showed a decided unwillingness to insist upon any particular form of church polity as a *sine qua non* of union. He was quite willing that the united church should permit variations in polity among the national churches and that the negotiators should work out a scheme for a central organization by accepting any one of the existing forms of polity or by combining several of the existing forms. Against Brandes' claim that Dury would insist on the acceptance of the Presbyterian polity there also stands the fact of Dury's willingness to accept Anglican reordination in 1634. In 1641 Dury issued a pamphlet, entitled *The Several Forms of Government received in the Reformed Churches Beyond the Seas*, in which he minimizes the essential points of difference in polity among the various branches of Protestantism. In this pamphlet (pp. 1–5) he attempts to prove that the Continental Protestant Churches either had episcopal forms of government or forms with features analogous to the episcopal polity. This pamphlet was frequently cited in tracts designed to champion the cause of episcopacy in England.

there might be an equal division of honors between the Lutheran and
the non-Lutheran churches. One president should be chosen from
the Church of Saxony as the representative of the Lutherans, and one
from the Church of England as the representative of the non-Lutheran churches.

The two tracts reveal the fact that Dury had made significant
changes in his union plans since he first began to advocate the cause
of Christian reunion in 1628. In planning his first efforts he had
thought in terms of establishing "ecclesiastical pacification" between
the churches of war-torn Germany. Next he had attempted the promotion of union between the Lutheran and the Reformed Churches
of Germany. Now he was working toward the ultimate goal of a union of all the Protestant churches. He had also adopted the use of
new methods in the advocacy of the reunion project. He was now advocating the call of a General Assembly, composed of representatives
of all the Protestant churches, which should deal with the problem of
working out a connectional polity and a common confession of Christian faith and duty. As Spinka says: "He proposed the first Conference on Faith and Order."[36] The proposal for the preparation of a
common confession of faith, containing all the essential elements in
the existing confessions and eliminating all nonessentials, was the
basis of much of Dury's later union activity.[37]

Many of Dury's contemporaries regarded his proposals as altogether impractical. Dury frequently admitted that it would require
much "persuasive work" to put them into operation, but he was always optimistic in his hope for the ultimate success of his plans.
However, the course of events in Germany ruined all chances for the
immediate realization of the union plans which he had elaborated in
the two tracts. The death of Gustavus Adolphus, November 16,
1632, made Dury's task most difficult. Likewise the death of Frederick V, November 29, 1632, further impeded the progress of the
proposed program. Dury had hoped to enlist the support and patronage of the dominant party at the court of Charles I by persuading the English leaders to believe that the restoration of the Palatinate to Frederick V would come as the inevitable result of a successful attempt to unite the Protestants in opposition to the Roman

---

[36] Matthew Spinka, "John Dury, the Peacemaker," *Christian Union Quarterly*, XIII (1924),
376.

[37] In 1887 Philip Schaff proposed that this plan for the preparation of a harmony of confessions should be made the basis of a new effort toward Christian reunion (see *The Harmony
of the Reformed Confessions*, pp. 1–60).

Catholic Reaction.[38] These losses forced him to revise his plans for future union activities. He thus expressed his sense of loss and his resolve to continue the work despite all difficulties:

> While this was in agitation and I was bethinkinge myself how to extend the worke further . . . . and afterwards how to goe to the King of England for his Promotoriall Letters towards ye Lutheran princes, the doleful newes of his [Gustavus'] death afflicted us all which afflicion was redoubled by a second blowe in the Losse of the Kinge of Bohemia. These great chaunges brought a great stop to our delibera-cions, yet the worke being Gods rather than mans, wee trusted to him, and confirmed one another in ye firste purposes not to leave of so longe as any thinge could bee attempted seasonably or hopefullie.[39]

Oxenstierna was now the dominant political figure in Germany. Dury at once attempted to secure from him the indorsement and support for his union project which Gustavus Adolphus had prom-ised. He had every reason to expect the co-operation of the Chan-cellor, who had repeatedly professed an interest in the union move-ment. At Elbing, in 1630, he had promised to co-operate with Dury.[40] After Dury's interview with Gustavus at Würzburg, he had another conference with Oxenstierna. Dury reported that Oxenstierna was then

> very forward to profess his love to mee, and expresst his desire to further myne in-tention of seeking peace and unitie, but because the K[ing] and hee were both over-laden with affairs of state, with treaties and visits of ambassadors from all partes both farre and neare, he willed me to stay till the most pressinge businesses should bee dispatched, and then hee would give mee all possible furtherance and assistu-ance.[41]

In 1632, John Bovidius, a Lutheran clergyman in charge of the staff of chaplains in the Swedish army, condemned Dury's union pro-

---

[38] While Dury was pleading his cause in Germany, Roe was making repeated attempts to persuade Charles I to support Dury's union project and to co-operate with Gustavus Adolphus. He relied chiefly on the argument that the reconciliation of Protestants and the success of Swedish intervention in Germany would make possible the restoration of the Palatinate to Frederick V. Roe's letters give frequent references to his activities in support of Dury's schemes. Thus the *Calendar of State Papers, Domestic Series, 1631–1633*, p. 401, summarizes a letter from Roe to the Earl of Holland, under date of August 6, 1632, as follows: Roe "has moved his majesty long since and often concerning a reconciliation of all the Protestant Churches of Europe. Since, there has been much progress made that it seems merely the mo-tion of the Prince of Peace. Has had freshly so large an account that he beseeches the Earl to let his Majesty know, that it may by his help be done, and not without it. If the king take not care of the King of Sweden, not so much by money, or that only, as by countenance and reputa-tion of unity, though an enemy cannot beat him out of Germany friends may undermine and undo him" (see also the text of the Dury-Roe correspondence as given by Westin, *op. cit.*, pp. 200 ff.).

[39] Dury, "Summarie Relation," *Presbyterian Review*, VIII, 303.

[40] See W. C. Dowding, *German Theology during the Thirty Years' War*, pp. 170, 171.

[41] Dury, "Summarie Relation," *Presbyterian Review*, VIII, 302.

posals on the ground that they were impractical and would provoke further strife among the churches. Thereupon Oxenstierna defended Dury against these criticisms and again expressed a friendly interest in his union program.[42]

After the death of Gustavus Adolphus there was a marked change in Oxenstierna's attitude toward Dury. He refused to furnish the "Promotoriall letters" which Gustavus had promised as an aid in securing the support of the Lutheran clergy.[43] Dury was informed that he would not be given public support in his union efforts. The reasons for the sudden change in attitude are apparent. The conduct of both the foreign and the domestic affairs of Sweden was now in the hands of the Chancellor. He found it difficult to work out a satisfactory domestic policy because of the ill-defined character of the Swedish constitution and the disorganized condition of the Swedish Church.[44] Any move toward reconciliation with the Reformed Churches would arouse opposition among the strict Lutheran clergy in Sweden and thwart the Chancellor's plans for the settlement of the Swedish constitution and the reorganization of the Swedish Church. Moreover, the Swedes now occupied a precarious position in Germany. Gustavus had built up an alliance between Sweden and the Lutheran and Reformed princes of Germany with great difficulty.[45] Oxenstierna's hopes for a successful foreign policy were dependent upon the continuation of this alliance, which was now threatened with dissolution because of the mutual jealousy of the Electors of Saxony and Brandenburg and the growing German distrust of the Swedes. Oxenstierna thought that the discussion of religious differences at this juncture would create further distrust and make it impossible to continue the existing alliance.

In order to strengthen the alliance between Sweden and the Protestant princes of Germany, Oxenstierna secured, through the cooperation of Landgrave William of Hesse-Cassel, a summons for a Convention of the Protestant Estates at Heilbronn on April 23, 1633.[46] As soon as Dury learned of the plans for this meeting he be-

---

[42] *Ibid.*, p. 303.

[43] See Brandes, *Evangelischen Union in Preussen*, I, 278, 279.

[44] Wordsworth, *op. cit.*, pp. 283–86.

[45] Gardiner, *op. cit.*, p. 138.

[46] Georg Mentz, *Deutsche Geschichte im Zeitalter der Reformation, der Gegenreformation und des Dreissigjährigen Krieges*, pp. 409, 410; see also Westin, *op. cit.*, pp. 139 ff.

gan anew to plead with Oxenstierna to make a public indorsement of his union plans. In the *Summarie Relation* he says:

This . . . . gave mee some boldness to entreate more freely the Lord Chauncellor to performe now that which hee often had promised unto mee. But hee beinge then more than ever before busy to frame a new state which was afterwards and now is called the Evangelicall League could not intend my requests. . . . . Thus hee delaied the matter so long yt I was wearie and out of hope to obtaine it, yet before I would desist wholie from yt purpose I used means to speake with the Lord Chauncellor myself to knowe wherefore the promise was delaied, and to shew how much harm that dilation did unto the cause; hee gave mee large audience, and pretended many causes why he was scrupulous to undertake the worke soe publickely, whereof the chief was yt hee feared his owne countrey clergie who would misinterpret this action as a thing disadvantagious to their religion; secondlie that alreadie the Saxon Court havinge heard of this Intention was jealous of him, as if hee would presume to rule all affaires as well in religion as State, and yt hee would make himself unfitt to doe anie good in the busines if hee did not goe warilie to worke.[47]

Despite this failure to secure the support of the Chancellor, Dury continued his efforts. In a letter which he wrote to Christian Beckmann, under date of November 25, 1632, he indicated that he was still hopeful that the plan for a gradated system of conferences, culminating in a General Assembly of representatives of all the Protestant churches, might be put into operation.[48] This letter also indicates that Dury was now relying upon the hope that Charles I and Archbishop Abbot would officially sponsor the promotion of his union plan and that their support would compensate for the loss of patronage from the Swedish authorities.[49]

In the months which intervened before the date set for the Heilbronn Convention, Dury hastened from one conference to another. Thus far he had labored, for the most part, with the princes, clergymen, and statesmen of the Reformed Churches. Now he attempted to win the favor of the Lutheran leaders. His first interviews were arranged with Lutherans whom he considered favorably disposed toward irenic efforts. By April 26, 1633, he was able to inform Roe

[47] *Presbyterian Review*, VIII, 304, 306.

[48] See Hering, *op. cit.*, II, 97–99.

[49] Letters written by Dury at this phase of his negotiations indicate his increasing hopes for English mediation. Thus, Dury to Roe, January 28, 1633: "I am now dealing with every province severally, and if they entreat our church to join in this work and take the lead in it, I hope it will not be refused" (*Calendar of State Papers, Domestic Series, 1625–1649*, p. 444). Dury to Roe, February 4, 1633: "I have yet hope of a general meeting, at which the direction of the matter may be offered to our king. The Lutherans must be brought together by Denmark, Saxony, and the Lord Chancellor Oxenstierna, and if his majesty speaks in the name of the Reformed side, viz. the Low Countries, France, and Helvetia, the matter may come to a happy issue" (*ibid.*, p. 445).

that "he had opened the matter to the best affected of the Lutheran side"; had met with a "reception in all cases favorable"; and had gained the support of Dr. Richter of Nuremberg, Colonel Bunick-hausen of Württemberg, John Valentine Andreae of Calw, Dr. Dunner of Mainz, and Dr. Gerard.[50]

On April 23, 1633, Dury, traveling in company with the English ambassador, Sir Robert Anstruther, arrived at Heilbronn. He states that he "tooke advise of friends what to doe and how yt I might not let the diet slipp without anie speciall benefit unto the cause I had in hand."[51] His friends suggested that he should present a petition to the Convention, asking that his union proposals be referred to each of the states in the Convention with the request that the clergy of each state should be asked to give their opinions on these proposals and that Dury should be given permission to treat with the divines of the different states. Such a petition was drafted, and Dury thus relates its reception by the Convention:

> By generall consent they graunted my desire, and promised to recommend it by an act . . . . of this tenour. . . . . Mr. John Durie an English Divine hath desired . . . . permission to treate with the chief divines and Prelats of the confederate states, concerninge the meanes how Ecclesiasticall unitie might bee established betwixt the Evangelicall Churches. Now although the deputed Amabssadores have gotten no Pticuler instruction concerninge this business yet they conceive yt if the Ld Chaunceller Excellencie would be pleased to further by his eminent authoritie this matter, that their most gracious and favourable Lord principalls and masters, as from their hearts wishing for such an agreement will be so much ye more bent to do all what can be done on their pts to set forward such a worke accordinge to the preparation made at ye conference at Leipsicke, whereunto also the states at this time nowe present doe offer and professe themselves noe lesse every way willinglie disposed.[52]

As the members of the Heilbronn Convention were not instructed to negotiate on the subject of the union of the churches, their in-dorsement of the continuation of union activity was only semi-official in character. Yet their action indicated a genuine interest in the problem of reunion, and their resolution was one of the most important indorsements which Dury was able to secure during his stay in Germany. Dury was enthusiastic over the progress made at Heil-

---

[50] *Calendar of State Papers, Domestic Series, 1633–1634*, p. 31. Dury made detailed notes of the views regarding Christian reunion which were held by these and other Lutheran leaders (see his "Summarie Relation," *Presbyterian Review*, VIII, 305; *Calendar of State Papers, Domestic Series, 1625–1649*, p. 447; and Historical Manuscripts Commission, *Report IV*, Part I, p. 159).

[51] "Summarie Relation," *Presbyterian Review*, VIII, 307.

[52] *Ibid.*, pp. 307, 308.

bronn. He was especially delighted to find that the Lutherans did not publicly oppose his plans during the Convention, as he had expected such opposition on their part. During the remainder of his stay in Germany he sought, by means of conferences and correspondence, to give wide publicity to his plans and to secure the appointment of representatives who should be definitely instructed to support reunion negotiations at the next Convention of the Protestant Estates.

Dury's new series of conferences and his letters pleading for further advance in union effort met with varied response. The Lord Chancellor of Brandenburg, says Dury, "did oblige himself, assuringe mee yt he would cause his master never leave to stirre in this busines."[53] Oxenstierna informed Dury that, "although he could not undertake the worke in publicke as yet, that never the les he would give all ye private assistance he could." At the Heilbronn Convention, Dury had become acquainted with John Jacob Breitinger, the representative of the Swiss cantons. He secured from him the promise that he would inform the Protestant Churches of Switzerland regarding the union proposals and would secure expressions of their opinions.

After Breitinger's return to Switzerland, Dury received letters from the Churches of Geneva, Zurich, Bern, and Basel. These letters indicated a friendly interest, but the letter from the Bernese church authorities suggested an attitude of suspicion toward the participation of the English Church in such union negotiations because of the increasing use of "half-Catholic" ceremonial practices by the High Church party in England and the disposition of that party to interfere with the liberties of the Calvinistic Churches of Scotland.[54]

The letters which Dury addressed to the French Protestants at this time did not meet with enthusiastic reception. The Academy of Sedan was the only French Protestant school that expressed a willingness to co-operate.[55] The response from the Reformed Churches

[53] *Ibid.*, p. 308.

[54] See the discussion of the attitude of Breitinger toward Dury's union program and the summary of the letters from the Swiss Churches as given by E. Bloesch, *Geschichte der schweizerisch-reformierten Kirchen*, I, 443-45.

[55] Brandes, "John Dury and His Work for Germany," p. 30; cf. also Hering, *op. cit.*, II, 99 ff. It was probably due to Dury's influence that Peter du Moulin wrote to Abbot in the name of the pastors, professors, and clergy of the academy and churches at Sedan, under date of June 13, 1633, requesting him "to promote the meeting of a general synod of representatives from the Protestant Churches for the purpose of reconciling their differences." After the death of Abbot this letter was given to Laud, who replied, under date of October 7, 1633, that "he has received their letter . . . . has laid the matter before the king, who after deliberation,

of Germany was more cordial. Dury received letters promising co-
operation from the Reformed Churches and divines of Anhalt, Strassburg, Nuremberg, Hamburg, Cassel, Nassau, Deuxpont, Isenberg,
and the Palatinate.[56] But the Lutherans, with only a few exceptions,
indicated their opposition to his proposals. The Saxon theologians
promptly refused to co-operate, and the Universities of Jena, Wittenberg, and Leipzig subjected Dury's plans to severe criticism.[57] In
some cases the Lutheran theologians replied to the pacific proposals
of Dury by issuing bitter countercharges to the effect that the Reformed Churches alone were responsible for the divided state of
Protestantism because they refused to accept the "Unchanged Augsburg Confession."[58] Mosheim refers to this opposition of the Lutheran leaders to Dury's proposals and adds: "Some, suspecting that the
fervent and extraordinary zeal of Duraeus arose from mysterious and
sinister motives, and apprehending that he had secretly formed a
design of drawing the Lutherans into a snare, attacked him in their
writings with animosity and bitterness, and loaded him with the
sharpest invectives and reproaches."[59]

The Lutheran statesmen and princes were more favorably disposed toward union effort than the Lutheran clergy. Among the
Lutheran clergy, only the irenic party led by George Calixtus, of the
University of Helmstadt, gave Dury cordial and public support during the closing months of his mission to Germany. After the Heilbronn Convention, Duke Frederick Ulrich requested the theological
faculty at Helmstadt to consider Dury's proposals and to indicate
"their opinion how most conveniently the unity of the Church might
be to the uttermost secured; and especially whether (or how easily)
a junction could be made with the Calvinists."[60]

---

desired that this answer should be returned; that as concerned their plan for a conference of
divines he thought that men's minds were not yet enough prepared, but recommended that a
confession of faith should be composed, drawn from the fundamental tenets on which both
parties agree" (see Historical Manuscripts Commission, *Report IV*, Part I, pp. 159, 160).

[56] On the contents of these letters see Brandes, "John Dury and His Work for Germany,"
p. 30; *Calendar of State Papers, Domestic Series, 1633–1634*, p. 149; and Historical Manuscripts
Commission, *Report IV*, Part I, pp. 159, 160.

[57] See Dowding, *op. cit.*, p. 172; and Brandes, *Evangelischen Union in Preussen*, I, 283. The
text of the reply by the Jena theologians was published by Dury in his *De pace ecclesiastica*,
pp. 110 ff.

[58] Brandes, "John Dury and His Work for Germany," p. 31.

[59] J. L. Mosheim, *Ecclesiastical History*, II, 266.

[60] Dowding, *op. cit.*, p. 173. The text of the letter of Duke Frederick Ulrich to the Helmstadt
theologians is quoted in part by E. L. T. Henke, *Georg Calixtus und seine Zeit*, I, 503 ff.

In response to this request the Helmstadt theologians, under the leadership of Calixtus, drew up a reply in which they stated their conviction that "divisions in matters of faith are not only an evil to Christians and utterly contrary to Christianity, but do also bring upon nations and governments confusion, detriment and damage—the healing whereof is a work pleasing to God and useful to the secular power." They regarded the foundation principle of unity to be the acceptance of the Holy Scriptures according to the consensus of antiquity as set forth in the creeds, "all by-questions unknown to the ancients, unessential to true Christianity, inflated, over subtle and in great measure unlearned—being set one side, or relegated to the schools." Proceeding on this basis, immediate efforts should be made to effect a union of the Lutheran and Reformed Churches.[61] The Helmstadt theologians also wrote to Dury expressing their approval of his irenic activities and promising further co-operation.[62] But the friendly advances of Calixtus and his associates only served to arouse more bitter opposition on the part of many Lutheran theologians.

Under these circumstances Dury realized that he could accomplish very little in Germany until the next meeting of the Protestant Estates of the Empire, which was to be held at Frankfort in 1634. Several considerations prompted him to decide to visit England at this time. He had incurred a heavy indebtedness, and it was necessary for him to make some arrangement for financial support if he was to continue in the work.[63] Moreover, he hoped that a series of conferences with English leaders would enable him to gain their active co-operation in union efforts. The death of Archbishop Abbot, August 4, 1633, also necessitated his return, as he could no longer use the letters which he had received from Abbot as evidence that he was authorized by the English Church to negotiate in the interest of the union of the churches. He was especially anxious to gain the favor and support of Laud, who had been advanced to the see of Canterbury after the death of Abbot. Always optimistic, Dury now believed that his union program could be put into effect if he could persuade Laud and Charles I to become its sponsors.

[61] Dowding, *op. cit.*, pp. 174, 175. Cf. Henke, *op. cit.*, I, 506–8.

[62] For the text of this letter see Henke, *op. cit.*, p. 506.

[63] During the years 1631–33, Dury was supported by small gifts from English friends. Sir Thomas Roe was active in soliciting funds for his support. In his letters Dury frequently mixed petitions for personal assistance with his appeals for support in behalf of the cause of Christian reunion; for example, see *Calendar of State Papers, Domestic Series, 1633–1634*, pp. 36, 329; *Calendar . . . . , 1625–1649*, pp. 446, 447.

Before leaving Germany he made detailed arrangements to keep his union project under discussion during his absence.[64] En route to England he passed through Holland, where he made numerous visits to leaders among the Dutch clergy. At Utrecht he had an interview with Buschoen, whom he describes as "the chief preacher of the place, and a man of great counsell and credit with the Prince of Orange." Dury reported the interview as follows:

> I laid open ye state of ye Ecclesiasticall busines in Germanie unto him, and asked what assistance hee thought I could expect from theis quarters of the Lowe Countries, he sayd hee could not yet tell, but suspected yt some factious spirits would be averse from it, never the les hee made no doubt of many well affected with whom in due time hee for his parte woulde labour to concurre and contribute such talents as god had given him.[65]

Thus Dury ended his first major effort at "ecclesiastical pacification" by laying the foundation for new negotiations in which Dutch support might prove of great value. After a number of conferences with Dutch leaders, he returned to England. His *Summarie Relation* concludes with the words: "I took shippinge at Flushinge and arrived here prosperouslie at London the 8th of this month of November for which I praise the Lord to whom bee all thankes and glorie for ever and ever Amen."

[64] Dury, "Summarie Relation," *Presbyterian Review*, VIII, 308, 309.

[65] *Ibid.*

CHAPTER IV

FURTHER NEGOTIATIONS WITH THE CHURCHES OF ENGLAND AND GERMANY

DURY was in England from November, 1633, to April, 1634. During these months he was constantly occupied with efforts to gain support for his union program. He was now thoroughly convinced that its ultimate success depended entirely upon the possibility of winning the patronage and support of Charles I and Laud.[1] Roe, at Dury's request, had continued his attempts to persuade the English authorities to take an active interest in the plans for the union of the Protestant churches.[2] Now Dury sought to plead his cause in person. In order to do this more effectively he prepared an account of his activities since his last visit to England. This narrative, the *Summarie Relation*, was to be presented to the Archbishop, together with a statement of the points of difference which were in dispute between the Lutheran and the Reformed churches and copies of letters from churches and theologians of Germany requesting Laud to take a position of leadership in the union movement.[3] Hitherto Laud had disregarded all such appeals. He had been too busy, as Gardiner indicates, with affairs in England to take part in any attempted solution of the difficulties which confronted the Continental Protestants.[4]

[1] On July 31, 1633, Dury had written Laud: "Since the death of the King of Sweden the churches of Germany look to the Church of England to mediate ecclesiastical matters" (Historical Manuscripts Commission, *Report IV*, Part I, p. 159).

[2] See *Calendar of State Papers, Domestic Series, 1633–1634*, pp. 149, 161, 162, 403. A letter from Roe to Laud, under date of January 30, 1634, is calendared in the Historical Manuscripts Commission, *Report IV*, Part I, p. 160, as follows: "It is well advertised that the French king will attempt to enlarge himself upon the Rhine, at the expense of the Palatinate, and if once he get a hold there, he will never give up again. . . . . There will be as little hope for religion under the French as under the Austrians. The only remedy is in the power of the Archbishop, viz., by uniting the churches to fortify the temporal powers of our friends, so that all should be equally balanced and the proudest brought to moderation."

[3] See the calendar of these papers in the Historical Manuscripts Commission, *Report IV*, Part I, pp. 159, 160. These documents, found among Laud's papers, constitute the most reliable source of information regarding the indorsement of Dury's reunion program by Continental theologians and churches prior to 1634 (cf. Dury, *The Unchanged Peacemaker*, pp. 3, 4).

[4] S. R. Gardiner, in his *Personal Government of Charles I*, II, 18, 19, says: "Laud's anxiety to secure uniformity in England led him to cast suspicious glances across the sea. It is true that he never troubled himself with the condition of the Continental Protestants. . . . . Laud

This time, however, Dury met with a friendly reception from the Archbishop. Laud invited him to dine at Lambeth Palace, manifested deep interest in his account of Continental affairs, and remarked that he would have taken Dury for a German, as he spoke the German language as readily as the English.[5] Encouraged by this reception, Dury made frequent visits to the Archbishop and pleaded persistently for a promise to the effect that he would serve as the patron of his union program and furnish financial assistance that would enable him to continue his negotiations on the Continent. In a letter to Sir Thomas Roe, under date of January 9, 1634, he gave an account of an interview with Laud which is summarized in the *Calendar of State Papers* as follows:

Durie went to Archbishop Laud. Inquired whether he should give attendance on his Grace oftener than heretofore or not. He answered he could not tell which was most expedient, but that Durie should come when he would and should always be welcome. Durie inquired whether he might not write something to encourage the divines to go further on in Durie's business, giving them assurance of help from hence. The Archbishop answered that, as for the King, he found not that he was willing to declare himself as yet, for causes which he kept to himself, and that Durie had done well in writing hitherto nothing unto them, lest in writing before things be resolved upon, he should be forced to retract; that between this and spring things would frame themselves otherwise in those parts, and according to their state a course may be taken.[6]

Dury was impatient at this delay. He had received news that there might be a meeting of the Protestant Estates of the Empire at Frankfort as early as February 24. Puritan leaders, such as Pym, Lord Brooke, Nathaniel Rich, and Richard Sibbes, urged him to continue to solicit the Archbishop's support.[7] Contrary to their expectations, Laud finally began to manifest more interest in Dury's program. In a conference with Dury he expressed his desire to promote the peace of all the churches but indicated that it would be necessary for Dury to receive episcopal ordination if he wished to carry on his

---

held it his business to reduce the Church of England to order, not to meddle with other churches. He could speak without irritation of Presbyterianism beyond the sea so long as the Presbyterians were not subjects of King Charles. But it was altogether another matter if Englishmen acquired Presbyterian habits abroad. It might be of little importance to him how men prayed or preached at the Hague or Rotterdam. But they would some time or another return to England, bringing with them an infection which might taint the flock under his care."

[5] "Dury, Calixtus, and the Peacemakers," *Christian Intelligencer*, XXIX, 19.

[6] *Domestic Series, 1633-1634*, p. 406.

[7] Dury, in his *Unchanged Peacemaker*, pp. 4, 7, says: "Although they expected little good from the Archbishop, yet they did incourage me in my application towards him, for the churches sake to try the utmost."

irenic program as an accredited representative of the Anglican Church. For years Dury had expressed doubts as to the validity of his ordination, owing to some irregularities connected with it. These doubts probably influenced the Archbishop in his favor. It was now evident that he could never secure Anglican support unless he complied with Laud's demand for his reordination. Roe urged him to accept episcopal ordination on the ground that this would increase his usefulness in union work.[8]

Dury finally decided to comply with Laud's demand. His decision was announced in a dramatic interview. In this interview the Archbishop stated his determination to withhold letters recommending Dury's project to the Lutheran and Calvinistic churches of the Continent unless he would submit to episcopal ordination. He promised to provide Dury with moral support and financial assistance if he would receive ordination and accept a benefice in the Anglican Church. Dury states that Laud suggested this bargain and,

with a serious look fixed upon me, asked whether I would, if the king should be pleased to bestow a parsonage upon me, receive it or not. I stayed a while in deliberation and said, I thanked his Grace, to which he replied that was no answer to the question, but he would know whether or no I would accept a benefice. . . . . I said yes . . . . and that I would wait upon him when he should be pleased to appoint me. . . . . Perhaps all this while they do but sift me, and try how I am inclined.[9]

Such was the occasion of Dury's ordination in the Anglican Church. On February 24, 1634, he was ordained in the Cathedral of Exeter by Bishop Hall, "with the imposition of the hands of several presbyters together with himself."[10] Briggs states that "he did not renounce his previous ordination but seems to have had some scruples about it on account of some irregularities in connection with it. And then he viewed his reordination as giving him an office in the Church of England, holding very much the same views as his friend Baxter on the subject."[11] Dury thus justified his action:

As for the Church of England . . . . I did look upon it as a Church of Christ, true in respect of the doctrine professed therein, and eminent for all spiritual gifts bestowed upon it; that I judged the government thereof by bishops with indifference, and that I took them as men commissioned by the king to be his delegates.

[8] *Ibid.*, p. 5.

[9] The full text of Dury's account of this interview with Laud is quoted in the *Calendar of State Papers, Domestic Series, 1633–1634*, Preface, p. xxxvi.

[10] Dury, *Unchanged Peacemaker*, p. 8.

[11] C. A. Briggs, "The Work of John Durie in Behalf of Christian Union in the Seventeenth Century," *Presbyterian Review*, VIII, 298.

. . . . I did not think that the Ordination which I had to a particular place beyond the Seas, by men who were under another kind of Church-Government could sufficiently authorize me to administer a public charge in this place, and under this Government, where the Law of the Land had provided another way of authorizing men to their places.[12]

To him the unity of the church was much more important than questions of orders and forms of church government. Accustomed for years to seek real conformity in spirit and agreement between religious bodies, he was able to regard such matters with indifference when the substance of the creeds of the churches was the same. He hoped that his decision in the matter would secure both moral and financial support and enable him to represent both Presbyterian and Episcopal groups.

But Laud was slow in fulfilling the promises which he had made to Dury. Shortly after receiving ordination, Dury was notified by the Archbishop that he had been granted a living in Devonshire with the understanding that he could have permission for nonresidence if he would provide the services of a curate. Dury, eager to settle his affairs in England as soon as possible in order that he might resume his work in Germany, went at once to Devonshire to take possession of his benefice. On arrival he found that the living had been granted to another, the Archbishop having been misinformed as to the vacancy. Laud then paid the expenses of Dury's trip to Devonshire and refused further help until a suitable vacancy should occur.[13] Later Dury was given the living of Saxebye in Lincolnshire with a license to be absent from his cure, but this arrangement neither relieved him from the pressure of debt nor furnished means for further travel as the living scarcely paid sufficient funds to provide the services of a curate.[14]

Dury's correspondence during the next six years abounds in appeals to Laud for adequate financial support, together with requests to Roe, Hartlib, Secretary Windebank, and others that they use all

[12] *Unchanged Peacemaker*, pp. 5, 15. Newman Smyth ("John Dury: A Peacemaker among the Churches," *Constructive Quarterly*, IV, 410) says of Dury's reordination: "In order that he might represent the Episcopal Church in the further prosecution of his undertaking he received additional ordination . . . . without renouncing his previous ordination. In so doing he seems to have anticipated the act of John Humfreys, a Congregational minister of London, in 1678, who was willing to receive episcopal ordination on the express understanding that he did not renounce his previous ordination, but accepted it as conferring additional jurisdiction, his previous ordination being *in foro Dei*, the second *in foro Ecclesiae Anglicanae*."

[13] See *Calendar of State Papers, Domestic Series, 1633–1634*, Preface, pp. xxxvii, xxxviii.

[14] Historical Manuscripts Commission, *Report IV*, Part I, p. 162. The benefice at Saxebye was reported in 1680 as having the value of only £12, 18s., 6d. (see *A Book of the Valuation of All the Ecclesiasticall Preferments in England and Wales*, sec. "Lincolnshire").

possible means to persuade Laud to grant him such support.[15] But these appeals were made in vain. Sir Thomas Roe provided the money needed to clear Dury's indebtedness and to pay the expenses of his next journey to the Continent. During the next six years Dury was supported chiefly by funds which Roe contributed personally or solicited from friends who were interested in Dury's union program.[16]

Likewise the hope that Laud would become "the prime mover in establishing ecclesiastical peace" was doomed to disappointment. Despite Dury's anxious pleadings, the Archbishop refused to answer each of the many letters on Christian reunion which Dury had persuaded the Continental churches and theologians to address to him. He told Dury that he would write only two letters in reply—one addressed to the Reformed churches and one to the Lutheran churches. The text of these letters is preserved and, although the letters contain, as Dury says, "strong expression of love towards the work, and some commendations of my labors," it is evident that the Archbishop was anxious to avoid, rather than assume, a position of leadership in the union movement.[17]

In the letter to the Calvinistic churches on the Continent, Laud stated that he had received the letters sent by the brethren of the Palatinate and elsewhere and had learned from those letters of Dury's efforts in behalf of peace ecclesiastical; he wished Dury to go on and prosper in the work under God's blessing; for his own part, he was willing to do all that could be done to promote the work in a country so remote from the disputants; he desired Dury to continue in the work and at the proper time he would come forward to help him. He wished to send greetings to the brethren in Christ, especially to those who had written him and to assure them that, although he did not have sufficient time to answer them individually, they might trust in his fidelity to the cause which under God he committed to Dury and to those who seek peace in the midst of war.

[15] See *Calendar of State Papers, Domestic Series, 1633–1634*, pp. 329, 406, 417, 427 ff.; *Calendar . . . ., 1640*, pp. 320 ff., 443 ff.; *Calendar . . . ., 1640–1641*, p. 183 and *passim*.

[16] Among the lists of those who assisted Roe in financing Dury in this period we find the names of Elizabeth, Queen of Bohemia, Sir Nathaniel Rich, Bishops Hall and Bedell, Lady Waller, Lady Barnardiston, and Lord Craven.

[17] See *Calendar of State Papers, Domestic Series, 1633–1634*, Preface, p. xxxvii. For the Latin text of these letters see *The Works of William Laud*, VI, 410; VII, 112, 113. For the text of the Roe-Laud correspondence concerning Dury's negotiations at this time see *ibid.*, VII, 48, 73, 74, 86, 87. Laud's obvious efforts to avoid a position of leadership in the union movement stand in sharp contrast to the attitude of Cranmer toward the Continental churches (cf. John T. McNeill, *Unitive Protestantism*, pp. 221 ff.).

In a similar letter, addressed to the Continental divines who accepted the Confession of Augsburg, Laud stated that he had learned from their letters both Dury's zeal for the peace of the church and also the perils and conflicts that threaten its life. These are due chiefly to the dissensions within the church. So much the more ought Dury's efforts for peace to be encouraged; though both the Archbishop and the whole English Church approved them, he could do nothing openly without considering some peace which might embrace the several parties within the churches of Germany. Meantime he wished Dury to continue his efforts. He hoped that he would remember Christ's blessings on the peacemaker and that he would signify to the churches of Germany his zeal for reconciliation lest the church get a bad name on account of dissensions and party strife.[18]

This was all that Laud would do in support of Dury. When Roe again appealed for more effective help, he was told that the Archbishop's letters indicated his interest in the matter so far as was in "any ways fit" and that he hoped that Dury would be successful. He thought that a public expression of interest in reunion on the part of the approaching Frankfort Convention might furnish a basis for further proceedings, but, until such an expression could be secured, he saw little hope of success. He informed Roe that the King highly approved of the movement in the interest of the peace of the churches, but considerations of state made it impossible for him to take public part in the negotiations; and, although he was at court, he could offer no more practical assistance than Roe could give, as business of this kind was handled by a committee on foreign matters of which he did not happen to be a member.[19] About the same time that Laud was thus expressing to Roe a friendly interest in Dury's reunion negotiations, he wrote to Sir Robert Anstruther, who was to represent English interests at the Frankfort Convention, instructing him to "show Dury no countenance whatever."[20]

Anthony à Wood states that Dury received encouragement from Laud in his efforts to establish the peace of the churches and settle a Protestant union but adds: "Tho' Prynne his [Laud's] inveterate enemy saith not, but found so small encouragement from him, that

[18] The two letters were drafted on February 10, 1634. The original drafts, in the handwriting of Dell, Laud's secretary, and signed by Laud, are preserved in the collection of Laud's papers (see Historical Manuscripts Commission, *Report IV*, Part I, p. 160).

[19] *Calendar of State Papers, Domestic Series, 1633–1634*, p. 562.

[20] David Masson, *The Life of Milton*, III, 195.

he oft complained thereof to his friends."[21] Wood here refers to circumstances connected with the trial of Laud in 1643–44. One of the
charges made against the Archbishop was to the effect that he had attempted to sow "division and discord between the Church of England and foreign Protestants."[22] In proof of this charge William
Prynne, who was in charge of the prosecution, attempted to show
that Laud had discouraged Dury in his schemes for conciliation between the churches because he regarded the Calvinistic churches as
alien from the true faith. Dury's intimate friend, Hartlib, who was,
as Masson says, "a most competent witness in this matter," was
called upon to give evidence against the Archbishop.[23] In answer to
this charge Laud contended that he did not discourage Dury but
rather encouraged him, as he could prove by letters from Dury which
he had in his possession. Thereupon Prynne attempted to show that
Laud's claim was false and that Dury had often complained to his
friends because of the Archbishop's failure to give effective support.[24]

The evidence preserved in Dury's letters indicates that Prynne
was absolutely correct in his statement that Laud had failed to give
effective support to Dury. But it does not necessarily follow that
Laud withheld his support because he regarded the Calvinistic
churches as alien to the true faith. On the contrary, his refusal was
due to the fact that his primary interests were centered in the settlement of the problems of the Church of England; to his conviction
that the churches of the Continent should work out the solution of
their own problems; to his desire to keep out of any reunion negotiations which might prove a hindrance to the government in its efforts
to work out a satisfactory foreign policy; and to his suspicion that
the reunion plans of Dury were too impractical to accomplish lasting
results.

During the months of his stay in England, Dury was also making
persistent attempts to enlist the help of English clergymen and laymen of all parties. Few influential men escaped his earnest appeals.
The responses to his appeals were now more cordial than on the occasion of his previous visit to England. His work on the Continent had

---

[21] *Athenae Oxonienses*, I, 230.

[22] See the account of the charges against Laud as given by Daniel Neal, *History of the Puritans*, I, 518 ff.

[23] Masson, *op. cit.*, III, 229.

[24] See the text of the documents connected with this part of the trial of Laud, as given by William Prynne, *Canterburies Doom* (1646), pp. 539–42.

aroused the interest of many Englishmen. He had been able thus far to secure the cordial indorsement of his plans by Archbishop Ussher; by Bishops Hall, Morton, Davenant, and Bedell; by the London ministers, William Gouge, John Downame, George Walker, Adoniram Byfield, Sidrach Simpson, and Obadiah Sedgewick; by the Puritan divines, John White of Dorchester, Richard Sibbes, and John Cotton; and by many other ministers of the most varied party affiliations.[25]

Among the laity Dury counted Sir Thomas Roe and Samuel Hartlib as his most dependable supporters. He was also able to enlist the interest and help of Sir Nathaniel Rich, a wealthy layman who was noted for his opposition to the growth of Roman Catholicism in England and for his encouragement of the spread of Presbyterianism in Bermuda.[26] Edward Montagu, second earl of Manchester, was at this time interested both in Dury's scheme for the union of the churches and in his plans for the introduction of improved Continental methods of education in the schools of England.[27] Earl William Craven, son of the lord mayor of London and earnest champion of the claims of Elizabeth of Bohemia, also favored Dury's union plans. His interest was probably due to the fact that he shared with Roe the hope that the successful realization of Dury's plans would make possible the restoration of the Palatinate to Elizabeth of Bohemia.[28]

Dury was a firm believer in propaganda by means of the printed page. During his residence in England he sought to secure the preparation and publication of a "Body of Practical Divinity"—a work which was to include the best English discussions on the subject and present the material in such a way that it could be introduced into the curriculum of the schools as a theological discipline.[29] He had brought to England a letter, dated from Hanau, February 24, 1633, in which a number of German divines asked for the preparation of

[25] C. A. Briggs, "The Work of John Durie in Behalf of Christian Union in the Seventeenth Century," *Presbyterian Review*, VIII, 299; cf. also B. Brook, *The Lives of the Puritans*, III, 370 ff.

[26] Historical Manuscripts Commission, *Report VIII*, Part II, pp. x, 51.

[27] *Ibid.*, pp. 10, 54.

[28] *Calendar of State Papers, Domestic Series, 1636–1637*, p. 400.

[29] As early as April 12, 1633, Dury had written from Germany urging Sir Thomas Roe "to help Mr. Hartlib with a petition of those quarters concerning an edition of a Body of Practical Divinity, gathered out of English authors, a work which will be exceeding profitable, but will require diverse agents and an exact ordering of the work" (see *Calendar . . . . , 1633–1634*, p. 2).

such a work by English scholars. They indicated their conviction that a book of this kind would be most useful in discounting the influence of the prevailing type of scholastic and controversial divinity. They also asserted their belief that

in the churches of Great Britain the doctrine of Practical Divinity, by the publique writings of many wise, godly ministers of your churches, is brought to great perfection, and that it is excellently fitted for the use of the common people, but yet it is kept up as a hidden treasure from the eyes of forreine nations within the bounds of your language alone.[30]

At Dury's suggestion a group of London ministers requested Archbishop Ussher to supervise the preparation of such a work in Latin, which was to be translated into German. Ussher stated: "I was very glad of the notion and laid it very seriously to heart and conferred with some of my brethren about it that we might bring it to some perfection."[31] The outbreak of the Civil Wars rendered the preparation and publication of the work impracticable at the time, but this scheme for the publication of a "Body of Practical Divinity" was revived at a later date.[32]

Dury was more successful in his next venture. This was an effort to persuade leaders of the English Church to prepare and publish treatises on the subject of Christian reunion, which might be circulated in Latin among the churches of the Continent for propaganda purposes. Bishops Davenant, Morton, and Hall—three typical representatives of a party which would now be designated as "Low Church"—prepared such treatises. Dury published the treatises of the three bishops in 1634 under the title *De pacis ecclesiasticae rationibus inter evangelicos usurpandis.*[33] In their writings in behalf of Dury's program these English bishops held that the Leipzig Collo-

---

[30] For the full text of this letter see Dury, *Earnest Plea for Gospel Communion*, pp. ix–xvii.

[31] *Ibid.*, pp. 81–84.

[32] See below, pp. 92, 133.

[33] John Wordsworth (*The National Church of Sweden*, p. 293) states that a second edition of this work was printed at Amsterdam in 1636 under the title *De pace ecclesiastica inter evangelicos procuranda sententiae quattuor.* In this edition Dury added a fourth treatise, written "ab ecclesiae in Gallia pastoribus," and a useful syllabus of writings in favor of ecclesiastical peace. A third edition was published at London in 1638. This was also translated into English in 1641 and published at Oxford under the title *Good Counsels for the Peace of the Reformed Churches.* This Oxford edition presented, in addition to the earlier treatises, the "Opinion of James Ussher, Archbishop of Armagh, with some other bishops of Ireland." Davenant's contribution was published separately in Latin (Cambridge, 1640) and in English (London, 1641) as an introduction to his *Exhortation to Brotherly Communion Betwixt the Protestant Churches.* Bishop Hall's statement was reprinted in his *Works*, XI, 488–501.

quy had produced evidence of complete agreement between the
Lutherans and Calvinists on all except three of the doctrines of the
Christian faith; that their views on these doctrines did not differ so
widely as to preclude the possibility of mutual agreement; that
Lutherans and Calvinists should grant intercommunion with each
other, as they were both willing to grant intercommunion with the
English, Scottish, and Irish Protestant churches; that earnest efforts
should be made to reach more complete doctrinal agreement; and
that all should co-operate in Dury's plans for reunion negotiations,
which would be conducted in a brotherly spirit and with strict avoid-
ance of bitter controversies and disputations about scholastic subtleties. Frequent use was made of these treatises in later reunion
negotiations on the Continent.

Dury was now of the opinion that he had accomplished all that
was possible in England at this time. He had kept in close touch
with developments on the Continent. Oxenstierna had succeeded at
Heilbronn in uniting, under his direction, the four upper circles of
Germany, despite the opposition of Saxony.[34] He had summoned a
Convention of the Protestant Estates of the Empire to meet at
Frankfort on the Main, in March, 1634, in order that new measures
might be taken to meet the common dangers. Dury and Roe considered this a most opportune occasion to present anew the proposals
for union negotiations. When it became evident that the Convention would extend its sessions over a period of months, Roe redoubled
his efforts to secure additional support for Dury.[35] In May, 1634,
John Oxenstierna, son of Axel Oxenstierna, arrived in England to
serve as Swedish ambassador. Roe immediately arranged a conference with him and later reported that he was "most glad of the Ambassador's good disposition to the ecclesiastical treaty" and that he
had asked him to aid Dury in his work.[36]

Dury, in letters to Roe, dated March 27 and April 24, 1634, announced his intention to visit the Frankfort Convention despite his
lack of funds and his failure to gain official authorization. These letters, as summarized in the *Calendar of State Papers*, indicate the

---

[34] Georg Mentz, *Deutsche Geschichte im Zeitalter der Reformation, der Gegenreformation und
des Dreissigjährigen Krieges, 1493–1648*, pp. 409 ff.

[35] See the letters of Roe to Laud and Elizabeth of Bohemia, *Calendar of State Papers, Domestic Series, 1634–1635*, pp. 11, 349.

[36] *Ibid.*, pp. 18 ff.

spirit which prompted him to continue his reunion negotiations regardless of all handicaps:

> If he be not prohibited to act in this work, he will never give over, and where he cannot ride he will go afoot, and when he cannot go on foot he will creep on all four, rather than not proceed. It is grievous to see so good enterprises so little cherished. He suspects a main stop . . . . because they fear the relation which this matter has to matters of state, wherein they will have no meddling, this he gathers from words let fall by Archbishop Laud and Sec. Windebank. . . . . If Durie can subsist in a mean way a year or two, his heart tells him that this seed may spring up, although no sunshine nor shower from England upon it. . . . . Hopes the churches will bless Roe's name for being a patron, and the only patron, of so good a work. So long as Durie sees appearance to do God service, he will not be wanting to the occasion, and hopes Sir Thomas will not discontinue his support so long as God shall give apparent blessings to these attempts.[37]

With this determined spirit Dury returned to the Continent. In May, 1634, he was at Hamburg on his way to the Convention of the Protestant Estates, which was continuing its sessions at Frankfort. Poverty was a constant handicap in his travels at this time. At Hamburg he met with the British ambassador, Sir Robert Anstruther, who allowed him to travel with him to Frankfort in his coach— Dury's man being shifted "sometimes in the baggage wagons, and sometimes afoot, and sometimes in the second coach." En route Dury held conferences with a number of Lutheran leaders in the towns through which he passed.[38]

Arriving at Frankfort, he found that lodgings were expensive and that he did not have sufficient funds to "put himself in some fashion for clothes."[39] Immediately after his arrival he began to hold conferences with divines and ambassadors from the various states. The letters of recommendation, which had been furnished by Roe, Laud, and others, were presented to all the representatives whom he could approach. The Latin edition of the treatises of Davenant, Morton, and Hall was freely distributed to all who were in position to help his cause. Another pamphlet favoring his reunion proposals, drafted and signed by pastors of varying denominational affiliation from the churches of Transylvania, was also given wide circulation at this time.[40]

But Dury soon found that conditions were unfavorable for the suc-

---

[37] *Calendar* . . . . , *1633–1634*, pp. 525, 566.

[38] *Ibid.*, p. 18.   [39] *Ibid.*, pp. 18, 148.

[40] The text of this pamphlet is reprinted by Dury in his *Irenicorum tractatuum prodromus*, pp. 50–87.

cess of his mission. He was seriously handicapped by Laud's action
in ordering Anstruther to give no countenance to his efforts. The
alliance between Sweden and the German Protestant princes was
threatened with dissolution in the face of the increasing strength
on the part of the imperial and Roman Catholic powers. Leaders
were of the opinion that the inclusion of a discussion of religious issues as a part of the agenda of the Convention would prove a hindrance to the establishment of political unity and effective military
co-operation.[41] Dury soon discovered that his proposals for reunion
negotiations were actively opposed by the Landgrave of Darmstadt
and that there was "no more hope of assistance from Lord Chancellor
Oxenstierna than formerly."[42]

However, the most active opposition came from the Saxons. The
Elector of Saxony was engaged in negotiations with the emperor and,
as he was breaking with his Protestant allies, steadily became more
pronounced in his hostility toward the Calvinists.[43] The anti-Calvin-
ist and antiunion arguments of the Elector of Saxony were given
forceful expression in a number of pamphlets by his court chaplain,
Hoë von Hoënegg. In these pamphlets Dury's union plans were subjected to severe criticism.[44] On the other hand, the Elector of Brandenburg was favorably inclined toward the union movement.

In July, 1634, Dury presented his proposals to the Convention
"with the foreknowledge of various ambassadors who had promised
to second it." He expressed the hope that the Convention would decide to "authorize certain deputies to prosecute the matters, and invite the foreign churches to consultation."[45] From this statement
it is clear that Dury was continuing his efforts to secure the call of a
general assembly of representatives of all the Protestant churches
which should be empowered to settle upon terms of union. Despite

---

[41] F. H. Brandes, *Geschichte der evangelischen Union in Preussen*, I, 285.

[42] *Calendar of State Papers, Domestic Series, 1634–1635*, pp. 96, 179, and *passim*.

[43] *Ibid.*, p. 55.

[44] See *ibid.*, p. 196. Dury sent a copy of one of Hoë's pamphlets to Roe. Roe forwarded it
to Laud with this comment: "It is the perfect dialect of Rabshekah, without learning or proof,
but by bitter invectives and railing presumptions, the question being always begged and then
concluded. This lightning was shot to blast our best endeavors." After reading the pamphlet,
Laud stated that he had "in his time read much bitterness, but [had] hardly seen more gall drop
from any man's pen." Roe wished to answer the pamphlet, but Laud dissuaded him (see
Calendar . . . . , 1625–1649, pp. 476, 477; *Calendar . . . . , 1634–1635*, p. 196). On Hoë's
opposition to Dury's program see also Pierre Bayle, *Dictionnaire historique et critique*, I, 1095,
1096.

[45] *Calendar of State Papers, Domestic Series, 1634–1635*, p. 148.

the opposition which had been maintained for weeks by the Saxons, the Convention, on September 14, 1634, adopted resolutions which Dury regarded as one of the most important indorsements of his work that he had been able to secure.

Dury, in his *Briefe Relation*, quotes the full text of the resolutions of the Frankfort Convention.[46] These resolutions state that Dury was heard by a committee of the Convention which "did judge his work most laudable, most acceptable to God, and most necessary and useful to his Church." However, since many of the ambassadors had no instructions on the subject, they were unwilling to take immediate action on his proposals. Some members of the Convention thought that a series of conferences, patterned after the Leipzig conference, should be held to settle "a Fundamentall agreement on points necessary for salvation." Some thought that a general assembly of divines from all Protestant churches should be called to draft a common confession of faith. Pending advances along these lines, some, but not all, of the members of the Convention believed that "all Christian moderation was to be used on both sides, as well in Preaching as in Writing." There was general agreement that prayers should be offered "in the churches of both sides to intreat Almighty God to blesse these attempts."

Dury was pleased to secure this official indorsement of his work. But his Lutheran opponents, particularly the Saxon delegation, had prevented action which might have resulted in an early union of the Lutheran and Calvinistic churches. The Calvinists were responsible for the cordial approval of Dury's objectives; the Lutherans were responsible for the expressions of divided opinion and the suggestions for the postponement of definite action. The resolutions received wide publicity and helped to develop a new interest in unity among some of the Protestant churches, notably in France.[47] Dury began to hope that they would pave the way for significant advances. He continued his stay at Frankfort and made new efforts to win the support of the ambassadors through private conferences. At this time he formed a friendship with Hugo Grotius, who became one of his most influential supporters.[48] Before he was able to secure further official

---

[46] Pp. 11–14.

[47] See M. Tabaraud, *De la réunion des communions chrétiennes*, pp. 70, 71; cf. also Hugo Grotius, *Hugonis Grotii . . . . epistolae quotquot reperiri potuerunt*, p. 165.

[48] On Grotius' interest in the movement toward reunion and his relations with Dury see Tabaraud, *op. cit.*, pp. 313–24.

indorsement for his program, the Swedish army was defeated by the
imperial forces in the battle of Nördlingen (September 6, 1634). This
defeat of the Protestant forces and the establishment of peace between the Elector of Saxony and the emperor forced the dissolution
of the Frankfort Convention and destroyed all hope for the immediate realization of the union schemes. Dury was convinced that
he should return to England, report on his mission to Germany, and
seek further instructions from the English authorities. After a brief
visit in Holland, he returned to England toward the close of the year
1634.

Dury was delighted with his reception in England. Archbishop
Laud presented him to the King. Roe was able to report that Dury
was "well received of his majesty and well accepted by the archbishop of Canterbury, who had obtained from the king a good retreat with a dispensation to return to his labor."[49] Dury presented
to the Archbishop a detailed account of his activities during his last
visit to the Continent.[50] With the assistance of Sir Thomas Roe, he
drafted and presented to the King a paper in which he advocated the
adoption of a new foreign policy by the English government. He
suggested that the central feature of this new policy should be the
establishment of a "Protestant League as a counterpoise to France
and Spain, the King of England being its head and director to his
own ends and the common safety."[51] He hoped that the adoption of
such a policy would provide a promising field for a new approach to
the solution of the problem of the reunion of the churches. However,
this proposal met with no favor at court, as Charles I was then negotiating for an alliance with Spain to offset the proposed partition of
the Spanish Netherlands between France and Holland.

Dury spent the winter of 1634–35 in efforts to win additional support for his union program. He visited Edinburgh and Aberdeen for
the purpose of interviewing leaders of the Scottish Church.[52] It is
probable that this visit to Scotland was suggested by Laud, who was
then busily engaged with plans for securing conformity of the Scot-

---

[49] This "good retreat" brought no financial assistance to Dury. The benefice sometimes
failed to pay the expense of providing a curate. Roe states that, when Dury started out on his
next mission, "he went out like an apostle with scrip and staff and in that poverty" (*Calendar
of State Papers, Domestic Series, 1635*, pp. 138, 139).

[50] This document of twenty-two pages is summarized in the *Calendar . . . . , 1634–1635*,
p. 530; see also *The Works of Joseph Hall*, XI, 501–11.

[51] *Calendar of State Papers, Domestic Series, 1635*, pp. 10, 11.

[52] George Grub, *Ecclesiastical History of Scotland*, II, 371.

tish Church to the Church of England.[53] Dury's proposals met with
varied response in Scotland. Archbishop Spottiswoode was favorably
impressed and presented Dury with letters indorsing the movement
toward reunion. These letters proved to be of value to Dury in his
later reunion activity in Sweden.[54] Spottiswoode, keenly sensitive to
the signs of the coming storm in the Scottish Church, advised Dury
to avoid a public discussion of his union plans at this time on the
ground that many of the Scots would regard his scheme as a proposal
to yield first to the Lutherans and then to the Papists.[55] He suggested
that it would be more advisable for Dury to present his proposals in
a private way to Scottish clergymen and laymen who were known to
be interested in irenic endeavors and secure their indorsement of his
project.

However, Dury's visit to Scotland and its purpose were soon well
known to men of all parties within the Scottish Church. The more
uncompromising type of the advocates of Presbyterianism were
suspicious of Dury because he had accepted reordination at the hands
of an Anglican bishop. Thus Samuel Rutherford, in a letter written
in 1637, mentioned the proclamations regarding the introduction of
the new liturgy into Scotland and added:

> Our service Book is ordained, by open proclamation and sound of trumpet, to be
> read in all the kirks of the kingdom. Our prelates are to meet this month for it and
> our canons, and for a reconciliation betwixt us and the Lutherans. The professors of
> Aberdeen University are charged to draw up the articles of an uniform confession,
> but reconciliation with popery is intended.[56]

On the other hand, Robert Baillie, a Presbyterian of more irenic spir-
it, cordially approved of Dury's efforts but was of the opinion that
Spottiswoode had acted wisely in curbing popular discussion of
Dury's proposals during his visit to Scotland.[57]

The most important indorsement which Dury was able to secure as

---

[53] P. Hume Brown, *History of Scotland*, II, 298.   [55] Grub, *op. cit.*, II, 370.

[54] Wordsworth, *op. cit.*, p. 293.   [56] *Letters*, p. 362.

[57] Baillie, in a letter to his friend, William Spaing, made the following comments on Dury's
efforts: "Concerning Duraeis business, whenever I hear of the advancement of it I am re-
freshed, you neid put no questions on our side, for we did ever earnestlie fute it. . . . . I was
much bettered by the wreit of the thrie Inglish bishops. . . . . However it be now two years
since Dureae wreit to St. Andrews of that purpose, yet never did I hear of any such purpose,
no, not to this day, but from you, albeit in such purposes, I am curious of intelligence. I
approve weill the Bishops' wisdome in concealing that from our people, for they would not
faill to tak it for a policie of them, to bring us on that farr, to yield first to the Lutherans and
then to the Papists, so if they saw any such matter in hand, they would by that means, be
more concerned in standing still where they are" (*Letters and Journals*, I, 9).

a result of his visit to Scotland was a carefully prepared statement regarding reunion problems, which was furnished to him by the theological professors of the University of Aberdeen and the ministers of the city of Aberdeen. These men, known as the "Aberdeen Doctors," took a mediating position on most of the issues which were under discussion amid the bitter partisan strife then prevailing in the Scottish Church.[58] Spottiswoode had requested the Aberdeen Doctors to prepare a statement of their views regarding Dury's proposals. Two years later they presented their opinion in a long letter to Archbishop Spottiswoode.[59]

In this statement the Aberdeen Doctors cordially approved Dury's reunion efforts. Deploring the consequences of discord among the churches and acknowledging the many obstacles to union, they maintained that union was possible if the parties involved would emphasize the doctrines which they held in common rather than those about which they differed. A distinction must be made between the primary doctrines of the Christian faith and other doctrines of lesser importance. Effort must be made in a conciliatory spirit to secure a common confession of faith which should state the primary doctrines of Christianity in a way that would be acceptable to all branches of the Protestant churches. Christians must be persuaded to agree on this common confession of faith. They should be willing to allow a wide variety of opinion about the less important doctrines which are not essential to salvation.

This document was of no service in settling the discord which prevailed in the Scottish Church. The Aberdeen Doctors were discredited during the strife over the National Covenant because of their irenic attitude, which ran counter to the spirit of the times. But their opinion was of great service to Dury in his later negotiations. He frequently cited the arguments of the Aberdeen Doctors in his efforts to persuade the leaders of the different branches of Protestantism to undertake the preparation of a common confession of faith.

[58] Three of the Aberdeen Doctors (John Forbes, Robert Baron, and William Leslie) were teachers in the university; and three (James Sibbald, Alexander Scroggie, and Alexander Ross) were ministers in the city. An interesting account of the views of the group is presented by D. Macmillan, *The Aberdeen Doctors* (London, 1909).

[59] For the text of the opinion of the Aberdeen Doctors see John Forbes, *Instructiones historico-theologicae*, Book XIV, chap. vii; cf. Macmillan, *op. cit.*, pp. 158 ff.

CHAPTER V

"A TRAVELLER IN THE WORK OF PEACE"

RETURNING from Scotland, Dury found little chance of promoting his cause in England. He was restless and eager for a new opportunity to negotiate with Continental leaders. In July, 1635, he left England for the Continent, where he was to spend the next five years as "a traveller in the work of peace among the churches" of Holland, Sweden, Denmark, and Germany. He began this new mission with buoyant enthusiasm. His previous mission to Germany had been thwarted by Saxon opposition to his union proposals, but he dared to hope that "by this means the rest will be soldered more strictly together to maintain their liberties and religion and so his propositions will strengthen their politic considerations."[1]

This time Dury started his travels with a royal safe conduct and with letters of indorsement from a number of the English bishops.[2] He also carried letters of recommendation from the distinguished Cambridge scholar, Joseph Mede, and from other influential English educational and religious leaders.[3] He planned to begin his work with a visit to the Dutch churches. It is probable that Laud suggested this procedure, hoping that Dury would be able to provide the government with information regarding the churches of Holland which would be of service in shaping a more effective English foreign policy.[4]

Dury hoped that his negotiations in Holland would enable him to make peace between the contending factions in the Dutch churches and then secure the support of the united Dutch Church in behalf of his program for the union of all Protestants. But the situation in Holland was unfavorable for the success of his mission. The old hatred between Remonstrants and Counter-Remonstrants continued

---

[1] Dury to Roe, July, 1635 (*Calendar of State Papers, Domestic Series, 1635*, p. 265).

[2] Karl Brauer, *Die Unionstätigkeit John Duries unter dem Protektorat Cromwells*, p. 4.

[3] B. Brook, *Lives of the Puritans*, III, 371.

[4] Throughout Dury's stay in Holland he was frequently criticized by Laud because of his failure to send reports on religious and political conditions. Dury was often in difficulties with the Dutch authorities because they believed that Laud had sent him to Holland for other purposes than the conduct of reunion negotiations (see *Calendar of State Papers, Domestic Series, 1635–1636*, pp. 167, 168).

without abatement, although Frederick Henry had reversed the policy of religious persecution which had characterized the reign of Maurice and had adopted a policy of toleration. Political strife between the republican and monarchistic factions intensified the disputes about religious affairs.[5] Moreover, the Dutch regarded Dury with distrust because England had recently joined Spain in an alliance against France and Holland.

Despite these handicaps Dury spent a year in Holland. He began his union activity by visiting the synods of North Holland, South Holland, Zealand, Leyden, and Utrecht in an effort to persuade the leaders of the Dutch Church to indorse his union program.[6] He met with little success. In most cases the synods declared that the consideration of proposals in the interest of the peace of the churches "belonged not to them but to the National Church."[7] Dury believed that his failure to secure the indorsements of the synods was due, in large measure, to the influence of "Dr. [Jan] Bogermannus, who presided at the Synod of Dort and still exercises (though in secret) the authority of a perpetual dictator, [and he] has put this answer in the mouths of the synods of North and South Holland, according to which all the rest will conform their resolutions."[8] Only the Walloon Synod was willing to give a cordial indorsement of his union program.[9]

Dury next attempted to secure the support of the Dutch political authorities. He had hoped that his plans would be "much furthered" by the Prince of Orange, but he soon discovered that Frederick Henry was too busy with military affairs to concern himself with the problem of the union of the churches.[10] Dury informed Roe that "his next course is to deal with the states to obtain their recommendation of the matter, either to some choice divines or to the universities, and this last is likely to be obtained, although Dr. Bogermannus will

[5] F. H. Brandes, "John Dury and His Work for Germany," *Catholic Presbyterian Review*, VIII, 91.

[6] For Dury's accounts of his visits to the Dutch synods see *Calendar of State Papers, Domestic Series, 1635*, pp. 265, 337, 338, 345, 395. Resolutions regarding Dury's proposals which were passed by the Dutch synods are quoted by W. P. C. Knuttel, *Acta der particuliere Synoden van Zuid-Holland*, II, 56, 69, 70, 87, 88.

[7] Dury to Roe, August 17, 1635 (*Calendar of State Papers, Domestic Series, 1635*, pp. 337, 338); cf. also J. Lindeboom, "Johannes Duraeus en zijne werkzaamheid in dienst van Cromwell's politiek," *Nederlandsch Archief voor Kerkgeschiedenis*, N.S., XVI, 259.

[8] Dury to Roe, August 20, 1635 (*Calendar of State Papers, Domestic Series, 1635*, pp. 344, 345).

[9] "Dury, Calixtus, and the Peacemakers," *Christian Intelligencer*, XXIX, 21.

[10] See *Calendar of State Papers, Domestic Series, 1635*, pp. 337, 338.

labour against it."[11] Making his headquarters at Amsterdam during the winter of 1635–36, he made numerous trips to the different states and universities, but he was unable to secure a favorable hearing. In the intervals between these trips he spent much time in literary work. Many of the books and pamphlets which he published in later years were planned and written in part during his stay in Holland.[12]

Dury was poverty stricken at this time. He informed Roe that his finances were in a "terrible state" and added that "if no other help may be had he purposes to contract his fardells, selling some of his books and hopes that the rent of his living will furnish him with clothes and so much as will pay the postage of his letters."[13] However, he expressed the determination that "he will not leave off as soon as outward supports seem to fail, but as at first he spent all his own when he ventured upon the attempt, so before he leaves off he cares not although he becomes as bare as when he first came with staff from Cologne after he had served the French Church in secret."[14] Just at the time he was most in need of money an opportune gift from Elizabeth, Queen of Bohemia, furnished him with sufficient funds to meet his expenses during the winter in Holland.[15]

But Dury's troubles did not end with this temporary solution of his financial problems. He had incurred the marked displeasure of Laud during his residence in Holland. It seems evident that Laud sought petty means of annoying Dury. Thus, in December, 1635, Dury informed Roe that the Archbishop had reported him to the English ambassador, Sir William Boswell, because he had preached at Amsterdam. Dury observed that he was like "a grain of corn bruised between two millstones, and oppressed in those parts [Holland] because he came last from England, and in England because he is silent. But he is not at all troubled. His cause in Germany will gain more by this opposition."[16]

But Laud had what he regarded as a far more serious charge against Dury. Under orders from the Archbishop, the study of the Puritan divine, John White of Dorchester, had been searched.[17] The officers who conducted the search found letters addressed to

---

[11] *Ibid.*, pp. 344, 345.

[12] *Ibid.*, p. 535.   [13] *Ibid.*, p. 539.

[14] Dury to Roe, November 23, 1635 (*ibid.*, p. 500).

[15] *Ibid.*, p. 460.

[16] *Ibid.*, p. 605.

[17] *Ibid.*, pp. 435, 459, 506; cf. also *Calendar . . . . , 1636–1637*, p. 545.

Dury by White and also papers which indicated that White had recommended to Lady Barnardiston that she should provide in her will
for a legacy which could be used in the advancement of Dury's project for the union of the churches.[18] When Dury learned that these papers were in the hands of Laud, he sent Roe a letter in which he defended himself and revealed something of his breadth of view, his indifference to party spirit, and his eagerness to secure the co-operation of men of the most varied party affiliations in forwarding the
cause to which he had devoted his life. The contents of this letter are
summarized in the *Calendar of State Papers* as follows:

> Dury imagines the Archbishop will be offended at his intimacy with such men as
> if he had not dealt faithfully with him, he would say that from the beginning he has
> haunted all sorts of men, and chiefly those who seemed most partial in their courses,
> laboring to gain them to his purpose; neither did he take notice of their particular
> humours, which he hoped might be swallowed up in thoughts of peace.[19]

It was useless for Dury to seek further help from the Archbishop.
Laud's ecclesiastical policies in England tended to nullify his peace
negotiations in Holland. The Dutch were displeased by news of the
High Church innovations in England. Dury reported to Roe that
"odious tales are spreading concerning the defection of the Church of
England, and the State and Church of Holland are jealous of an intention to work the ceremonies of England upon them. They are exceeding shy to concur in anything wherein England seems to have a
hand."[20] Dury's hopes for a Protestant "political alliance supported
by the King of England to second the Prince Elector in the recovery
of his Palatinate" were likewise doomed to disappointment, as
Charles I was again negotiating with Spain regarding a plan for the
partition of Holland between England and Spain.[21] After the Dutch
learned of these negotiations, it was impossible for Dury to make further advances in his work in Holland. Dury concluded that he had
thus far depended too much upon political agencies and resolved to
rely more upon spiritual means for the advancement of his cause.
One of his letters to Roe, written during the latter part of his stay in
Holland, is summarized in the *Calendar of State Papers* as follows:

> So long as they trust in the arm of the flesh he doubts their prosperity, not that
> they ought to neglect means, but he fears that they trust too much in them. . . . . He

[18] *Calendar* . . . . , *1636–1637*, p. 545. Lady Barnardiston made a gift of £150 to Dury.

[19] *Domestic Series, 1635*, p. 500.

[20] *Calendar* . . . . , *Domestic Series, 1635–1636*, p. 142.

[21] On this plan of Charles I for the partition of Holland by England and Spain see G. M.
Trevelyan, *England under the Stuarts*, pp. 162, 163.

hopes to come to an end with his adversaries in that country [Holland] by printing certain papers explaining his real objects, which he purposes to distribute in every consistory. He hopes thus quietly to put his enemies to shame. The more he enters into the spiritual way and presses things belonging to conscience, the more he shall perhaps be left by men, and yet advance the business more than any other way.[22]

Dury now sought a new field of labor where there would be more chance of success in union activity. He was especially interested in renewing his negotiations in Germany in order to conserve the progress already made in that quarter.[23] But friends in Germany warned him that it would be well for him to delay his visit to Germany until conditions were more favorable for the success of his mission.[24] While he was attending a meeting of the Synod of the French churches at Utrecht, he received an invitation to come to Sweden.[25] This invitation, which prepared the way for a new series of union negotiations, came from John Matthiae, who assured Dury that the time was opportune for union activity in Sweden.[26] As the Swedish Church was in process of reorganization, Dury believed that he could persuade the leaders to indorse his irenic program as an enterprise worthy of the support of the reorganized church.

The English authorities were now interested in forming a closer political alliance with Sweden. John Berkeley, a kinsman of Sir Thomas Roe, had been sent to Sweden to negotiate an alliance which would commit England and Sweden to a policy of co-operation in securing the recovery of the Palatinate for the son of Elizabeth of Bohemia. Roe thought that Dury should undertake the mission to Sweden at once in order that the project for the union of the Protestant churches might be considered while the proposed political alliance was under discussion.[27] Dury was also urged to come to Sweden by Lewis de Geer, who was deeply interested in his irenic program.[28] It is probable that De Geer gave Dury financial support during his stay in Sweden, as his complaints about his failure to secure support

[22] *Domestic Series, 1635–1636*, pp. 207, 249.

[23] See *Calendar . . . . , 1635*, pp. 538, 539.

[24] *Ibid.*, pp. 419, 420.

[25] Historical Manuscripts Commission, *Report IV*, Part I, p. 160.

[26] Brandes, *op. cit.*, p. 91.

[27] John Wordsworth, *The National Church of Sweden*, p. 289; and *Calendar of State Papers, Domestic Series, 1636–1637*, pp. 292, 293.

[28] See J. Kvačala, *Korrespondence Jana Amosa Komenského*, p. 9.

are less frequent in the letters which he wrote during his residence in that country.[29]

Dury was also encouraged to undertake the work in Sweden by Hugo Grotius, who was then serving as the Swedish ambassador at Paris.[30] Since the meeting of the Frankfort Convention, Grotius had manifested a genuine interest in Dury's union program. He had repeatedly recommended the Scottish peacemaker to men who were in position to advance his cause.[31] Masson believed that Dury was responsible for Grotius' interest in the union movement, and he discovered evidence which indicates that Grotius, while serving as Swedish ambassador at Paris, had made ineffectual attempts to persuade Laud to give more hearty support to Dury.[32] He advised Dury to emphasize the necessity of preparing a confession of faith which would be acceptable to the Protestants of England and Sweden. Acceptance of a common confession of faith by the Churches of England and Sweden, he argued, could now be secured more readily as the two nations were moving toward a closer political alliance. If England and Sweden could agree upon a common confession of faith, Denmark and Norway could easily be persuaded to accept this confession, and it would ultimately be adopted by all those countries which had accepted the Reformation.[33] Grotius promised Dury that he would make persistent efforts to persuade Oxenstierna to give effective support to the reunion movement.[34]

[29] Lewis de Geer, a Dutchman, had settled in Sweden, where he had become wealthy through profits from munitions trade and the operation of mining concessions. As a former friend of Gustavus Adolphus, he was influential in political circles. He was noted for his philanthropic interests. He also provided financial support for Comenius during the latter's stay in Sweden (see Matthew Spinka, *John Amos Comenius, That Incomparable Moravian*, pp. 90 ff.; and W. S. Munroe, *Comenius and the Beginnings of Educational Reform*, pp. 57 ff.; cf. also S. S. Laurie, *John Amos Comenius*, pp. 41–45).

[30] F. Sander, "Comenius, Duraeus, Figulus nach Stammbüchern der Familie Figulus-Jablonski," *Monatshefte der Comenius Gesellschaft*, III, 312, 313.

[31] See M. Tabaraud, *De la réunion des communions chrétiennes*, pp. 70, 71, 301–4, 316–21.

[32] David Masson (*Life of Milton*, II, 368) states that "by the year 1637 he [Durie] had access to the great Grotius, and had . . . . innoculated him with the idea. . . . . Grotius was then in earnest communication on the subject with Lord Scudamore, the English ambassador at Paris. Though Durie was not named in the account of the correspondence between Grotius and Laud, my authority for the account (Gibson's *Parochial History of Door*, etc., 1727) contains ample proof that Durie was in the background all the while, inspiring Grotius, and what Grotius urged upon Laud and Laud thought visionary nonsense, was but a Grotian modification of Durie's idea."

[33] Grotius, *Hugonis Grotii . . . . epistolae quotquot reperiri potuerunt*, Ep. 866, p. 380.

[34] *Ibid.*, Ep. 821, pp. 357, 358. Grotius to Dury, September 11, 1637: "Ego ut antehac feci ita nunc quoque Magno D. Cancellario, tuam pietatem, tuam eruditionem, tuique animi in hoc proprio purum et sincerum studium commendare non desinam, successum ardenter optabo, et quid quantumque promoveris quoque tempore gaudebo cognoscere."

When Dury left Holland for Sweden, he was accompanied by Peter Figulus, a ward of John Amos Comenius.[35] For seven years, 1636–43, Figulus was associated with Dury as traveling companion and amanuensis. During these years Figulus kept a Stammbuch which furnishes materials that are most useful in efforts to trace the travels and labors of Dury. The entries also furnish imposing lists of persons from all walks of life who were interviewed by Dury in the course of his varied negotiations.[36] The fact that Comenius intrusted his ward to Dury's care is indicative of a close friendship between Dury and Comenius at this time. Comenius, as bishop of the Moravian Brethren, was in thorough sympathy with the irenic attitude of the Brethren, who held that only the fundamental doctrines of the Christian faith should be stressed; that emphasis should be placed upon Christian life rather than upon dogma; and that the major Protestant bodies should make formal recognition of their essential unity.[37] As a pioneer in the work of educational reform Comenius was drafting plans for new developments of far-reaching importance in the field of educational method. By connecting and co-ordinating his irenic and educational interests in a unified program, he was able to make a distinctive contribution in the field of irenics as well as in the field of education.[38]

Comenius adopted the theory that efforts to promote unity in knowledge would also promote unity in faith. Spinka says:

He hoped to bring about an organic unity in culture and religion, both in spirit and in organization. The religious instruction which he proposed to be taught to children was purely Biblical, i.e., nonconfessional. It was to consist of the general truths of Christianity without confessional interpretation. By training children from infancy in the same system of religious ideas and ideals, gradually the conflicting confessional interpretations would cease to divide Christendom, and unity would be thus obtained.[39]

[35] Matthew Spinka ("John Dury, The Peacemaker," *Christian Union Quarterly*, XIII, 377) states that "Peter Figulus later married Comenius' daughter, Elizabeth. Their renowned son, Daniel Ernest Jablonski, became a Berlin court preacher. It was through him that the present day Moravian Church derived its Episcopal ordination, for he had consecrated Count Zinzendorf in the episcopal succession of the Unitas Fratrum."

[36] For an account of Figulus and a summary of the Dury material contained in his Stammbuch see Sander, *op. cit.*, pp. 310–26.

[37] Matthew Spinka, "The Irenic Program and Activity of John Amos Comenius" (typed Ph.D. diss., University of Chicago, 1923), p. 13.

[38] Munroe (*op. cit.*, p. 172) says of Comenius: "As a philosopher and divine, in union with Andreae, Dury, Milton and others, he devoted his life to a work of peace. He placed the weal of man, as he termed it, above the respect for languages, persons and sects; thus his energies were directed toward restraining wrangling people, churches and classes from the violent utterance of their differences, and leading them on the ground of the early Christian views to mutual peace and forbearance."

[39] "The Irenic Program and Activity of John Amos Comenius," pp. 37, 38.

Dury was indebted to Comenius for this idea of the possible combination of irenic and educational effort. Throughout the remainder of his life educational reform had a prominent place in his interests. He attempted, through the agency of his friend Hartlib, to arouse the interest of English educational leaders in the program of educational reform sponsored by Comenius.[40] He centered his own efforts upon the advocacy of educational reform whenever he found it impossible to make progress in more direct union negotiations.[41] On the other hand, Dury's plans for establishing the peace of the churches and promoting Christian reunion received the hearty indorsement of Comenius. When Dury appealed to the Unitas Fratrum Bohemicorum, then in exile in Poland, for an indorsement of his union program, Comenius used his influence to secure an expression of cordial approval. The Synod of Thorn, in July, 1636, approved resolutions which promised co-operation to Dury, requested that prayers be made in all the churches for the success of his enterprise, and appealed to all princes to give their assistance to the union program.[42]

Dury and Figulus arrived in Sweden early in June, 1636. Matthiae had prepared the way for a favorable reception by his frequent appeals to the Swedes to favor Dury's program.[43] Dury's reception was most cordial, and he was convinced that his mission would be successful.[44] On July 19 he informed Laud that "he had begun action in Sweden, having made some acquaintance amongst the clergy and administrators of state, and having received some countenance from

---

[40] See Friedrich Althaus, "Samuel Hartlib, ein deutsch-englisches Charakterbild," *Historisches Taschenbuch*, pp. 206 ff.; Spinka, *John Amos Comenius, That Incomparable Moravian*, pp. 62 ff., 72 ff.; R. F. Young, *Comenius in England*, pp. 5 ff.; and Munroe, *op. cit.*, pp. 51–54 and *passim*.

[41] In 1636, before examining several of the more important writings of Comenius, Dury wrote to Hartlib from Stockholm as follows: "I cannot give you satisfaction upon . . . . the papers which you have sent me of Comenius and the bookes. I cannot spend my judgment because of my distractions and weakness. . . . . I will set a month apart to digest all Pansophicall and Pedagogicall notions and give you my thoughts upon them" (Kvačala, *op. cit.*, p. 12). In 1637, after studying the writings of Comenius and after meeting with considerable opposition during the course of his negotiations in Sweden, Dury again wrote Hartlib from Stockholm as follows: "I have a mind to retire myself to a settled way of writing and meditation to elaborate my own and some of Mr. Comen. Pansophicall taskes as God shall enable me" (*ibid.*, p. 14).

[42] Sander, *op. cit.*, p. 312. The text of the resolutions of the Synod of Thorn is presented by D. E. Jablonski, *Historia Consensus Sendomiriensis*, pp. 128–30.

[43] Brandes, *op. cit.*, p. 92.

[44] On Dury's reception in Sweden and the favorable prospects for the success of his negotiations see Wordsworth, *op. cit.*, pp. 296 ff.; F. H. Brandes, *Geschichte der evangelischen Union in Preussen*, I, 287 ff.; and C. W. Hering, *Geschichte der kirchlichen Unionsversuche seit der Reformation bis auf unsere Zeit*, II, 106 ff.

Oxenstierna."[45] On November 12, 1636, he wrote Laud from Stockholm, assuring him that "the negotiation with the Swedish clergy had been more successful than ever he had expected. There is a general resolve to form a 'fundamental confession.' Expects still further progress if there should be a meeting of the states of the kingdom this winter. Meanwhile there is a general softening of feeling, and some have preached in favor of unity."[46]

Dury was in Sweden from July, 1636, to August, 1638. For slightly more than two years his efforts were directed toward four well-defined objectives: first, he sought to win the indorsement and active support of Oxenstierna in behalf of his union program; second, he attempted to persuade the Swedish leaders who were planning the reorganization of the Swedish Church to adopt a type of polity which would bring that church into closer conformity to the Church of England; third, he conducted a constant succession of conferences with Swedish clergymen and statesmen in an effort to win their support; and, fourth, he labored to secure the co-operation of Swedish theologians in the preparation of a common confession of faith.

Oxenstierna had returned to Sweden in 1636. During the years 1636–44 he was in complete control of the foreign and domestic policies and exercised practically all the powers of kingship. Dury renewed his attempts to secure the support of the Chancellor, but political considerations once more made it difficult for Oxenstierna to support the union program in an effective manner, although he continued to profess a genuine interest in the realization of the program. In 1634 the Chancellor had provided the Swedish nation with a Form of Government. The Preamble to this new constitution attributed the past difficulties of the nation to disputed succession, the lack of a well-organized government, and religious disunion. The constitutional provisions of the Form of Government provided a safeguard against the evils of disputed successions and furnished a plan for a well-organized central government. At the time of Dury's arrival the Chancellor was interested in improving religious conditions by drafting a new type of organization for the Swedish Church.

The chief feature of Oxenstierna's plan for the reorganization of the Swedish Church was his scheme to centralize its administration by the establishment of a General Consistory Court. His plan involved the formation of a Consistorium generale, which was to be intrusted with power to act as a court of appeal in all ecclesiastical

[45] Historical Manuscripts Commission, *Report IV*, Part I, p. 160.　　[46] *Ibid.*, p. 161.

matters and with the oversight of the educational system of the nation, as well as the worship, doctrine, and discipline of the church. Gustavus Adolphus had hoped for the establishment of such a system, but he had found no opportunity to reorganize the church.[47] Oxenstierna, realizing that the defeat at Nördlingen and the later reverses which the Swedish armies had suffered in Germany had brought him to the verge of ruin, was extremely careful to avoid unnecessary opposition on the part of the Swedish clergy, who might be in position to secure his overthrow in a political crisis.

The Chancellor was, therefore, cautious in his advocacy of Dury's union plans. He was insistent that Dury should be given a hearing and that he should have ample opportunity to plead his cause, but he steadfastly refused to give the union program his official and public indorsement lest he should arouse the opposition of the Swedish clergy.[48] The Chancellor allowed Dury to travel with him from place to place; invited him to his home; furnished him with letters of introduction to bishops, clergymen, and statesmen; and, when Dury's proposals encountered opposition, he attempted to restrain the bitter attacks of his opponents.[49] Knowing Laud's unwillingness to give effective support to Dury, the Chancellor finally took the position that he could not publicly indorse Dury's project until it had been officially indorsed by the English authorities.[50]

One of Dury's efforts to win the favor of Oxenstierna has escaped the notice of all his biographers. He knew that Oxenstierna was preparing plans for the reorganization of the Swedish Church and that he wished to embody in these plans legislation which would centralize the control of the church in the hands of a Consistorium generale. Dury urged the Chancellor to reorganize the Swedish Church after

[47] Wordsworth, *op. cit.*, pp. 283–86.

[48] Brandes, *Evangelischen Union in Preussen*, I, 287.

[49] The attitude of Oxenstierna toward Dury is clearly reflected in the summary of the Dury-Laud correspondence (Historical Manuscripts Commission, *Report IV*, Part I, pp. 160 ff.). Dury to Laud, November 26, 1636: "[The Chancellor] is well affected but exceeding wary; as good reason he should be in a matter of such importance and so ticklish to be meddled with in the Church." Dury to Laud, September 9, 1637: "Hopes the Chancellor will interfere. He is slow in all things, but I fear in this he will be too slack for as the clergy doth stand in awe of him, so he of them, and perhaps more than they of him. The opposition of the bishop of Westerose has upset the Chancellor's plans in Dury's favor." Dury to Laud, December 9, 1637: "With regard to his own business of pacification the Chancellor said he would try to restrain the boisterousness of the Bishop of Westerose" (cf. "Dury, Calixtus, and the Peacemakers," p. 93).

[50] Historical Manuscripts Commission, *Report IV*, Part I, p. 161. Dury to Laud, April 14, 1637: "[The Chancellor] is willing to take up the matter of pacification publicly with the countenance of England."

the model of the Church of England and to provide for centralization and state control by erecting a new court modeled after the English Court of High Commission. In making this suggestion he was motivated by the idea that the establishment of closer conformity in government between the two churches would increase the chances for the favorable outcome of his union activities.

On July 19, 1636, shortly after Dury arrived in Sweden, he informed Laud that "many changes are intended in Sweden; some provincial courts will be erected; an ecclesiastical court is thought of, for which he has suggested the English Court of High Commission as a model."[51] On November 26, 1636, Dury again wrote to Laud, urging him to send "authentic information respecting the High Commission Court."[52] Sir Thomas Roe sent letters to both Laud and Oxenstierna, pleading for their co-operation in this proposed plan to secure conformity between the church governments of the two realms.[53] Oxenstierna was interested in Dury's suggestion and attempted to use some of the materials furnished by Dury when he was drafting his plans for the reorganization of the Swedish Church.[54] But the Chancellor failed to put his new plans into operation. "The Swedish clergy," as Reddaway says, "defeated an attempt of the state to reduce the church to order by the establishment of a General Consistory Court."[55] The High Commission Court was responsible at the time for much of the rising discontent against the Laudian regime in England. The fact that Dury was willing to suggest the introduction of the Court of High Commission into Sweden is indicative of his attitude of utter indifference toward forms of church government and administration, provided the cause of union could be advanced by proposed changes in organization.

In addition to the conduct of these negotiations with Oxenstierna,

[51] Historical Manuscripts Commission, *Report IV*, Part I, p. 160.

[52] *Ibid.*, p. 161.

[53] On January 21, 1637, Roe informed Laud that Dury was hoping the Archbishop would soon fulfil his promise "that he would assist to build up the government and discipline of that Church [the Church of Sweden] by communicating a pattern of this, which will be very acceptable to them and, he thinks, to the Church of England, and a strong bond of that unity they seek." Five days later Roe informed Oxenstierna that Laud would "send by the next occasion a model of our government ecclesiastical, in which a conformity will give great strength to both kingdoms" (see *Calendar of State Papers, Domestic Series, 1636–1637*, pp. 378, 392).

[54] Dury to Laud, May 6, 1637: "The Chancellor and the senior professor of Upsal are very anxious to see copies of the English Ecclesiastical Courts with a view to reforms in Sweden." Dury to Laud, July 29, 1637: "The short draft respecting the English Ecclesiastical Court has met with favor" (see Historical Manuscripts Commission, *Report IV*, Part I, p. 161).

[55] *Cambridge Modern History*, IV, 570.

Dury attempted to enlist further interest in his union program by means of conferences with outstanding leaders of church and state in Sweden. Shortly after his arrival he held a number of interviews with clergymen at Stockholm. The friendly offices of Matthiae gained him ready access to the Swedish leaders.[56] At Stockholm he met Jacob Zebracynthicus, a court preacher and pastor of the most important church in the city.[57] Here he also interviewed Laurentius Paulinus, who shortly afterward received appointment as the archbishop of the Swedish Church. This kindhearted preacher expressed a favorable judgment of Dury's program.[58] He also provided Dury with a letter of introduction to the theological faculty of the University of Uppsala. In this letter he expressed the hope that Dury would succeed in his union efforts and indicated his willingness to act as Dury's patron.[59]

After a series of conferences with the clergy of Stockholm, Dury made an extended tour of Sweden for the purpose of holding conferences with church leaders throughout the kingdom. By October 12, 1636, he was able to inform Laud that "he has had good success in three of the chief episcopal sees, Upsal, Westerose, and Strengnas; to keep up interest has sent them two treatises, one concerning points fundamental in religion, the other on means of advancing the work."[60] After a visit to Oxenstierna at his home in Tido, Westmanland, he went to Uppsala, where he spent considerable time in discussions with the members of the theological faculty of the University of Uppsala.[61] His negotiations with this group form one of the

---

[56] John Matthiae was Dury's closest friend and most consistent supporter among the Swedish clergy. Later, as bishop of Strengnas, he continued to advocate the cause of Christian reunion. Toward the close of his career he was persecuted because of his irenic activity. Tabaraud (*op. cit.*, p. 305) says: "Duraeus avoit inspiré ses sentimens à Jean Matthiae, Chaplain de Gustave-Adolphe, précepteur de la reine Christine, et évêque de Strengnes en Suede. Ce théologien les exposa dans un ouvrage intitule: *Ramus olivae septentrionalis*. La publication de ce livre devint funeste à son auteur. Il eut doleur de le voir supprimé par un acte de l'autorite royale; ayant été lui-meme déposé de son siège par les Etats de 1664, il fut constraint d'aller le reste de ses jours dans la retraite, où ses ennemis le laissèrent enfin tranquille."

[57] Brandes, *Evangelischen Union in Preussen*, I, 287.

[58] Brandes, "John Dury and His Work for Germany," p. 92.

[59] Hering, *op. cit.*, II, 110, 111.

[60] Historical Manuscripts Commission, *Report IV*, Part I, p. 161; cf. also Hering, *op. cit.*, II, 110, 111. It is evident that Dury often regarded general expressions of interest in Christian unity as specific indorsements of his own plans for securing the reunion of the churches. Bishop John Rudbeck of Westeras, whose support Dury thought he had gained on this visit, later became a most pronounced opponent of his union plans.

[61] Wordsworth, *op. cit.*, pp. 296 ff.

most important phases of his work in Sweden and gave direction to much of his later union activity. The professors at Uppsala gave Dury a cordial personal welcome but presented him with a reply to his union proposals which was strikingly like the replies which he had already received from the Lutheran theologians of Jena and Leipzig. They indicated their unwillingness to form a union with the Reformed churches unless those churches should become Lutheran; expressed their judgment that Dury's proposals were impractical; and pointed out the fact that there was no competent authority to decide the issues on which the churches differed.[62]

Not content with this rebuff, Dury persistently appealed to the Uppsala professors to "set down the conditions upon which they were ready to agree, and joyn with the reformed side." Finally they yielded and presented a list of these conditions which Dury quotes in his *Briefe Relation* as follows:

1. That a full agreement should be made on all the fundamentall articles of faith.
2. That all errors overthrowing the foundations, or tending to overthrow the same, should be condemned.
3. That in matters Ceremoniall and of indifferency, there should be mutuall toleration.
4. That betwixt the parties united sincerity and uprightnesse should be maintained, lest ancient errors might be upheld under doubtful speeches.
5. That when peace is made, none should be suffered to maintain, excuse, or spread any more of the errors once condemned.
6. That ambitious and needlesse disputes and bablings should be inhibited on all sides.
7. That former reproaches and injuries should be put in oblivion.
8. That the Church-government should be setled according to Apostolicall Rules.[63]

Though the list was obviously drafted with the idea of obstructing union based on mutual concessions, the ever optimistic Dury indicated his willingness to accept these principles as a basis for negotiations. He drew up and presented to the Uppsala professors a paper in which he gave his interpretation of the meaning of these conditions.[64] He was especially interested in the suggestion that there should be a full consensus on all fundamental articles of faith. He invited the Uppsala faculty to co-operate in the formation of a common

[62] Hering, *op. cit.*, II, 107. In 1641 Dury published an account of his negotiations with the Uppsala professors under the title, *Consultatio theologica super negotio pacis ecclesiasticae promovendo, exhibita, submissaque judicio Rev. Facult. theologicae in Academia Regia Upsaliensi.*

[63] P. 17.

[64] See Brauer, *op. cit.*, pp. 225, 226.

profession of faith and submitted a paper, in which he discussed the problem of determining what should be regarded as the fundamental articles of faith that should be accepted by all.[65] In this paper he took the position, as suggested by the Aberdeen Doctors, that the consensus should be limited to "those heads of Christian doctrine which are necessary to be known and believed by all the faithful for obtaining eternal salvation, and without which no one could be saved."[66] He thought the new confession of faith should put emphasis upon practical Christian truths which would promote Christian living and fellowship instead of requiring intellectual assent to metaphysical theories of the schoolmen. Equal emphasis should be placed on faith and duty in this new consensus.

On January 24, 1637, Dury wrote a letter to Lord Forbes, in which he announced his intention of making the preparation of a common confession of faith the immediate objective of his union negotiations. In this letter he said:

One position is laid as the ground-worke of all this negotiation, which is that the onely Meanes to reunite devided Protestants, and knit their Churches together in a bond of brotherly love, is to bring them to make a publick profession of one and the same Confession of Faith in respect to Fundamentalls. For I find it to be agreed upon, and yielded on all sides, that if the Fundamentall Truthes of Faith and Practice be acknowledged and professed by two Churches, that those Churches ought for this cause to profess sisterly love one towards another, and they ought not for some differences in things not fundamentall, to break the unitie of the spirit through unprofitable debatements. . . . .

For I know that the Communion of the Saints (Beleeved in in the creed verbally by many, but practised in effect by very few) amongst men that have a special care to deny themselves as well in spirituall as in temporall things of a present nature, is the only Instrument which God doth make use of to builde up his Church.[67]

Dury thought that the new confession of faith should be derived from the Bible, the ecumenical symbols, and the catechisms. In treating with the Uppsala theologians he expressed a willingness to use the Augustana as the basis for the new creed.[68] Brandes states

[65] Hering, op. cit., II, 107, 108.

[66] On Dury's use of the statement of the Aberdeen Doctors during his mission to Sweden see D. Macmillan, The Aberdeen Doctors, pp. 168, 170.

[67] Dury, A Copy of John Duries Letter Presented in Sweden to the truly Noble and Religious Lord Forbes, pp. 2, 7, 8.

[68] See Brauer, op. cit., p. 225. Dury's idea of the best method of procedure in preparing a common confession of faith was somewhat different from that suggested by Calixtus, who took the position that the Christian churches should unite in adopting the Apostles' Creed and the consensus of the first five centuries as the dogmatic norm (see the exposition of his views by H. Friedrich, Georg Calixtus, der Unionsmann des 17. Jahrhunderts). At this time Dury was primarily interested in preparing a new confession by harmonizing the teaching of the more important existing confessions. However, Dury and Calixtus were in complete agreement on the view that both faith and duty should be stressed in the common confession.

that "Dury was looking for a formula which would satisfy all the different theological parties, and could not be persuaded that such a formula was itself an impossibility. To satisfy everyone it must be as indefinite as possible."[69]

It is true that Dury wished to have the new confession "as indefinite as possible" in its treatment of many of the doctrines which were being debated in scholastic and theological circles, as he did not consider these doctrines as of primary importance. It is noteworthy that when, years later, he prepared a list of twenty doctrines which he thought should be incorporated in a common confession of faith because they were concerned with beliefs and practices which were essential to Christian life and salvation, he made no reference to the three doctrinal issues on which the Lutherans and Calvinists were unable to agree at the Leipzig Colloquy.[70] He held that a wide variety of opinion should be allowed on these doctrines and championed the idea that "it is the mind of Christ that his servants in all matters merely circumstantiall by him not determined, should be left free to follow their own light, as it may be offered, or arise unto them from the general rules of edification, and not constrained by an implicit faith to follow the dictates of other men."[71]

But the theological professors at Uppsala, adhering to the stricter type of Lutheranism, refused to co-operate with Dury in promoting the union movement.[72] Although courteous and considerate in their discussions with Dury, they declined to take part in the preparation of a new confession on the ground that such an effort would lead to unsafe compromises. They reasserted their opinion that Dury's proposals were impracticable and also dangerous because the adoption of a new confession, designed to place major emphasis upon Christian life rather than upon Christian teaching, would result in the detachment of ethics from dogmatics and a consequent effort to build up a system of Christian ethics without the necessary religious foundations.

After his failure to gain the support of the Uppsala professors, Dury renewed his attempts to enlist the support of the Swedish clergy. He was able, through the influence of Oxenstierna, to secure

[69] "John Dury and His Work for Germany," p. 30.

[70] See Dury's list of the fundamental articles of faith as quoted by Brauer, *op. cit.*, pp. 217–19.

[71] Dury, quoted by C. A. Briggs, "The Work of John Durie in Behalf of Christian Union in the Seventeenth Century," *Presbyterian Review*, VIII, 300.

[72] See Dury, *Briefe Relation*, pp. 18–20; Wordsworth, *op. cit.*, p. 296; Brandes, "John Dury and His Work for Germany," p. 92; and Hering, *op. cit.*, II, 108. Cf. the discussion of the characteristic features of Swedish Lutheranism by W. Elert, *Morphologie des Luthertums*, II, 224 ff.

a hearing before a synod of the clergy of the whole nation which was held at Stockholm on July 8, 1637. Dury's friend and patron, Laurentius Paulinus, now archbishop of the Swedish Church, presided at this synod. Here Dury's proposals met with vigorous criticism from the Swedish clergy.[73] His opponents questioned the willingness of the Reformed Churches to unite with the Lutherans. They held that union was possible only on condition that the Reformed should become Lutheran, just as Dury, formerly a Presbyterian, had now become an Anglican. Dury's proposal for the preparation of a common confession of faith was rejected by the synod. Approval was given to resolutions which denounced any union proposals that did not require the common acceptance of the "unvaried Augsburg Confession."[74]

In contrast to the kindly treatment which Dury had thus far received in Sweden, the synod subjected him to an extended examination regarding his views about the doctrines on which the Lutheran and Reformed Churches disagreed.[75] The leader of the opposition against Dury in the synod was John Rudbeck, Bishop of Westeras. Rudbeck had been the choice of the clergy for the position of archbishop, but the government had appointed Paulinus instead. The mass of the clergy promptly rallied to the support of Rudbeck in his attacks on Dury. Bitter personalities figured prominently in these attacks. Rudbeck gave public expression to his hatred of Dury as a "stranger confessing the cursed heresy of Calvinism."[76] Despite Oxenstierna's request that he should desist from personal attacks on Dury, Rudbeck continued his opposition throughout the remainder of Dury's stay in Sweden.[77]

Dury next attempted to interest the laity in his project, hoping that he could secure an indorsement of his union plans by the Riksdag. In this effort he was assisted by Hugo Grotius, who addressed

73 Hering, op. cit., II, 111 ff.; Wordsworth, op. cit., p. 297.

74 Brandes, "John Dury and His Work for Germany," p. 92.

75 Wordsworth, op. cit., pp. 297 ff. Dury gave an account of this synod in a letter to Laud, July 29, 1637. The summary of this letter in the Historical Manuscripts Commission, Report IV, Part I, p. 162, reads, in part, as follows: "The long expected meeting of divines has taken place, and his business, recommended by the regents, has been considered. By the wish of the meeting he was called and examined as if he had been a witness. . . . . In their report to the Lords regent they said they could not decide anything with him, as he avoided discussing particulars of doctrine, and came with no public authority."

76 See T. A. Fischer, The Scots in Germany, p. 179.

77 Brandes, Evangelischen Union in Preussen, I, 287.

letters to his friends in Sweden, urging them to aid Dury.[78] Dury was able to win the support of two of the state councillors, Smolch and Müller.[79] Encouraged by these influential laymen, he appealed to the Riksdag at Stockholm in 1638 for an indorsement of his program. But Rudbeck and the clerical estates secured a declaration from the Riksdag to the effect that it was opposed to any union with the Reformed Church so long as the Reformed theologians refused to abjure their errors; that it regarded the Augsburg Confession, the Apology, and the Formula of Concord as necessary doctrinal standards, which must be accepted by any church seeking union with the Swedish Church; and that it was the judgment of the Riksdag that Dury should be sent out of the kingdom.[80] Dury's work in Sweden was now at an end. Oxenstierna thought that it was necessary for him to yield to the demand of the Riksdag. A decree of banishment was issued against Dury and proclaimed in the name of Queen Christina on February 7, 1638.[81]

Despite the vote of censure by the Riksdag and the decree of banishment which followed, Dury did not leave Sweden until August, 1638. Oxenstierna granted him permission to stay until he could recover from a serious illness.[82] This illness was caused partly by climatic conditions, but it was due chiefly to overexertion during his mission in Sweden and to his anxiety and disappointment over the failure of his negotiations. Although disappointed, Dury continued steadfast in his conviction that he was called of God to negotiate in the interest of the reunion of the churches and that he would ultimately be successful in this work. During his illness he consecrated himself anew to the task and made a solemn vow to the effect that he would continue his union efforts until the end of his life.[83] When he had recovered and was preparing to leave Sweden, he sent a copy of

[78] A summary of these letters by Grotius is presented by Hering, op. cit., II, 113 ff.; see also Fischer, op. cit., pp. 307, 308.

[79] Brandes, Evangelischen Union in Preussen, I, 287, 288.

[80] Wordsworth, op. cit., p. 297.

[81] The author of the article, "Dury, Calixtus, and the Peacemakers," p. 22, states that the royal decree against Dury read, in part, as follows: "It is the pleasure of Queen Christina that John Dury, a British preacher, who has resided in this country for some months, not without great scandals to our ecclesiastics, should depart without any delay from this kingdom"(cf. also Hering, op. cit., II, 117).

[82] Wordsworth, op. cit., p. 298; and Sander, op. cit., p. 313.

[83] For the text of this vow see Dury, Irenicorum tractatuum prodromus, pp. 196–99.

this vow to Oxenstierna with the request that he should communicate it to the Swedish clergy as evidence of his determination to continue his advocacy of Christian reunion despite such opposition as he had encountered in Sweden.[84]

Leaving Sweden in August, 1638, Dury proceeded by way of Lübeck to Hamburg. Sir Thomas Roe was then at Hamburg, and Dury was anxious to secure his advice as to where he should next attempt to carry on his reunion negotiations.[85] Roe advised him to seek the support of the civil authorities and the clergy of Denmark. After a short stay in Hamburg, Dury went to Denmark. Through the influence of Sir Thomas Roe he was able to secure an audience with Christian IV.[86] The eccentric and visionary King of the Danes and his Chancellor, D. Reventlow, expressed themselves publicly as favoring Dury's union proposals.[87] It is probable that Christian IV, foreseeing the danger of an impending war with Sweden, thought that an indication of interest in Dury's union schemes might prove helpful toward gaining English support in the approaching struggle.[88] Although the King and his Chancellor expressed an interest in the project, the clergy of the church of Denmark were committed to the stricter type of Lutheran views, and they were unwilling to co-operate in reunion efforts. Dury presented memorials and papers to the University of Copenhagen and to other Danish Lutheran groups.[89]

In order to promote his negotiations with the Danish clergy he prepared and printed a treatise under the title *De omnipraesentia corporali manducatione*, in which he made such liberal concessions to Lutheran opinion on the Lord's Supper that Hartlib was compelled to defend him against attacks from Calvinists by citing the fact

[84] Hering, *op. cit.*, II, 117. For Dury's account of the last months of his stay in Sweden see his letter to Laud under date of June 21, 1639 (Historical Manuscripts Commission, *Report IV*, Part I, p. 162).

[85] Dury, *Briefe Relation*, pp. 22 ff.; Mrs. M. A. Everett Green, *Elizabeth, Queen of Bohemia*, pp. 341 ff.; and Kvačala, *op. cit.*, p. 15.

[86] "Dury, Calixtus, and the Peacemakers," p. 22.

[87] See Hering, *op. cit.*, II, 118. Dury to Roe: "I hear the King of Denmark talks publicly of my work, commending it, and declaring it to be a thing to be sought for . . . . he having urged his divines to more forwardness than they have yet shown. . . . . I find the inclination of Mons. Reventlow very real and perceive that if statesmen did not fear to offend their clergy by being too forward in this business, they would of their own accord press it more than they do" (*Calendar of State Papers, Domestic Series, 1640*, p. 510).

[88] *Calendar of State Papers, Domestic Series, 1640*, p. 510.

[89] These memorials and papers are presented by Dury in his *Irenicorum tractatuum prodromus*, pp. 116–89.

that Bucer, whose attitude had been approved by Calvin, had taken the same position as Dury.[90] Until the close of the year 1640, Dury was busily engaged in visiting and interviewing church leaders in Denmark. But the Danish clergy finally took the position that they would entertain no proposals for union negotiations with the Calvinists until the latter had made formal renunciation of all their errors.[91] When they announced that they had taken this extreme position, Dury almost lost patience. In a letter to Roe, dated October 20, 1640, he said: "As for the Danish and other Lutherans, I know they all seek their own end, but there is a possibility of proceeding with them to prevent the inconveniences which arise from the same, and to correct that stiffness wherewith they cleave to Luther and to their belly, which is the great idol of many more than the Lutherans."[92]

After the failure to win the support of the Danish clergy, Dury centered his efforts upon attempts to secure the indorsement of his project by the cities and principalities of North Germany. He had hoped that his program would meet with a favorable reception in Lübeck because Nikolaus Hunnius, the influential Lutheran superintendent in that city, had long concerned himself with the solution of the difficulties which hindered the union of the Lutheran and Reformed Churches and had issued several treatises on the subject of Christian reunion.[93] The methods which Dury used at Lübeck may be regarded as typical of his procedure in union negotiations in many of the cities of North Germany.[94]

Arriving in Lübeck on October 6, 1639, he gave notice to the Council of the purpose of his visit and asked that he be allowed a hearing before the clergy of the city. The Council and the ministers of the city heard Dury's explanation of his reunion program, and both groups seemed to be interested in his proposals. Dury sought to intensify this interest by circulating irenic literature and by holding personal conferences with influential clergymen. He was especially anxious to secure the support of Hunnius. An interview was arranged; but Hunnius, while expressing interest in the union of the

[90] See *Calendar of State Papers, Domestic Series, 1640*, pp. 568, 569.

[91] Sander, *op. cit.*, p. 317.

[92] *Calendar of State Papers, Domestic Series, 1640–1641*, p. 185.

[93] See H. Schmid, *Geschichte der synkretistischen Streitigkeiten in der Zeit des Georg Calixt*, pp. 321, 322.

[94] On Dury's activities at Lübeck see Ludwig Heller, *Nikolaus Hunnius: Sein Leben und Wirken*, pp. 121–34.

churches, took the position that Dury's schemes were impracticable at the time as there were too many hindrances in the way of the type of union which he proposed.

Hunnius soon began to take an active part in securing the rejection of Dury's plans by both the Council and the Ministerium of Lübeck. In public discussions he maintained that Dury's plans were impracticable; that the obstacles in the way of reunion were too great to be overcome; and that the situation at Lübeck was of such a nature that it would be well for the Lutherans of the city to suppress the Calvinistic churches instead of uniting with them on equal terms. He drew up a paper discussing the obstacles in the way of the union of the Lutheran and Reformed Churches. This paper was presented to the Council and Ministerium in 1641. It was adopted by both bodies as a suitable explanation of their unwillingness to undertake union negotiations.[95] After Hunnius took over the leadership of the opposition, Dury could make no further progress in his negotiations at Lübeck. Years later, when he attempted to renew union propaganda in this city, the Ministerium sent him a copy of Hunnius' paper, together with an exhortation designed to persuade him to relinquish his errors.[96]

When Dury began similar negotiations in Bremen he met with a favorable reception.[97] Bremen had been a storm center in the earlier struggles between the Lutheran and Reformed Churches. Since 1568 the Reformed party had dominated the situation and had retained possession of all the churches in the city with the exception of the cathedral, which remained under Lutheran control.[98] The people of Bremen, wearied by the strife of the churches which had continued for more than three-fourths of a century, showed a genuine interest in Dury's reunion proposals. The leaders of the Reformed Churches of the city requested Dury to make further efforts to secure the preparation of irenic literature by English authors. They hoped that this would serve to deepen interest in reunion projects and that the English Church would offer its services as mediator between the Lutheran and Reformed Churches. The request of the Bremen divines was

---

[95] This paper by Hunnius was printed at Lübeck in 1671 under the following title: *Ministerii ecclesiastici Lubecensis theologica consideratio interpositionis, seu pacificatoriae transactionis, inter religionem Lutheranam ex una, et Reformatam ex altera parte profitentes, abs D. Johanne Duraeo, ecclesiaste Britanno, his temporibus tentatae.* Heller (*op. cit.*, pp. 124–33) presents an outline of the contents of the treatise.

[96] Heller, *op. cit.*, pp. 125–27.

[97] Brauer, *op. cit.*, p. 4.

[98] J. H. Kurtz, *Church History*, II, 382.

forwarded to Hartlib, who secured additional statements regarding Christian reunion from Bishops Davenant and Hall and also a statement from Dr. Prideaux, a distinguished teacher of Cambridge University.[99]

When Dury received the letters and treatises of his English friends, he attempted to use them in an effort to persuade the Lutheran archbishop of Bremen and his chancellor to support the union project. Although he had secured the indorsement of the Reformed pastors, he could make little progress in his negotiations unless he could gain the help of the Archbishop, who then figured as an important secular prince. The Archbishop refused to use his influence to enlist the cooperation of the Lutherans in the reunion movement, but he indicated his own wish to live at peace with the Reformed party in Bremen.[100] This was all that Dury could accomplish during his stay in the city. "Thus I keep their minds in a fit temper," he said in a letter to Hartlib, "and this is all that I can now intend, only I have, when last at Bremen, given a small paper to the press, wherewith I purpose to take my leave of the public agitation of the work till a fitter time, or else lay a ground to set the work forward if it be not found unreasonable."[101]

Meanwhile, Dury had visited the territories of the Welfian princes of Brunswick-Lüneberg. The principality of Brunswick-Wolfenbüttel-Lüneberg had been divided in 1635. When Dury visited this section of Germany in 1639, Duke Augustus the Younger ruled in Brunswick-Wolfenbüttel, and his brother, Duke George, ruled in Lüneberg. These princes were interested in promoting the union of the churches. The irenic spirit, sponsored by Calixtus and his associates at Helmstadt, prevailed throughout their territories. In December, 1639, Dury visited Duke Augustus at Hildesheim and asked his co-operation. The Duke called a synod of divines in order that they might hear Dury's union proposals and express their views regarding his plans. This synod cordially indorsed his union project and furnished him with a declaration expressing their views on the subject.[102] Dury reported to Laud that he had met with "great success" in his negotiations in Brunswick. He also sent the Archbishop a copy of a

[99] Calendar of State Papers, Domestic Series, 1640–1641, p. 186.

[100] Ibid., pp. 185, 186.

[101] Ibid., p. 186.

[102] See Historical Manuscripts Commission, Report IV, Part I, p. 162.

letter of indorsement and introduction which Duke Augustus had given him for use on his visit to Duke George of Lüneberg.[103]

On this visit to Brunswick, Dury became personally acquainted with Calixtus. A conference, attended by Dury, Calixtus, and other Helmstadt theologians, was held in the palace of Duke Augustus at Hildesheim on December 5, 1639.[104] In this conference Calixtus and his associates pledged Dury their co-operation in his reunion program. Here the idea was stressed that union effort was necessary not only as a measure for advancing the Protestant cause against Romanism but also as a means of protecting the churches against Socinian errors, which were regarded as destructive of the very essence of the gospel. In view of the current dangers, differences about minor matters, unknown to the ancients, should not keep the Protestant churches apart.[105] Calixtus and his associates promised to seek support for Dury's union plans in the churches of neighboring principalities and in the Lutheran universities.[106]

Dury also received a cordial welcome from Duke George of Lüneberg, when he visited that prince at Zelle. The Lutheran divines of Lüneberg promptly followed the example of Calixtus and his associates by giving their indorsement to Dury's reunion proposals.[107] However, indorsements by followers of Calixtus were of little service to Dury in his efforts to win the support of other Lutheran princes and theologians, as Calixtus and his associates were generally regarded with suspicion by the strict Lutheran party. After the rise of the Syncretistic controversy, Dury found that the support of the Helmstadt theologians was in reality a hindrance rather than a help in his negotiations with the larger Lutheran groups.

After two years of such union negotiations in Denmark and North Germany, Dury was convinced that he had accomplished all that

[103] Dury to Laud, December 8, 1639 (Historical Manuscripts Commission, Report IV, Part I, p. 162). The summary of the letter reads, in part, as follows: "John Durye, an English priest, has come over with letters . . . . showing the desire for ecclesiastical union in England, Scotland and Ireland. He wants to find out whether the same feeling prevails in Germany. His plan is much to be praised if it might tend to pacification between Lutherans and Calvinists, and a general modification towards papists. The Duke has put Durye into communication with the divines [of Brunswick] who have given the adjoined 'declaration and contestation towards unity.' Prays the Duke to allow Durye a conference with his divines."

[104] E. L. T. Henke, Georg Calixtus und seine Zeit, II, 108 ff.

[105] For an account of this conference and a summary of its conclusions see F. U. Calixtus, Via ad pacem, pp. 97–100.

[106] Henke, op. cit., II, 109.

[107] "Dury, Calixtus, and the Peacemakers," p. 22.

could be done at the time by means of public negotiations. He was of the opinion that, under the circumstances, further progress could be made only by quiet attempts to prepare the minds of men for new advances in union effort when conditions should prove more favorable. He wished to settle at Hamburg and devote his time to the preparation of new materials for propaganda purposes. Lack of financial support was the chief obstacle in the way of this plan. In a letter to Roe, dated October 20, 1640, he said:

I confess that till the work be countenanced by authority it cannot be effected; but yet I uphold that neither policy nor power, the two legs of authority, can make it take effect without the preparation of the minds and method of working, which by spiritual policy and strength is able to conquer the souls of men, and bring them to yield willingly for conscience sake to the duties of righteousness in the profession of the gospel. . . . . I know God's work cannot be hastened before time. You may be confident that if I can but have meat, clothes and lodging without being in debt, and not want what is requisite for printing some things for distribution, that I shall be as contented as any man that hath ten thousand a year, then I will rid my hands fairly of the negotiations till God show a time more seasonable or send some countenance to the work.[108]

At Dury's request, Roe asked Laud to appoint Dury as chaplain to the English ambassador at Hamburg. When Laud refused this appointment, Dury decided to return to England. He made his way to Bremen, where he remained fourteen days and visited all the pastors in the city. From there he went to Oldenburg, where he had a long interview with the Lutheran superintendent.[109] He traveled through Hanover and spent some time at Emden. From Emden he passed through Holland, stopping for conferences with theologians of Groningen and Zealand. He arrived in London in August, 1641.[110]

[108] *Calendar of State Papers, Domestic Series, 1640–1641*, pp. 183, 185, 186.

[109] On Dury's itinerary from Bremen to London see "Dury, Calixtus, and the Peacemakers," p. 22.

[110] Many sketches of the life of Dury give 1640 as the date of his return to England. The entries in the Stammbuch of Figulus indicate clearly that he arrived at London in August, 1641 (see Sander, *op. cit.*, p. 34).

CHAPTER VI

"A PEACEMAKER WITHOUT PARTIALITY"

THUS far Dury had concerned himself chiefly with projects for the establishment of peace and unity among the churches of the Continent. Conditions in Britain now prompted him "to study for peace and unity at home."[1] The attempt of Charles I to impose the modified Anglican liturgy upon the Church of Scotland, in 1637, had caused a rebellion that ultimately necessitated the call of the Long Parliament, which was to voice the general reaction against both the civil and the religious policies of the King. The consequent bitter strife of parties caused Dury to center his attention upon affairs at home.

However, for years prior to his return, Dury had manifested increasing interest in the situation in England and Scotland. During the crisis occasioned by the introduction of the new liturgy into Scotland, he had expressed a desire to return to his native country in order that he might try to reconcile the contending parties. He decided against this plan when the Covenanters passed from a policy of protestation to acts of rebellion against the Crown.[2] On October 20, 1640, after receiving news that the Scottish army had invaded England, he wrote Sir Thomas Roe as follows: "As for the public distractions proceeding from my countrymen's coming into England, I can but deplore them and hope that the nearer matters draw to an extremity, the nearer we shall be able to change for the better."[3]

Dury believed that his proposed method of adjusting differences by conference and mediation would solve many of the problems which were dividing the English and Scottish churches and threatening disastrous civil war. At his suggestion the Swiss Protestant churches addressed letters to Archbishop Laud and the Scottish Presbyterians, offering their services as mediators. This offer occasioned an ex-

[1] Dury, *The Effect of Master Dury's Negotiations*, p. 4.

[2] Historical Manuscripts Commission, *Report IV*, Part I, p. 162. On June 21, 1639, Dury wrote Laud that "since coming to Hamburg he had been in doubt what steps to take next, being most of all perplexed by the insurrections in Scotland, which he would have attempted to have appeased had he means to pay for travelling, and if the insurrection, at first merely ecclesiastical, had not changed to political rebellion."

[3] *Calendar of State Papers, Domestic Series, 1640*, p. 510.

change of correspondence among Anglican, Scottish, and Swiss leaders regarding the issues involved.[4] Though the offer of mediation was not accepted, this correspondence established a precedent, which prompted the struggling parties in England and Scotland to make frequent efforts to justify their views and policies to the Continental Protestant churches.

Two years before Dury's return to England he had reached the conclusion that the most effective method of promoting a spirit of unity in England and Scotland would be the advocacy of the formation of a civil confederation among Protestants to offset the Roman Catholic alliance under the leadership of Austria. Interest in such a project would promote unity at home and develop co-operation with Protestants on the Continent. Such a confederation, he argued, could save the Protestant interest in Germany and secure the restoration of the Palatinate. The restoration of the Palatinate was an objective which appealed with equal force to the King, the High Church Anglicans, the Moderate Anglicans, the English Puritans, and the Scottish Presbyterians.

Dury's ideas on the proposed civil confederation of Protestants were developed in detail in a paper which he presented to Roe at Hamburg in 1639.[5] Protestantism must be saved, he states in this paper, by "joyning the Protestant states together in counsels and actions of peace and war tending to their mutual preservation."[6] Negotiations should be undertaken "to stirre up a necessary mutuall care, and to establish a conjunction of endeavors amongst all Protestants for the preservation of the liberties and rights civill, religious and Ecclesiasticall, of Protestants in Germany, lest the House of Austria lay for itself a foundation of an universall monarchy on their ruins."[7] But the civil confederation of Protestants is impossible unless peace can be established among the Protestant churches: "The ground of this position is clear from reason backed with experience, which hath taught us for the space of these hundred years by-past, that except the schisme Ecclesiastical and the causes thereof be taken out of the way, it will not be possible either to make a true and constant league or to confirm it when it is made."[8] He urged the English

---

[4] E. Bloesch, *Geschichte der schweizerisch-reformierten Kirchen*, I, 444, 445.

[5] This paper was printed at Cambridge in 1641 under the title *A Summary Discourse concerning the work of Peace Ecclesiasticall: How it may concurre with the aim of a civill confederation amongst Protestants.*

[6] *Ibid.*, p. 1.   [7] *Ibid.*, p. 8.   [8] *Ibid.*, p. 3.

leaders to champion the Protestant cause and aid in the effective promotion of the movement in behalf of the peace of the churches and the formation of a strong Protestant alliance—thus proposing to Charles I a type of foreign policy which was ultimately to be adopted under the Cromwellian regime.

In support of this idea Dury also prepared and published a pamphlet entitled, *Motives To Induce the Protestant Princes to Mind the Worke of Peace Ecclesiasticall* (London, 1641). Here Protestantism is represented as a house divided against itself.[9] In this condition it is powerless to oppose the Austrian schemes for its suppression. A united Protestantism would be sufficiently strong to secure the restoration of the Palatinate and guarantee the future security of German Protestantism.[10] Therefore, Protestant princes should make

the re-establishment and conservation of the reformed churches in Germany no less [than] a fundamental reason of state in all their conjoint or severall proceedings. . . . . And to doe this, there is none other way so likely, or so sure to doe good, or so safe without danger, or so lawful and laudable before God, as this is of procuring a reconcilement of differences in Religion, that the body and cares of all Protestants being made one and the same, their unitie may be their strength and their Religion may be their preservation.[11]

Thus, while occupied with his negotiations on the Continent, Dury attempted to bring his program for peace at home and for the support of the Protestant interest abroad to the attention of the leaders of all parties in England and Scotland. The appointment of his friend, Sir Thomas Roe, as a member of the privy council (June, 1640) encouraged the hope that his suggestions would be given favorable consideration by that body.[12] Letters asking the support of Moderate Anglicans in behalf of his program brought favorable responses from such leaders as Dr. Prideaux and Bishops Hall and Davenant.[13] By direct appeals Dury also sought to win support for his program from Alexander Henderson, the outstanding leader among the Scottish Covenanters.

The third of a series of letters addressed by Dury to Henderson is preserved.[14] In this letter Dury describes the dangers which were

<hr>

[9] *Motives To Induce Protestant Princes*, pp. 1 ff.

[10] *Ibid.*, p. 3.

[11] *Ibid.*, p. 5.

[12] *Calendar of State Papers, Domestic Series, 1640*, p. 464.   [13] *Ibid.*, p. 568.

[14] This letter was printed in 1643 under the title, *The Copy of a Letter Written to Mr. Alexander Hinderson*. David Masson (*Life of Milton*, III, 220) incorrectly ascribes this letter to Hartlib. Masson had seen only a part of the letter. The printed copy in the Library of Union Theological Seminary bears the autograph signature of Dury.

threatening German Protestantism; pleads for the establishment of peace at home in order that king and people might co-operate in an effort to secure the restoration of the Palatinate and the preservation of German Protestantism; discounts the current tendency to put undue stress upon minor matters of worship and church discipline; and suggests the immediate establishment of a "theological correspondency" between divines who are interested in the "work of reconcilement." Dury later asked Henderson to communicate his proposals to the General Assembly of the Church of Scotland.[15] Although Henderson was occupied with other affairs at the time, he was genuinely interested in the union of the churches, and it is probable that this correspondence with Dury intensified his interest in the cause of Christian reunion. A few years later he emerged as one of the most zealous advocates of a project for uniting the churches of England, Ireland, and Scotland into one church and stressed the idea that this united church should maintain close association and correspondence with the Protestant churches of the Continent. However, Henderson differed from Dury in that he insisted upon the general acceptance of the Presbyterian type of church organization as the necessary basis for the union of the churches.[16]

Dury also made a direct appeal to the King and the Scots. In July, 1641, he addressed *A Memoriall Concerning Peace Ecclesiasticall Amongst Protestants* to the King and the General Assembly of the pastors and elders of the Kirk of Scotland. In this document, after describing his own efforts in the interest of Christian reunion, he appeals to the Protestants of England and Scotland to learn to "live in the communion of the saints one toward another." Minor differences should be forgotten in an effort to place new emphasis upon the doctrines and practices in which the Protestant churches "do fully agree betwixt themselves and disagree from Papists." This consensus should be embodied in a common confession of faith. Correspondence between the churches should be inaugurated as a means of advancing the cause of peace, spreading scriptural knowledge, increasing interest in practical divinity, and promoting educational reform.[17] When

---

[15] Dury, *A Memoriall Concerning Peace Ecclesiasticall*, Preface, p. iv.

[16] The evidence of Henderson's interest in the union of the Protestant churches on a Presbyterian basis is presented in the writer's "Life of Alexander Henderson," *Journal of the Presbyterian Historical Society*, IX (1918), 229 ff., 236 ff., 269 ff.; see also the text of a paper by Henderson on "Unity in Religion," as quoted by W. M. Hetherington, *History of the Westminster Assembly of Divines*, pp. 382–92.

[17] Dury, *Memoriall Concerning Peace Ecclesiasticall*, pp. 1–12.

this *Memoriall* was discussed in the General Assembly at St. Andrews, there was a disposition on the part of some of the members to criticize Dury's union efforts, but Robert Baillie was able to persuade the Assembly to present a reply which professed a general interest in the proposals which Dury had presented.[18]

Before Dury returned to England, he had also made attempts to interest members of the Long Parliament in his union projects. As soon as he received the news that the personal government of Charles I was to be ended by the meeting of Parliament, he prepared a narrative of his union negotiations, which he forwarded to Hartlib with the request that it should be circulated among the members of Parliament and the Convocation.[19] In 1640 he made a direct appeal to Parliament for support of his union plans, addressing to the House of Commons a *Petition*, in which, after mentioning his ten years of union activity, he asked that

some Act or Declaration might be made, First, That the blessed and long sought for union of Protestant Churches may bee recommended unto the publick prayers of the Church. And secondly, That either an Evangelical correspondency for mutuall edification, for healing of breaches, for taking away of scandals, and for the advancement of the Gospel of Jesus Christ amongst Protestants should henceforth bee entertained with forraigne Churches, by those to whom the care of so blessed a worke may be with authority referred: Or that his majesty with your Honours advice and grave counsell, might be moved to call together a generall Synod of Protestants in due time, for the better setling of weighty matters in the Church, which now trouble not onely the consciences of most men, but disturb the tranquility of publick States and divide the Churches one from another, to the great hinderance of Christianity, and the dishonor of Religion. All which evils by this means may bee taken out of the way, and from hence a great blessing of God, and much honour amongst men will redound to this Church and Nation.[20]

Meanwhile, Hartlib was again busy with efforts to win the support of men of all parties in behalf of the union project. His letters during

[18] See Robert Baillie, *Letters and Journals*, I, 364-65.

[19] *Calendar of State Papers, Domestic Series, 1640*, p. 185.

[20] *John Dury His Petition to the Honourable House of Commons*, pp. iii, iv. The suggestion that Englishmen of all parties should unite in intervention in behalf of the German Protestants and in support of the claims of Elizabeth of Bohemia awakened a sympathetic response from a number of the Puritan members of the Long Parliament. On July 9, 1641, Denzil Holles spoke in the House of Commons advocating English intervention in Germany. Daniel Neal (*History of the Puritans*, I, 387) quotes the speech of Holles as follows: "There is another motive which has an irresistible operation with us, which is the advancement of the Protestant religion. The Protestant religion and this kingdom must live and die together; and it is madness to suppose that the Protestant religion can continue here, if we suffer it to be destroyed and eradicated out of neighboring countries. Religion is the heart of England, and England is the heart of the Protestant religion in all other parts of Christendom; let us, therefore, like wise men, that foresee the evil afar off, rather meet it at a distance, than stay until the Austrian ambition and popish power come to our door."

the years 1639 and 1640 indicate that he was in close association with leaders of the Moderate Anglican group.[21] He also attempted to interest the Scottish Presbyterians and the English Puritans in Dury's union program.[22] The suspicions of the authorities were aroused by his negotiations with these groups. On May 1, 1639, Secretary Francis Windebank issued an order for the arrest of Hartlib. He was freed after examination and promptly renewed his activities. He was able to gain support for Dury's plans from Edward Montagu, duke of Manchester and prominent Puritan leader in the House of Lords.[23] Hartlib was also in communication with Alexander Henderson, who was in London from November, 1640, to June, 1641, ostensibly for the purpose of negotiating a peace between the King and the Covenanters but really for the purpose of arranging a plan for united action between Scots and Puritans.[24]

When the Long Parliament opened, Hartlib was enthusiastic in the hope that it would inaugurate a new and better era for England. In order to enlist public interest and attract the attention of the members of the new parliament to his favorite schemes, he issued tracts which presented his views regarding the formation of an ideal state, the promotion of the union of the Protestant churches, and the reform of the English educational system.[25] Since 1636 Hartlib had advocated the introduction of the Comenian program of educational reform into England.[26] He shared Dury's view that a thorough reform of the educational system would advance the cause of religion and promote Christian unity.[27] When the new parliament indicated

[21] See *Calendar of State Papers, Domestic Series, 1640*, pp. 568 ff.; *Calendar . . . . , 1641*, p. 186.

[22] On the activities of the Scottish Commissioners in London at this time see W. S. Hudson, "The Scottish Effort To Presbyterianize the Church of England during the Early Months of the Long Parliament," *Church History*, VIII (1939), 255–82.

[23] Historical Manuscripts Commission, *Report VIII*, Part II, pp. 10, 54, 55.

[24] Masson, *op. cit.*, III, 215 ff.

[25] F. Althaus, *Historisches Taschenbuch*, VI (1884), iii, 212 ff. The three tracts issued by Hartlib in 1641–42 were as follows: *A Brief Description of the Kingdom of Macaria* (London, 1641), an attempt to picture Hartlib's plans for an ideal commonwealth, following the literary models furnished by More's *Utopia*, Bacon's *New Atlantis*, and Andreae's *Christianopolis*; *A Brief Relation of that which hath been lately attempted to Procure Ecclesiastical Peace amongst Protestants* (London, 1641), a narrative of Dury's union activities, which was written by Dury and published by Hartlib; and *A Reformation of Schools* (London, 1642), a description of the Comenian program of educational reform.

[26] Althaus, *op. cit.*, pp. 204 ff.

[27] See the Dury-Hartlib correspondence regarding the educational program of Comenius in J. Kvačala, *Korrespondence J. A. Komenského*, pp. 11, 12, 16.

an interest in educational reform, Hartlib redoubled his efforts to keep the names of Dury and Comenius before the public eye. It was largely due to his efforts that Dury and Comenius were later called to England by members of the Long Parliament to serve as advisers of that body in its efforts to reform the educational system of England.

John Gauden, then chaplain to the Puritan leader, Robert Rich, second earl of Warwick, became interested in Hartlib's proposals. On November 29, 1640, Gauden preached a sermon before the House of Commons on "The Love of Peace and Truth." In the course of his sermon he developed the idea that peace must be founded on the basis of truth and that the knowledge of truth could be secured and preserved only through the use of correct educational method. He recommended the educational and irenic activities of Dury and Comenius, suggesting that Parliament should invite them to England to serve as an advisory commission to assist in drafting plans for the reform of the schools. In response to this suggestion, a small group of members of Parliament invited Dury and Comenius to England.[28] Both Dury and Comenius regarded the invitation as an official action of the Long Parliament.[29] Dury was pleased with the invitation, as he thought it would present an opportunity to try out his educational theories and also contribute toward the settlement of religious differences at home and the advancement of his irenic program abroad through the co-operation of English leaders. This invitation was directly responsible for his return to England in August, 1641.

The circumstances of Dury's call to England prompted him to concern himself with problems of educational reform immediately after his arrival. In his activity in this field he was closely associated with Comenius and Hartlib. Comenius arrived in London on September 21, 1641. By October 8 he had made a preliminary survey of the situation in England and had prepared a letter to his friends in Poland. This letter reflected the educational, religious, and political conditions in England with a clarity seldom found in documents of the period.[30]

---

[28] J. Kvačala, *J. A. Comenius*, p. 44. However, Kvačala is in error in referring to Gauden as a bishop at this time, as he did not attain episcopal rank until after the Restoration. He was for a time a zealous adherent of the Parliamentary party. Later he joined the Royalist party, asserted that he wrote *Eikon Basilike*, and was rewarded by appointment to the see of Exeter.

[29] See Matthew Spinka, *John Amos Comenius, That Incomparable Moravian*, pp. 73 ff.; R. F. Young, *Comenius in England*, pp. 39 ff.; and G. H. Turnbull, *Samuel Hartlib, with Special Regard to His Relations with J. A. Comenius*, pp. 30 ff.

[30] For the text of this letter see A. Patera (ed.), *Jana Amosa Komenského Korrespondence*, pp. 38–41.

Apparently England was on the eve of a great era of educational reform. Comenius was pleased by the increasing popular interest in projects for the reform of the schools. Interest in the subject was indicated by parliamentary action, as the House of Commons had voted that a large part of the revenues of the church should be confiscated and appropriated for the "advancement of piety and learning."[31] The triumvirate—Dury, Hartlib, and Comenius—stood ready to serve as a commission to direct the organization of a new educational system. But the commission had no opportunity to carry out its program. The Long Parliament was soon forced to give all its time and energy to the quarrel with the King. When civil war seemed inevitable, the funds assigned for the "advancement of learning and piety" were used for other purposes. Comenius, Dury, and Hartlib drew up elaborate plans, but there was no chance for the realization of these plans.[32] Comenius was soon convinced that the prevailing turmoil in England would make educational reform impossible. He left England for Sweden in August, 1642. In Sweden he inaugurated a new epoch in educational reform under the patronage of Lewis de Geer, to whom he had been recommended by Dury.[33]

Meanwhile, Dury was busily engaged in seeking solutions for some of the problems which were responsible for the prevailing unrest. After a year of study he published his conclusions in a tract entitled *A Motion Tending to the Publick Good of This Age, and of Posteritie* (London, 1642). In this tract he defines the public good as "nothing else than the universal private good of everyone in the life of God" and then develops the thesis that this public good can be secured only through efforts to advance peaceableness, piety, and truth.[34] The chief hindrance to civil peace and religious progress in England is described as the selfish spirit which prompts men to disregard the life of God in the soul and to devote themselves to party strife. To curb this spirit new efforts must be made to advance the cause of peace.

[31] This act of the House of Commons (June 15, 1641) is quoted by Foster Watson, "The State and Education during the Commonwealth," *English Historical Review*, XV (1900), 61.

[32] These plans included a project for the use of the Chelsea College building as a plant for experimental work in education; new methods for the instruction of children in the home; and new textbooks based on the Comenian principles (see Scougal, *Die pädagogischen Schriften John Durys*, pp. 22 ff.; Althaus, *op. cit.*, pp. 217–20; Masson, *op. cit.*, III, 199–215; Spinka, *op. cit.*, pp. 77 ff.; and Patera, *op. cit.*, pp. 38, 41, 46, 49, 50, 53).

[33] See the Dury–De Geer correspondence as printed in the *Monatshefte der Comenius Gesellschaft*, V, 101 ff.; cf. also Patera, *op. cit.*, p. 56; Spinka, *op. cit.*, pp. 90 ff.

[34] Dury, *Motion Tending to the Publick Good*, pp. 6, 17.

The endeavor of Peaceablenesse is a study whereby we are directed how to avoyd the occasions of strife, in respect of ourselves, and to bring others who are at variance unto a peaceable and harmless disposition. These endeavors are proper Characters of the sons of God; for . . . . the Apostle maketh the inoffensiveness of our conversation to be the property of the sons of God. And Christ saith, that the Peacemakers are blessed because they shall be called the sons of God. . . . . Thus then we must conclude that the endeavors tending to take away offences and scandalls from amongst Christians, and tending to cause them to avoyd strife and debates, and tending to make peace amongst them, and to bring them to the unity of the Spirit, by a reconcilement of differences in the truth, are undertakings and endeavors immediately conducing to the furtherance of the Gospel, and consequently the setting forward of the life of God amongst men.[35]

This cause of peace, he argues, can be advanced by efforts to secure a common confession of faith which would be acceptable to all Protestants; by granting official sanction to negotiations in the interest of ecclesiastical peace; by efforts to maintain a correspondency among the Christian churches; and by the circulation of literature in the interest of peace and Christian reunion. In addition to these suggestions, Dury made numerous proposals for measures designed to advance piety. Interest must be shifted from controversial divinity to practical divinity. A professorship of practical divinity should be established in each of the universities and also in London at Sion or Gresham College. A complete "Body of Practical Divinity" must be prepared for use both in English and in Continental schools. Popular lectureships should be established "to teach the common people the way how to make use of the Scripture by reading and meditating in their ordinary course." Research should be encouraged in an effort to discover more exact and helpful methods in the field of biblical interpretation.[36] Furthermore, the interests of peace, piety, and truth demand a reform of the whole educational system.

Then if we beleeve what hath been said and know that a man is first naturall, and then spirituall; I think it fit to move that assistance may be given, as well by way of counsell as by outward support, unto those that labour for the rectifying of men's natural parts, by reforming and facilitating all the means of humane learning for the schooles as well of old as young Schollers. For the great defects and errors in the manner of teaching, and in the matters which are taught, which . . . . breede evil habits, and make the soules of men unfit for the apprehension of the mistery of Godlinesse in the profession of the Gospel. Therefore to help the removeall of these, and to frame a right course for the education of children, and for the perfection of humane Learning, is a most laudable publique good worke as well for this age as for posterity.[37]

[35] *Ibid.*, pp. 18, 19.   [36] *Ibid.*, pp. 21, 22.

[37] *Ibid.*, p. 21; cf .also Scougal, *op. cit.*, pp. 27–29; and Matthew Spinka, *The Irenic Program and Activity of John Amos Comenius*, pp. 37, 54.

It is evident that Dury regarded improvement in educational method as a means for the promotion of the public good and for the ultimate establishment of Christian unity. The suggestions which he makes in this tract for the reform of education constitute a landmark in the history of English education. His proposals are presented in the form of outlines of treatises which should be prepared for use in the schools as textbooks and manuals of method.[38] Three treatises are outlined for use in planning a new system of elementary instruction for use in homes and in schools—a system based on the same fundamental principles of instruction as those underlying the modern kindergarten methods.

Likewise Dury is strikingly modern in his suggestions for treatises in the field of religious education. The biographical, historical, and religious materials which are available in the Bible must be presented in a form adapted to "childish simplicity." Since such procedure was altogether new, manuals must be prepared for the guidance of teachers. Revolutionary changes in the methods of teaching language and science by practice, experiment, and observation are advocated. The tract closes with an appeal for the establishment of a foundation devoted to the development of new educational methods in order that he, together with Comenius and Hartlib, might work out the details of the system which they had proposed.[39] While residing in England, Dury made varied attempts to secure new support for his church-union negotiations. Once more he solicited the help of men of all parties. He was in high favor in court circles at the time, as is evidenced by his appointment as a royal chaplain.[40] He was also highly

[38] Dury, *Motion Tending to the Publick Good*, pp. 23 ff.

[39] *Ibid.*, pp. 40, 41. Here Dury suggests that the details of the system could be worked out if means were provided "to have us set apart for our taskes and settled together. . . . . I meane Master Comenius, Mr. Hartlib and myselfe: For though our taskes be different, yet we are all three in a knot sharers of one anothers labours, and can hardly bee without one anothers helpe and assistance." John Pell and Theodore Haak were also associated with Dury, Comenius, and Hartlib in preparing these plans for educational reform. It was a definite part of the program of this group to establish an international academy of natural philosophers. Though their plans could not be realized at this time, they furnished the basis for the organization of the Royal Society in 1661 (see L. Keller, "Comenius und die Akademien der Naturphilosophen des 17. Jahrhunderts," *Monatshefte der Comenius Gesellschaft*, IV, 174 ff.). Held (*Christianopolis*, p. 124) states that the group was "responsible for the first agitation toward not only a better educational system, but also the founding of a college of science. Political conditions interfered with further developments. Had not this been the case, the Royal Society might well have been founded nearly two decades earlier than it was." F. R. Johnson ("Gresham College, Precursor of the Royal Society," *Journal of the History of Ideas*, I [1940], 413–38) presents forceful arguments in proof of his thesis that the influences contributing to the origin of the Royal Society may be traced back to the founding of Gresham College in 1598, its emphasis on scientific studies, and the informal scientific meetings sponsored by members of its staff.

[40] See Scougal, *op. cit.*, p. 23.

regarded by leaders of the Parliamentary party, as is shown by the fact that the House of Commons chose him as a member of the Westminster Assembly. He was in correspondence with Thomas Goodwin and Philip Nye, who were already assuming positions of leadership in the rising Independent party. In this period of bitter partisan strife he was determined to remain *extra partes* in order that he might serve as a peacemaker between all contending parties.[41]

Dury's method of presenting his cause varied from time to time. In 1642 he made two additional appeals directly to Parliament for support in behalf of his union program.[42] Recognizing the popular interest in the questions of the hour, he sought to bring his program to the attention of the public by preparing and circulating pamphlets which described his past negotiations and announced his plans for future union activities.[43] As the increasing factional strife gradually tended toward civil war, he realized that, under the circumstances, nothing could be accomplished in the interest of peace or educational reform at home and that there was no hope of obtaining documents which would authorize a renewal of his reunion negotiations on the Continent. In his *Summary Account*, Dury refers to his unsuccessful efforts in this period with the statement:

> Hee made his application to the King and Parliament, and to all that were in power and place to move them to countenance and assist his designe, but the division between the King and Parliament increasing daily; his motions though not unseasonable, yet were not effectively entertained by any either in England or Scotland. . . . . He found all to be vain, because everyone was intent upon his own particular occasions, and all minding onely their Domestick grievances, the common interest of Protestants could not be laid to heart.[44]

When Dury was thus troubled by the failure of his efforts in England and by the urgent need of financial support, a new field of service was opened to him. On May 12, 1641, Princess Mary, the nine-year-old daughter of Charles I, had been married to William, the fifteen-year-old son of the Stadtholder Frederick Henry of Orange.

[41] Writing in 1660, in his *Declaration of John Durie* (p. 3), Dury reviews the record of the strife of parties in England and adds: "I have walked harmlessly by provoking all different parties and chiefly their leaders in the Churches to love and good works toward each other"; see also Dury, *The Unchanged Peacemaker*, p. 1.

[42] In 1642 Dury addressed *A Petition to the House of Commons for the Preservation of the True Religion;* and also *A (second) Petition to the House of Commons; whereunto are added certaine considerations, shewing the necessity of a correspondence in spirituall matters betwixt all Protestant Churches* (see H. M. Dexter, *Congregationalism of the Last Three Hundred Years as Seen in Its Literature*, Bibliographical Appen., p. 47).

[43] At least twelve such pamphlets were issued by Dury in the years 1641 and 1642 (see the "Trial List of the Printed Writings of John Dury" as given below, pp. 214–15).

[44] *Summary Account of Mr. John Dury's Former and Latter Negotiations*, p. 1.

It is probable that Charles I arranged this marriage partly for the purpose of allaying the growing suspicion that the English Court was about to adopt the Roman Catholic faith.[45] According to the terms of the marriage contract, Princess Mary was to be taken to Holland by her mother, Henrietta Maria, in the year 1642 to assume her place at the court of Frederick Henry. When arrangements were being made for her departure, Dury was appointed a royal chaplain and assigned to duty at The Hague as tutor and chaplain of the Princess.[46]

This preferment, described by Dury as being "as honourable and as plentiful as any [that] could be bestowed on a man of my coat," was awarded on the joint recommendation of Sir William Boswell, the English ambassador at The Hague, and Sir John Dingley, the secretary of Elizabeth of Bohemia.[47] Dury was probably chosen for this post because of his thorough familiarity with Continental court procedure, his interest in educational methods, and his reputation on the Continent as an advocate of Protestant interests. Later Charles I, in an appeal designed to enlist the support of public opinion on the Continent, cited the marriage of Princess Mary to a Protestant prince and his selection of Protestant tutors for his children as evidence to disprove the Puritan and parliamentary accusations to the effect that he was planning the destruction of English Protestantism.[48]

By June 27, 1642, Dury had taken up his new duties at The Hague.[49] His position relieved him from the financial worries which had oppressed him for years. It also gave him some prestige, which he thought would prove valuable to him in the conduct of further reunion negotiations with the Continental churches. It provided opportunities for association with important leaders who might be in position to advance his cause, such as Elizabeth of Bohemia and the philosopher, René Descartes, who was then resident at court and was serving as tutor to the children of Elizabeth of Bohemia.[50] Dury was

---

[45] *Cambridge Modern History*, IV, 290, 702 ff.; and Mrs. M. A. Everett Green, *Elizabeth, Queen of Bohemia*, pp. 256, 345, 346, 356. The best detailed account of the life of Princess Mary is given by Mrs. M. A. Everett Green, *Lives of the Princesses of England*, VI, 100–339.

[46] Scougal, *op. cit.*, pp. 23, 24.

[47] Dury, *The Unchanged Peacemaker*, p. 13.

[48] See Neal, *op. cit.*, I, 470–72.   [49] Patera, *op. cit.*, p. 56.

[50] Scougal (*op. cit.*, pp. 23, 24) calls attention to the probability of association between Dury and Descartes at this time. There is some possibility that Dury's later educational theories were influenced by this association. The Cartesian philosophy, as fully developed, would tend to confirm Dury in his opposition to scholasticism—both Roman Catholic and Protestant (see Karl Müller, *Kirchengeschichte*, II, Part II, 715–18, 751–53).

well versed in the details of court procedure, and it is probable that his instruction was of benefit to the young princess.[51] But he was soon dissatisfied and complained of his "uncomfortable position." Perhaps his pupil, previously trained by Roman Catholic tutors, did not respond so readily to his instruction in other subjects as in the matter of court procedure. Contemporary accounts of Mary of Orange do not picture her as a promising pupil. Ruth Grannis is of the opinion that Dury's difficulties were due to the "uncompromising disposition of the high-spirited little Princess."[52] Elizabeth of Bohemia described her niece and Dury's pupil as "deadly lazy."[53]

But Dury's dissatisfaction with his position at The Hague was due to more important causes than the intractable disposition of his royal pupil. The central interest of his life was the advancement of the cause of Christian reunion. He soon discovered that, in his new assignment, he was to be seriously hampered in all his union activities. Henrietta Maria remained at The Hague for a year and made unwearied efforts to secure assistance for the King in the impending struggle with Parliament.[54] This placed Dury in a difficult position, as he was anxious to keep in favor with both the Parliamentary and the Royalist parties. Popular sentiment in Holland was inclined to favor the Parliamentary party.[55] Frederick Henry, despite the pleas of Henrietta Maria and his personal sympathy for Charles I, refused to assist the Royalist party in England, as he knew that public opinion in Holland would not approve such action. He attempted, therefore, to maintain a position of strict neutrality. On this account he was unwilling for Dury, as a resident at his court, to take any part in English affairs.

Meanwhile, Hartlib took care to inform Dury of the developments in England. Two events of the year 1643—the call of the Westminster Assembly and the adoption of the Solemn League and Covenant—seemed to indicate an increasing interest in the settlement of religious differences at home and the renewal of union

[51] Ruth Grannis, in her Preface to Dury's *Reformed Librarie-Keeper*, p. 26, suggests that "perhaps some of the pathetic gravity, ease and decorum with which shortly afterwards, at the mature age of thirteen, she gave audiences, received ambassadors, and mingled in court festivities, may be attributed to the gentle teachings of this kindly master."

[52] *Ibid.*, p. 25; cf. Theodor Klahr, "Johannes Duraeus; sein Leben und seine Schriften über Erziehungslehre," *Monatshefte der Comenius Gesellschaft*, VI, 69.

[53] Green, *Elizabeth, Queen of Bohemia*, p. 354.

[54] G. Mitsukuri, *Englisch-niederländische Unionsbestrebungen im Zeitalter Cromwells*, pp. 18 ff.

[55] *Ibid.*, p. 15.

negotiations abroad.[56] This apparent interest in causes which Dury had championed for years prompted Hartlib to make new efforts to give publicity to Dury's union proposals.[57] It was now evident to Hartlib that the schemes which he and Dury were sponsoring would receive more favorable consideration from the Presbyterian party than could be expected from the Episcopal party.

Therefore, he gradually shifted his allegiance from the Episcopal to the Presbyterian party. Masson states that, when the Westminster Assembly convened in July, 1643, Hartlib was fully convinced that Episcopacy was to be overthrown and that

it was to Parliament and an Assembly mainly Presbyterian that England was looking for a new system of church government. Hartlib's anxiety was, as Durie's also was, to make the best of the new conditions, and to instil into them as much of the Durie idea as was possible. Might it not even be (reasoned Hartlib and Durie) that a Reformed Presbyterian Church of England would be a more effective leader in a movement for the union of the Protestant Churches in Europe than the Episcopal Church had been?[58]

Hartlib was soon able to attract the attention of the Presbyterian and Parliamentary leaders. This is indicated by the fact that he was summoned as a witness in the trial of Archbishop Laud. When the trial finally began in November, 1643, Hartlib's testimony served to give some publicity to Dury's earlier union efforts.[59]

The call of the Westminster Assembly inspired Dury with new hope. His interest in developments in England was intensified when he learned that he had been appointed as a member of the Assembly. The first meeting of the Assembly was to be held on July 1, 1643. In the interim between the call of the Assembly and its first session, one of the members, Calibute Downing, died. On June 28, 1643, a

[56] The ordinance providing for the call of the Westminster Assembly, as passed by the House of Commons, June 12, 1643, professed an interest in religious peace at home and closer conformity with the Protestant churches abroad (see the text of this ordinance as quoted by A. F. Mitchell, *The Westminster Assembly: Its History and Standards*, p. xiii). Likewise, the Solemn League and Covenant professed a central interest in the unity of the churches at home and co-operation with churches abroad. The full text of the Solemn League and Covenant is given by H. Gee and W. J. Hardy, *Documents Illustrative of English Church History*, pp. 569–74.

[57] In 1643 Hartlib published a small tract advocating union efforts under the title, *A Faithful and Seasonable Advice, or the necessity of a Correspondence for the advancement of the Protestant Cause* (see Althaus, *op. cit.*, p. 220). Hartlib also printed and circulated Dury's *Letter to Lord Forbes*, hoping it might influence the Assembly to frame a confession of faith which would be acceptable to all Protestants.

[58] *Op. cit.*, III, 230.

[59] The documents relating to this part of the trial of Laud are given by William Prynne, *Canterburies Doome* (1646), pp. 539 ff.; see above, pp. 50, 51.

resolution was passed by the House of Commons providing for the appointment of Dury as a member of the Assembly to take the place made vacant by the death of Downing.[60] This appointment indicates that Dury was held in high regard by leaders of the Parliamentary party, despite his status as a royal chaplain.

Dury regarded his appointment as the providential opening of the way into a new field of union activity. He was eager to begin his work in the Assembly at once. He thought that his influence as a peacemaker in the Assembly would have more weight if royal approval could be secured for his participation in its deliberations. Immediately upon receipt of the news of his appointment, he wrote to Archbishop Ussher, who was with the King at Oxford, requesting him to secure permission from Charles I which would allow him to attend the Assembly. "I might be able," Dury said in his letter to Ussher, "to do his Majesty and the public more profitable service there by helping to reconcile differences at home, then I could do at the Hague." The requested permission was granted by Charles I, with the single proviso that Dury "was desired first to come to Oxford."[61]

Dury then asked Frederick Henry to allow him to leave The Hague and take his place in the Assembly. Frederick Henry refused to grant his request, as he was unwilling for any person connected with his court to take part in English affairs. Thereupon Dury resigned his position at The Hague but consented to remain until his successor could be appointed.[62] Because of this agreement he was not free to leave The Hague until January, 1644. At that time Dury realized that conditions were altogether unfavorable for his return to England. He knew that the King, who now faced a serious military situation, would be unwilling to sanction his participation in the debates of the Assembly. Furthermore, the dominant leaders of the Presbyterian party now regarded him with suspicion. Baillie, who had befriended him on previous occasions, took the position that

[60] On the date of Dury's appointment as a member of the Westminster Assembly see Historical Manuscripts Commission, *Report V*, Part II, p. 93.

[61] Dury, *Declaration of John Durie*, p. 5.

[62] *Ibid.*, p. 6. Later Continental friends of the Stuarts criticized Dury for resigning his position at The Hague and cited this as an act of disloyalty to the King. Dury answered these criticisms in a letter to John Bergius, dated January 1, 1656. For the text of this letter see T. Hasaeus, *Biblotheca Bremensis historico-philologica-theologica*, IV, 688, 689.

Dury, as a royal chaplain, was too much inclined toward Anglicanism to favor the program of the Presbyterian party in the Assembly.[63]

Under these circumstances Dury decided to delay his return to England. Meanwhile, he found employment as minister to the Anglican Church which was maintained at Rotterdam in connection with the factory of the English Company of Merchant Adventurers. He continued to serve this church until August, 1645. His willingness to accept the position indicates that he wished to continue in service as an Anglican minister. Among the numerous Anglican congregations in Holland, the English Merchant's Kirk at Rotterdam was the oldest and most important.[64] When Dury began his pastorate in this church he found that the congregation was divided on the issue of the propriety of using the liturgy in the services. Thus the controversies of the home church had spread to the Rotterdam congregation. Dury's ministry at Rotterdam furnishes an example of his efforts to reach a settlement of disputed points within the bounds of a single congregation. He says:

I therefore intending to unite them in the substance of their Gospell worship, followed a middle way, neither strictly formal, nor altogether informall; which did not offend the discreet and sober; but did not answer the expectation of the fiercer sort of either side, who were neither fully displeased nor well pleased with my moderation; and this I did . . . . to let them see that the true property of our Gospell-worship consists not in words and formalities but in power: for I conceive that the worship of God in public assemblies, may consist in set words and forms onely so far as these are subservient in an orderly way to beget and maintain in the soules of those that meet to worship God together the power of Godliness by the unity of the Spirit. . . . . The words then and the forms which are fittest to reach these endes, and to unite therein the spirits of those who are assembled to worship God together are the fittest to be used in a public assembly. . . . . And by this rule I made use of the Leiturgie at Rotterdam, neither laying it wholly aside in respect of the substance of the prayers; nor binding myself to the whole formality of it.[65]

Observation of worship in the Continental Protestant churches had convinced Dury that he should acquaint those churches with

[63] Baillie, op. cit., II, 163. Baillie to Spaing, April 19, 1644: "That any of the Assembly has written for Mr. Durie, its more than I know: that the Synod did never write for him, or any man else, I know assuredlie; for smaller actions exceeds their power. His letter to the Synod I heard read with no great regard; for it savored of somewhat. If he be pleased to come over to Oxford, he may resolve to be taken, while he lives, by us all here for a malignant; and if he should come to us with the least tincture of Episcopacie, or liturgie learning, he could not be welcome to any I know. As you love the man, persuade him to stay at this time where he is: he cannot be so well or honorablie imployed anywhere I know."

[64] On the English Merchant's Kirk at Rotterdam and Dury's ministry there see W. Steven, History of the Scottish Church at Rotterdam, pp. 2, 15, 264, 280, 325.

[65] Declaration of John Durie, pp. 6, 7.

the Anglican Prayer Book, hoping that the wider adoption of some of its features might serve as a bond of unity in worship among Protestants. As early as 1640 he had expressed the desire to secure the position as minister to the Anglican Church at Hamburg, promising Laud that, if he secured the place, he would make definite efforts to teach the Germans the merits of the Anglican Prayer Book.[66] While he was at Rotterdam he sought to acquaint the Dutch with the merits of the Anglican liturgy. A translation of the Anglican Prayer Book into the Dutch language was published at Rotterdam during the year of his ministry in the city.[67] Though Dury's connection with the publication of this book cannot be traced with certainty, it is clearly evident that he shared none of that aversion to the Anglican liturgy which had prompted his countrymen to revolt against the Crown.

After the outbreak of the Civil War, Dury looked to the Westminster Assembly as the agency which could most effectively negotiate the settlement of religious peace in England, Ireland, and Scotland. His hopeful spirit made him regard the Solemn League and Covenant as a national pledge for the settlement of religious and civil quarrels at home and the establishment of closer relationships between the Protestants of England and those of the Continent. The Covenant, he believed, would become a rallying standard for the advocates of peace and unity in the churches rather than the banner of a particular party within the nation. He hoped that Christians of all parties would join in accepting the Covenant as a pledge for co-operation in "lawful ways of advancing religion and righteousness, reformation and peace in Church and Commonwealth; and not to be serviceable to any one party."[68]

But, even before the close of the year 1643, it was evident that the Covenant was widely regarded as a badge of party allegiance rather than a pledge for the promotion of Christian unity. Dury had considered it his duty, despite the prohibitions of Frederick Henry, to protest against this tendency and to plead for a more impartial spirit among those who accepted the Covenant. This protest was forwarded to the Westminster Assembly, December 21, 1643. Its text

[66] *Calendar of State Papers, Domestic Series, 1640*, p. 320.

[67] Steven (*op. cit.*, p. 264) states that "for the use of such as chose to join, the Liturgy of the Church of England was translated into Dutch. . . . . The earliest copy which we have seen is in duodecimo, and printed at Rotterdam in 1645."

[68] Dury, "A Case of Conscience Resolved: Concerning Ministers Meddling with State Matters," *Harleian Miscellany*, VI, 204.

is preserved in the *Harleian Miscellany* under the title, "The Vow which J. D. hath made, and the covenant which he doth enter into with God, in reference to the national covenant of the kingdoms."[69] The document reveals Dury's attitude at the time. It indicates his willingness to take the Covenant but presents an earnest plea that the Covenant might be interpreted as a pledge for new and more consistent efforts to secure peace and unity rather than a pledge of support to a political party. It professes a willingness to sacrifice many of the characteristic features of the Anglican system in order that the nation, under the leadership of the Assembly, might adopt a new and more comprehensive system which would provide room for men of all parties within a single church. The replacement of the partisan spirit by conciliatory and Christlike attitudes was the necessary preliminary step toward such a union. According to Dury's interpretation, to take the Covenant was to make a public avowal of such attitudes, and he gladly vowed his acceptance of its principles.

Dury was especially concerned over the indications that the work of the Westminster Assembly might be rendered ineffective because of the strife between the Presbyterians and the Independents. He hoped to be able to serve as a mediator between these groups and thus promote the cause of unity. As early as 1642 he had been in correspondence with two of the leading Independents, Thomas Goodwin and Philip Nye. At the time he sought to inform them regarding his reunion efforts on the Continent in the hope that he might be able to enlist their support.[70] The Independent leaders, impressed by Dury's description of his conciliatory labors on the Continent, asked for an expression of his views regarding the toleration of Independency in England. Thereupon Dury asked them to give a concise account of their aims in order that he might be in position to present his views on their claims for toleration.[71] He regarded the *Apologetical Narration* of 1644 as a statement of the aims of the party. Here was a group which, if tolerated, might bring further division in the church life of England. He was of the opinion,

---

[69] Dury (*Declaration of John Durie*, p. 9) states that "this Declaration was read in the Assembly of Divines, and not contradicted by any; although (as I afterwards was told) some did grumble at the reading thereof, because they thought that it did not become any to put his own sense and limitations upon the covenant; and to publish that sense unto the Assembly"; for the text of this paper see *Harleian Miscellany*, VI, 208–12.

[70] For the text of this correspondence see Dury, *Epistolary Discourse*, pp. 1 ff.

[71] *Ibid.*, pp. 14, 16.

therefore, that the Independents must be persuaded to settle their differences with the Presbyterians and unite with them on a basis of comprehension.[72] In March, 1644, he sent Hartlib a letter in which he argued against the toleration of Independency and sought to point out a comprehensive basis on which the two parties could unite. This letter, which forms the major part of Dury's *Epistolary Discourse*, clearly indicates that Dury was convinced that the work of the Westminster Assembly would end in failure unless the two groups were reconciled.

In the *Epistolary Discourse* Dury expressed his opposition to the toleration of Independency unless the Independents could present better arguments in favor of their position. Thus far, he claimed, they had failed to prove that their new and untried system was more in accord with the ordinance of God than Presbyterianism, which had been tested by long usage in the Reformed Churches.[73] With a keener appreciation of unity than of liberty, he takes the position that two systems of church government should not be authorized in the same state and that the Independents, as they are few in number, should be willing to yield many of their distinctive views and join the majority group in the formation of one church. He answered the Independent claims for his own personal support by citing the fact that his previous efforts had been directed toward the promotion of brotherhood and unity rather than mere toleration.[74] Presbyterians and Independents should settle their differences without the necessity of the interference of the state authorities.[75] Unity could be obtained by the mutual exercise of a conciliatory spirit.

It is obvious that it was Dury's aim not to present arguments against toleration but to make a plea for union based on a policy of comprehension which would utilize the more desirable features of both systems of church polity. Only by the adoption of such a policy, he argued, could the centrifugal forces, which were then dominating the church life of the nation, be effectively curbed.

[72] *Ibid.*, pp. 17, 18.

[73] *Ibid.*, p. 21: "Except they can make it clearly appeare to the State that their Church way of non-communion (for I know not what else to call it) is the only true way of God, and that the Presbyteriall Way is not agreeable to the Word of God, in that wherein it differeth from them; I say, except they be able to make these two things clearly appeare, I think it would be no wisdom in the State to give them the Toleration which they do desire."

[74] *Ibid.*, p. 2.

[75] *Ibid.*, pp. 33 ff.

By the Grace of God I may be able to let them see that they really agree in all those meanes which are any way Fundamentall; and that the way of making use of the same may be intended uniformally by both sides each toward the other; then their difference may be composed, and their hearts joyned in the Lord for the advancement of his glorie, through the unitie of the Spirit, in the bond of peace. I am persuaded, then, that they both have the same sence of the New Covenant of Grace, whereby the Soules of believers are joyned to God in Christ. . . . . It is clear that to doe this [i.e., establish a workable form of church government on the basis of compromise and comprehension] they are obliged to maintaine the bonds of Ministeriall communion amongst themselves, which cannot be done more effectively then by such Consultations as are used in consistories, Presbyteries, and Synods, the true intention and nature of which, is not Coactive, but Auxiliary. And if to make up one single Congregation they require a Covenant betwixt each Beleever and his Brother, and betwixt them All and the Pastor that should watch over their soules; I see not why they should refuse the like Covenant to be established amongst the Pastors of severall Flocks.[76]

Dury's refusal to support the plea of the Independents for toleration indicates that he was less liberal than the many Englishmen who were at this time advocating liberty of conscience and the toleration of varying forms of church government.[77] Even his closest friend, Samuel Hartlib, was inclined to favor the plea of the Independents for toleration.[78] But Dury was convinced that the parties dividing the Parliament and the Assembly were in essential agreement and that a settlement could be reached which would be mutually satisfactory. A united church, established on a comprehensive basis and using a form of government which allowed large liberty to local congregations and also provided connectional unity through a system of church courts, might prove satisfactory to all. The peaceful union of Presbyterians and Independents on such a basis would curb the tendencies toward denominationalism which were steadily gaining force in England. He believed that he could contribute toward the establishment of harmony and union between the parties and thus secure results which were preferable to "bare toleration."

In February, 1645, two of the Scottish commissioners to the Westminster Assembly, Robert Baillie and George Gillespie, encountered storms while returning from Scotland to London, and their boat was driven to the coast of Holland. While in Holland, they visited Rotterdam and attended a Consistory of the Scottish

---

[76] Ibid., pp. 33, 36.

[77] W. K. Jordan, The Development of Religious Toleration in England, II, 255 ff., 364 ff., and passim; see also the views of Henry Robinson in answer to Dury's position as stated by W. K. Jordan, Men of Substance, pp. 91 ff.

[78] Masson, op. cit., III, 231.

Church in that city.[79] Dury was present as a visitor at this meeting. He now had opportunity to secure accurate information regarding the serious divisions which had arisen between the Presbyterians and the Independents in the Assembly. It is also probable that he was able to allay Baillie's suspicion that he was too strong in his Anglican sympathies to co-operate with the majority party in the Assembly. Prompted by his desire to make some contribution toward the settlement of the controversies which had arisen in Parliament and the Assembly and by a second request from Parliament that he should take his place in the Assembly,[80] he resigned his pastorate in Rotterdam and went to England, arriving at London in August, 1645. "I went thither," he says, "not to foment one party against another, but to do my Gospell work, and therein to serve his Majesty for the Kingdom's welfare; and this I did so as to keep an interest in all parties that I might do good offices between them."[81]

Dury states that he arrived in England "when the Parliament's affaires were at their lowest ebbs."[82] But the Battle of Naseby (June 14, 1645) had marked a new turn in events. This battle demonstrated the effectiveness of the New Model Army and gave the Independent party a more influential place in Parliament. The disastrous defeat of Charles I also indicated that the control of affairs in church and state would belong to Parliament rather than to the king. There was now no hope for an early restoration of the episcopal regime. But the parliamentary victory did not end religious conflict within the nation. The division of the Parliamentary party into hostile factions of Presbyterians and Independents was now the chief obstacle in the way of the establishment of religious peace and unity.

Here was an inviting opportunity for Dury to exercise his gifts as a peacemaker. For nine years (1645-54) he devoted himself unceasingly to the composure of "domestic differences." His efforts to promote the union of Protestants on the Continent were now discontinued, with the exception of an infrequent exchange of letters with Continental leaders who were in position to continue the agi-

[79] Steven, *op. cit.*, p. 15.

[80] Dury, *Unchanged Peacemaker*, p. 13.

[81] Dury, *Declaration of John Durie*, p. 10.

[82] Dury, *Unchanged Peacemaker*, p. 14.

tation in the interest of union.[83] This preoccupation with English affairs explains his failure to keep in touch with the prolonged negotiations which finally resulted in the Peace of Westphalia. In fact, Dury became so absorbed in efforts to solve problems of unity at home that many of his friends on the Continent believed that he was dead.[84] During this period of residence in England he was associated with leaders of all parties and attempted to serve as peacemaker between Parliament and the King, between Parliament and the Assembly, and between the Independents and the Presbyterians. He was convinced that he could do more efficient work as a peacemaker if he could remain *extra partes* and thus be in a position to serve all parties alike.[85] Discussing the current situation and the policy which he planned to follow amid the strife of parties, he says:

That we amongst ourselves, almost in respect of everything, are all broken to pieces in our affections, is very evident. That in this rupture of affections there is not only a distance of parties, but much heat of opposition, no man can deny. That by this heat, the alienations and thoughts of heart grow daily greater and greater, everyone can perceive. That few set themselves in the gap and labour to make up breaches, all must confess. . . . .

My aim shall be none other, but to stir up . . . . thoughts of brotherly kindnesse, of meekness, and of peace; to the end that some wayes may be taken up, which will help to reconcile the Affections of many divided about Circumstantials; to preserve and keep entire the Unity which remains about Fundamentals; and to prevent or cure the manifold Misprisions, which increase our confusions, and obstruct the Remedies of our diseases.[86]

Dury was certain that there could be no lasting settlement until ministers, civil authorities, and the masses of the people could be persuaded to adopt more conciliatory attitudes. He made his first attempt toward conciliation by negotiating for accommodation and union between the Presbyterian and Independent parties in the Westminster Assembly.[87] For a period of two years the work of the

---

[83] Dury, in his *Summarie Account*, pp. 23, 24, says: "The first Summons whereby hee was called unto the Assembly of Divines, being still insisted upon; he went from Rotterdam in the year 1645 and cam to London, where in the service of the churches, for the composure of Domestick differences, he imploied himself between all emergent parties, till the year 1654. So the work of his publick negotiations for the Unity of Protestants was suspended for . . . . years, wherein he entertained onely a correspondency by letters with some of the divines of his acquaintance beyond the Seas to keep the thoughts of so good a work a foot amongst them, so far as the times could permit."

[84] H. G. N. Tollin, "Johann Duraeus," *Geschichts-Blätter für Stadt und Land Magdeburg*, XXXII, 255; and Patera, *op. cit.*, p. 116.

[85] Dury, *Unchanged Peacemaker*, p. 11.

[86] Dury, *Model of Church Government*, pp. 8, 9.

[87] Dury, *A Demonstration of the Necessity of settling some Gospel-Government*, p. 53.

Assembly was his primary interest. He was admitted to the Assembly on August 12, 1645, and took the Protestation which was required of all members.[88] On August 29, 1645, he publicly subscribed to the Solemn League and Covenant, thus completing the requirements for admission.[89]

Prior to Dury's admission to the Assembly there had been a number of efforts to reconcile the Presbyterian and Independent factions. As early as March, 1644, Henderson, who was interested in Dury's union ideas, had suggested that a committee on accommodation should be appointed to adjust the differences which stood in the way of the union of the two groups.[90] The marked progress made by this committee in working out means of reconciliation was disregarded in the intense strife engendered by the Grand Debate and the bitter pamphlet warfare which followed. Shortly after Dury took his place in the Assembly a final effort was made to secure agreement. This took the form of the appointment of a new committee on accommodation. Parliament was responsible for its origin.

Presbyterian leaders in Parliament were alarmed by the prestige which came to the Independents as a result of the victories of the New Model Army and by the rapid increase in membership of the Independent party in the House of Commons. Under these circumstances Cromwell obtained an order from the House of Commons for the appointment of a committee of both kingdoms "to consider the differences of the Assembly in regard to church government, and to endeavor an union between them if possible, and otherwise to consider how far tender consciences, that cannot come up to the rule to be established, may be borne with according to the Word."[91] On November 6, 1645, this committee was named. Dury was one of the members which the Assembly was allowed to nominate for service on the committee.[92] As a member of this new committee on accommodation, Dury made his most earnest efforts to make peace between the factions into which the Assembly was divided. He served on this committee from November, 1645, until March, 1646.

During these months Dury used every opportunity to enlist public

[88] A. F. Mitchell and John Struthers, *Minutes of the Westminster Assembly*, pp. 121, 145.

[89] *Ibid.*, p. 126.

[90] Hetherington, *op. cit.*, pp. 202 ff.

[91] Mitchell, *op. cit.*, p. 205.

[92] W. A. Shaw, *History of the English Church during the Civil Wars*, II, 48.

interest in projects for the union of the churches in England and for co-operation and union with Protestants abroad. He was appointed to preach before the House of Commons on November 26, 1645—a day of public humiliation and prayer. The sermon which he delivered on this occasion, entitled *Israel's Call to March out of Babylon unto Jerusalem*, was printed by order of the House of Commons. In this sermon, after announcing that it was his object to show "the true relation wherein you [the members of the House of Commons] stand towards the Church of God; what the mystery of Babylon is; and what you ought to aim at in raising up the walls of Jerusalem," he turned his argument to his favorite idea of the union of the churches and sought to prove that the churches at home should be united on a broad basis of comprehension. He pleaded with the Commons to consider "the extent of your building that you must not make the walls of your Jerusalem too narrow in Compasse, but be mindful that ye ought to receive all those that are going out of Babylon with you." He also urged his hearers "to look with an eye of brotherly correspondency toward . . . . foreign Protestants, whose eyes are upon you, and whose peace and safety is wrapped up with your prosperity."[93]

After developing the argument that the Solemn League and Covenant was primarily a pledge for unselfish union efforts at home and abroad, he asked that he might be given further opportunity to present his views on comprehension at home and union with Protestants abroad.[94] He also suggested the outlines of a program for raising the standard of church life, including plans for educational reform, new methods for use in training ministers for service, and proposals for new emphasis on practical divinity.[95] To march out of Babylon and build a new and better social order there must be a spirit of co-operation among ministers, magistrates, and the common man. Co-operation must replace conflict in the relationships of these groups.

God hath distributed to every member of the body his faculty, charge and place, as he doth think good; therefore no member can effect the charge and place of another. . . . . So may not the Ministery incroach upon the Magistracy; nor the Magistracy upon the Ministery; nor may he who is called to bear the vessells only in a private way, take upon him the charge of a publike relation belonging to the Magistracy or Ministery. . . . . Let everyman abide in the sphear and calling wherein God hath set him.[96]

[93] Dury, *Israel's Call to March out of Babylon*, pp. iii, iv.   [95] *Ibid.*, pp. 45 ff.

[94] *Ibid.*, p. 24.   [96] *Ibid.*, p. 20.

In the meetings of the Committee on Accommodation, Dury soon discovered that his program in the interest of peace was handicapped both by the unyielding attitude of the Presbyterian leaders, who were now resolved to use their majority in the House of Commons and the Assembly to impose the establishment of an unmodified form of Presbyterianism, and by the determined attitude of the Independents, who had much to expect in their favor from the changing political and military situation.[97] However, Dury manifested his customary persistency. To the Committee on Accommodation he recommended a definite method of procedure, which involved the formulation of points of actual agreement between Presbyterians and Independents; the recognition of certain "Laws of Christian Brotherhood," which should be observed in dealing with the matters in dispute; and a concerted effort to arrange, on a basis of compromise, a system which would give complete freedom to the local congregation in the conduct of its own affairs and, at the same time, provide for "Brotherly Communion" through an association of churches.[98]

Despite the earnest efforts of Dury to secure a compromise along these lines, no agreement could be reached between Presbyterians and Independents either in the Committee or in the Assembly. The Committee on Accommodation held its last meeting on March 6, 1646. Thereafter, Dury was forced to make his appeal for the union of Presbyterians and Independents to the people through the medium of a series of pamphlets. He continued to serve in the Assembly, hoping that he might at least be able to revive the earlier interest of the Assembly in projects for closer co-operation with the Continental Reformed Churches.[99] This hope was likewise doomed to disappointment, as the Assembly was now centering its attention on affairs at home. After the rejection of his union proposals, Dury did not take a prominent part in the work of the Assembly. The *Minutes* indicate that he was in regular attendance until January, 1648, with the exception of two brief intervals when he was assigned

---

[97] See Hetherington, *op. cit.*, pp. 209 ff.; Mitchell, *op. cit.*, pp. 205 ff.; W. H. Stowell and D. Wilson, *A History of the Puritans and the Pilgrim Fathers*, pp. 270 ff., 275 ff.; and D. M. Wolfe, *Milton and the Puritan Revolution*, pp. 58 ff., 152 ff.

[98] Dury's proposals to the Committee were later elaborated in his pamphlet, *A Peacemaker Without Partiality*, pp. 47 ff.

[99] On the earlier interest of the Assembly in projects for co-operation with Continental Protestants see Hetherington, *op. cit.*, pp. 345 ff.; and John Aiton, *Life and Times of Alexander Henderson*, pp. 549–51.

to other duties by order of Parliament.[100] In a letter to Raumer he stated that he took part in the work of the Assembly in drafting the Westminster Confession of Faith, the Larger and Shorter Catechisms, and also in the preparation of the Book of Common Worship and the form for the ordination of ministers.[101]

Because of Dury's efforts to remain impartial amid the bitter partisan strife of the times, he was frequently selected to serve on committees which were appointed to present the views of the Assembly to the House of Commons.[102] He also served on numerous committees which were appointed to honor Continental guests and to examine the books of Continental authors—duties assigned to him because he was better informed regarding European affairs than most of his associates in the Assembly.[103] He attempted to secure the co-operation of the Assembly and the House of Commons in arranging for the publication of an English translation of the writings of Luther and a new edition of the Septuagint.[104]

It is probable that Dury was partly responsible for the emphasis on the Covenant theology which appears in the Westminster Standards, though it had not been incorporated in the earlier Protestant confessions.[105] As early as 1637, Dury had suggested the advisability of using the Covenant idea as the basic principle for the formation of a fundamental confession of faith which he hoped would be acceptable to all Protestants.[106] He was well acquainted with the Continental exponents of the Covenant theology, such as Amesius of Franeker and Cocceius of Leyden.[107] He favored the Covenant

[100] On Dury's participation in the work of the Assembly see Mitchell and Struthers, *op. cit.*, pp. 121, 126, 131, 160–68, 171, 182–84, 251, 252, 315–21, 338, 352–54, 477, 493, 501, 502, 505–7, 537.

[101] For the text of the letter to Raumer see J. Chr. Beckmann, *Histoire des Fürstenthums Anhalt*, VI, 156 ff.; cf. also C. W. Hering, *Geschichte der kirchlichen Unionsversuche seit der Reformation bis auf unsere Zeit*, II, 118, 119; and Hasaeus, *op. cit.*, VI, 683 ff.

[102] Mitchell and Struthers, *op. cit.*, pp. 164, 354, 493.

[103] *Ibid.*, pp. 167, 338, 352, 353.   [104] *Ibid.*, pp. 352, 353, 493.

[105] E. D. Morris, *Theology of the Westminster Symbols*, p. 822.

[106] Dury, *Letter to Lord Forbes*, pp. 5, 6: "I doe suppose, that two or three or more men spiritually affected and void of partiality may agree together to set upon this work of framing a Fundamental Confession. . . . . All the places of Scripture, chiefly in the New Testament, which speak of the Covenant of God should be brought together. . . . . [Thus] the chiefe matter and order of the parts of the fundamental Confession is found out, and is found out from Scriptures itself."

[107] F. Sander, "Comenius, Duraeus, Figulus nach Stammbüchern der Familie Figulus-Jablonski," *Monatshefte der Comenius Gesellschaft*, III, 318; cf. also John Worthington, *The Diary and Correspondence of Dr. John Worthington*, I, 280.

theology because he thought the acceptance of its principles would help to heal the divisions among the churches and give new impetus to the study of practical divinity and biblical theology and thus limit the current emphasis on scholastic and dogmatic theology.[108]

Mitchell has presented a labored argument to prove that the emphasis on the Covenant theology in the Westminster Standards was due to English rather than to Continental influences.[109] Strangely enough, he omits the name of Dury in his list of English writers who were interested in the Covenant idea. Yet it seems probable that Dury was the only one of the Westminster divines who had already suggested the Covenant theology as the basic principle for the formation of a fundamental confession of faith. The *Minutes* of the Assembly debates on doctrinal issues are scanty and defective. It is impossible to trace the details of Dury's participation in these debates, but it is probable that he was at least partly responsible for the Assembly's emphasis on the Covenant idea.

Dury was regarded with suspicion by many members of the Assembly. Evidence that he was in disfavor with his associates in the Assembly is presented in contemporary accounts which indicate that Dury was publicly censured by the Assembly because he had written a part of the Preface to an English translation of Jacob Acontius' *Satans Stratagems*, which was published at London in the year 1648.[110] This Preface contained letters from Dury and John Goodwin indorsing the book and its author.[111] Dury was attracted to Acontius because of his emphasis on subjective religious experience, his

---

[108] These ideas were further developed by Dury in his pamphlet, *An Earnest Plea for Gospel Communion*. In this tract (pp. 18, 19) he says: "Nor is it possible (as I conceive) ever to unite the Professors of Christianitie to each other, to heal their Breaches and Divisions in Doctrine and Practise, and to make them live together as brethren in one Spirit ought to do, without the same sense of the Covenant, by which they may be made to perceive the terms upon which God doth unite all those who are his children unto himselfe; and upon which everyone that is in Covenant with God, is bound in conscience, through love unto God, to maintain the unitie of the Spirit in the bond of peace with those that are his children, who all alike .... are in the same Covenant with him."

[109] *Op. cit.*, pp. 387–89.

[110] Müller, *op. cit.*, II, Part II, 477.

[111] Worthington (*op. cit.*, II, Part II, 143) states that Dury recommended the author of the book as "an excellent man, and thoroughly knowing in many sciences; his excellency did lie in the depth and solidity of his judgment in everything, and in the piety and moderation of his spirit in matters of religion..... To be carried along with the stream, or to be silent when matters are not carried according to our mind, is no hard matter to any that hath any measure of discretion; but to row against .... the current of an age, and that without offence to any, and that strongly and irresistibly, as in his age Acontius did, is not the work of an ordinary courage: therefore such as own him in his way are more to be commended."

championship of the view that only doctrines which are distinctly stated in Scripture should be regarded as necessary for salvation, and his interest in promoting unity among Protestant groups.[112] The fact that Goodwin, an outstanding Independent leader, had indorsed the book naturally aroused the suspicions of the strict Presbyterians.

Francis Cheynell, the most zealous heresy-hunter among the Westminster divines, denounced the book before the Assembly because of the latitudinarian and anti-Trinitarian views of Acontius. He also denounced Dury because of his indorsement of the book. Thereupon the Assembly appointed a committee to examine the book, and Dury was ordered to appear before the committee.[113] Although he was able to explain his action to the satisfaction of the committee, the Assembly ordered Cheynell to prepare an answer to Acontius.[114] Worthington concludes his account of the incident by stating that "the Assembly did snib [snub] Mr. Dury for writing a preface to the English translation."[115] Dury was convinced that there was no chance for the further promotion of his union ideas in the Assembly. Shortly after he had cleared himself of the charges presented by Cheynell, he ceased to attend the Assembly sessions.

In his efforts to secure support for his church-union projects Dury had enlisted the help of Lady Ranelagh, the daughter of Richard Boyle, who was the first Earl of Cork and Lord High Treasurer of Ireland. Masson describes this patroness of Dury as "one of the best educated women of her time, ... in religious matters a very liberal Puritan."[116] In 1645 Dury married an aunt of Lady Ranelagh. This marriage brought him within the circle of friends and relatives of Lady Ranelagh—a circle which included her brother, Robert Boyle the scientist, and John Milton. Boyle, Milton, and other in-

---

[112] See Müller, op. cit., II, Part II, 125-27, 135, 477 ff., 582 ff., 588, 731 ff.; and Jordan, The Development of Religious Toleration in England, I, 303 ff., and passim.

[113] Mitchell and Struthers, op. cit., p. 505.

[114] This answer was published by Cheynell in 1650 under the title The Divine Tri-unity of the Father, Son, and Holy Spirit. Cheynell's account of Dury's connection with the Acontius publication is given in pp. 453-56 of this work. He describes Dury's appearance before the committee as follows: "When Mr. Dury came among us and saw that he had given too fair a testimony to that subtle piece, he dealt as ingenuously with us as we dealt with him, and assured us that he would be ready to make his retraction as public as his recommendation had been made without his consent, because he clearly saw that they practiced upon his passionate love of peace to the great prejudice of truth, and that he was merely drawn in to promote a syncretism beyond the orthodox lines of communication."

[115] Op. cit., II, Part II, 143.   [116] Op. cit., V, 232, 233.

fluential friends of Lady Ranelagh became interested in Dury's church-union proposals and later helped to promote his efforts under the Cromwellian regime.

Dury's marriage also helped him in the solution of his financial problems. His wife possessed an estate worth more than £400 per year. Although the income from this estate could not be collected during the course of the civil war in Ireland,[117] it is probable that this income was later of great service to Dury in financing his union negotiations. That the marriage ultimately brought considerable wealth to the poverty-stricken minister is indicated by the fact that Dury's only child, Dora Catharine, who, prior to 1666, married Henry Oldenburg, the first secretary of the Royal Society, was provided with a dowry which consisted of £400 and an estate in the marshes of Kent worth £60 per annum.[118]

Dury's stay in England was marked by a renewal of his efforts to promote educational reform. Milton's tractate *On Education*, which was dedicated to Dury's friend, Hartlib, had aroused public interest in the subject. Dury now busied himself with the preparation of tracts on education with the hope that Parliament would undertake the reformation of the schools. Three of his treatises on education, which were prepared at this time, are preserved in manuscript form in the Sloane Collection. The first, entitled "Exercitation of Schooling," was probably written in 1646. It was designed to direct public attention to the whole problem of organized education.[119] Stressing "the Necessitie and Usefulnesse of the Worke of the Education of children to all societies of men, to the Church, and to the present reformation of the Church and State now intended," he urged the magistracy and the ministry to co-operate in the establishment of a universal system of public education. It should be the objective of this system of education "to make children's mindes sound and bodies healthful, [and] to set them in a way to become serviceable unto others publicly and privately."

To accomplish these aims Dury proposed that the primary and secondary schools should be public and common to all, with three types of curriculum, which should be designed to train "the vulgar for Trades and Servile worke, the Learned for the increase of science

---

[117] Dury, *The Unchanged Peacemaker*, p. 14.

[118] Worthington, *op. cit.*, I, 194.

[119] An outline of Dury's "Exercitation of Schooling" is presented by Klahr, *op. cit.*, pp. 199, 200.

and training up others thereunto, [and] the Nobles to fit them for public charges in Peace and Warre." Adamson regards this proposal for a system of universal public education, designed to meet the needs of all elements in society, as one of the most notable advances in seventeenth-century educational history.[120] A second tract, written in 1646 and entitled "The Heads of Matters to bee thought on Concerning the Education of Nobles and Gentlemen," was an attempt to give suggestions as to administrative policies, methods, and curricula which should be used in the new type of schools designed for the training of the children of the nobility.[121]

The third manuscript, entitled "A Transmarine School," was also written by Dury in the year 1646.[122] It seeks to inform English educators regarding the results of a survey of the educational methods employed in the Jesuit schools on the Continent.[123] Corcoran regards this Dury tract as the most important extant account of seventeenth-century school procedure.[124] Dury argued that the methods used by the Jesuits were worthy of study in connection with the proposed reform of education in England, because their system was designed not for the acquisition of fact knowledge but for the purpose of developing the students by exercising the powers of their minds in dealing with concrete life-situations.

Dury's educational theories attracted the attention of leaders in Parliament. Just as he had previously been appointed by Charles I to serve as the tutor of Princess Mary, so now he was appointed by Parliament to serve as the tutor of the younger children of the King. Prince Henry and Princess Elizabeth had been placed under the care of the Duke of Northumberland in 1645 and Prince James (later James II) was also placed under his care in 1646. Under orders from Parliament, Dury became the tutor of the royal children, despite the fact that his new duties occasioned some irregularity in his attendance on the sessions of the Assembly.[125] In addition to his duties as

---

[120] J. W. Adamson, *Pioneers of Modern Education*, p. 155.

[121] An outline of this tract is presented by Klahr, *op. cit.*, pp. 200–203.

[122] The full text of Dury's "A Transmarine School" was printed for the first time in T. Corcoran's *Studies in the History of Classical Teaching*, pp. 236–47. Apparently the two writers who have attempted studies of Dury's educational writings, Klahr and Scougal, overlooked this significant treatise.

[123] Dury's observations of the Jesuit methods show marked accuracy. Compare his account of the Jesuit schools in "A Transmarine School" with the description of these schools given by M. Siebengartner, *Schriften und Einrichtungen zur Bildung der Geistlichen*, pp. 81 ff., 366 ff.

[124] *Op. cit.*, p. 230.   [125] Dury, *Unchanged Peacemaker*, pp. 13, 14.

tutor and member of the Assembly, he also served for a time as one
of the ministers of Winchester—a post assigned to him by order of
the Committee for Plundered Ministers.[126]

Though engaged in these various activities, Dury continued his
interest in the problem of the union of the churches at home and
abroad. He prepared a number of pamphlets which were designed to
attract public support for the reunion movement. In 1646 he wrote
a pamphlet in answer to Saltmarsh's plea that the settlement of
church government in England should be delayed. Although this
Dury pamphlet was not published until 1654, when the issue was still
under discussion,[127] it indicates clearly that, in the year 1646, Dury
was already convinced and was seeking to convince others "that the
needless (that is to say, the meer Political, Subtile and Cunning) delay of settling that Church-Government which is most consonant to
the Word of God, and the example of the best reformed Churches
will not be found expedient, but hurtful to the whole state and members of the Houses."[128] This was the burden of his message to the
leaders of the Presbyterian and Independent parties whenever they
showed inclination to delay efforts at settlement until a new turn in
public affairs might produce a more favorable situation for one or
the other of the parties.

In 1647 Dury published his pamphlet entitled *A Model of Church
Government* as an attempt both to promote a new effort to unite the
Presbyterians and the Independents and to suggest a system of
church government which would be acceptable to both parties. In
an extended Preface to this book he pictures the destructive effects
of the current strife over religious issues in England and pleads with
the ministers to lead the way to a peaceful settlement of the existing
quarrels.[129] Despairing of any hope for union as a result of the deliberations of the Westminster Assembly, he suggests that there
should be an entirely new negotiation in the interest of reconciling
the various parties then contending for control of church life in
England.[130] In his own suggestions for the settlement of a new

---

[126] *Ibid.*, p. 13.

[127] Published at London in 1654 with the following entry on the title-page: *A Demonstration
of the Necessity of Settling some Gospel-Government Amongst the Churches of Christ in this Nation.
. . . . Written in the year 1646 by Mr. John Dury. . . . . And now Published for the Present Use
of these Times, wherein it may be seasonable to be taken into Consideration, for the preventing
of further Confusion and Disorder amongst the Professors of the Gospell.*

[128] *Ibid.*, p. 18.

[129] Pp. xix–xxiii.   [130] *Ibid.*, p. xxvii.

system of church government, Dury advises that care must be taken to avoid too high a degree of centralization of church authority, such as prevailed under the old episcopal regime; yet there must be connectional bonds between the churches in order that they may be held together in communion, fellowship, and effective co-operation in Christian service. He says:

I can see no way to prevent the growing effects of our fatal distempers, except God so blesse the Government by law established with that spirit of Discretion, of Moderation, of Equity, and of Lowlinesse in all things in which it doth act, that none shall be able to find any just grievance at it. And to this effect, the lesse the Classicall Presbyteries shall resemble the Civil Courts of Judicature, or the Bishops Courts in former times, the more they will be sutable to the end for which they are instituted, which is to entertain Brotherly conferences and consultations about spirituall matters for mutuall assistance and support in the wayes of God; and not at all to intermeddle with the Congregations in any of their particular affairs, which are not voluntarily brought unto them as a Case wherein their judgement is sought. . . . .

By which means all the Congregations of Professours will be, ... co-ordinate with each other, as companies of horses of Pharoahs chariots. . . . . Now this conjunction and co-ordination of churches, by the brotherly combination of their leaders; as it may not prejudge the liberty which they have in Christ, so it should oblige them to a right use of that liberty, to make it serviceable unto each other in the communion of the saints. . . . . To make this agreement free and mutual, there must be some Assemblies and Conferences setled; and these so ordered that all things shall be carried with that equality, that none shall have cause to think himself borne down or excluded from his right, or past by and concluded without his consent in matters which do concern him.[131]

Thus the system of church government must be settled on a basis of comprehension and must involve characteristic features of both the Presbyterian and the Independent systems. Such a settlement would bring peace, make possible the completion of the work of reformation, and prepare the churches to take a position of leadership in developing educational reform, religious education, and practical divinity.[132] In 1648 Dury issued another appeal for an entirely new effort at union on the basis of comprehension in a pamphlet entitled *A Peacemaker Without Partiality*. This pamphlet reveals the fact that Dury was beginning to look to Independent leaders in the army and in Parliament for the solution of the problem as to "How the means of Christian peace, as well Civill as Ecclesiastical, ought to be followed, and may be found among Professors." Cromwell and the Independents must, he argues, lead the way to a settled form of church government which would be acceptable to all.

If it be not now too late to quench this flame, or if it can be hoped that in the midst of our so great fears, so many jealousies, so different practises, and so loud

[131] *Ibid.*, pp. xxviii, 17, 18, 19.   [132] *Ibid.*, pp. xxxi ff.

clamours, and so sensible injuries, men's spirits can be brought to mutuall confidence and made susceptible of temperate thoughts towards one another, I would advise all, but chiefly such as have power in the Houses, in the Citie, in the Assembly, in the Army, and most of all the Generall and the Lieutenant Generall, on whom the eyes of most men are fixed, to proceed after this manner and lead us in this way.[133]

He suggested that the method of procedure employed in the Assembly should be discarded and that a smaller group, composed of men of more conciliatory spirit chosen from both parties, should be appointed to "discover the way towards an Accommodation which without prejudice to either side may be tendered to all."[134] Consistent with his previous suggestions, he advised that effort should be made to incorporate features of both the Presbyterian and the Independent systems in the formation of a new type of church government, which would allow large liberty of action on the part of local congregations and provide for the effective association of the churches on "the undeniable principle and maxime of Brotherly Communion."[135] Agreements reached in the Assembly's Committee on Accommodation would furnish a starting-point for further negotiations in the interest of such a union.

Meanwhile, the attention of Englishmen was called from matters of church government to significant political developments. In January, 1649, Charles I was placed on trial. Dury followed the reports of the trial with keen interest. True to his nonpartisan principles, he deplored the effort to bring the King to the scaffold and decided to make an attempt to save him. He took upon himself the task of securing the preparation of a brief which could be used by the King in his own defense. Dury describes his efforts to save the King in the following narrative:

I did conscionably judge myself bound to do for him, all which I could or should have done for mine own father if he had been in his case: Therefore I went to one of the Masters of Chancery, an able man, and an intimate friend of mine; whom I found no lesse troubled at those proceedings then I was; to consult him, what could be done for his majesty to prevent the sentence which was apprehended to be given against him; whereupon he resolved to write down such arguments as he conceived most effectual for his Majesty to use at the High Court in his own defense: Of these arguments I gave one Copy to the Lady Viscountes Ranalaugh, who with my wife furnished the Lady Monmouth therewith; that shee by Doctor Juxon his means might convey them to the king; and another Copy thereof I carried myself to the Prince Elector Palatine, that when he should be permitted to go to visit his Uncle he might give it unto him; which hee promised to do. This was to prevent the Sentence

[133] Dury, *A Peacemaker Without Partiality*, p. 1.

[134] *Ibid.*, p. 47.

[135] *Ibid.*, p. 48.

by Legall Plea; and then when the sentence was pronounced; I sate up a whole night and wrote about two sheets of Paper, wherein I did plead against the execution of that sentence, by eight classes of Arguments, which were inscribed and sent to the President and Judges of the High-Court to persuade them to suspend it. . . . . I am sure the President did receive them, for about a year and a half, or three quarters after that time; the President himself did shew me that Paper and did ask me if I did know such a hand, whereunto I did answer affirmatively, and looked him in the face steadfastly, whereupon he proceeded no further.[136]

But this appeal was without effect. Dury says: "When this wrought nothing upon them, nor any other means used by other ministers, nor the interposition of Holland's Ambassadors, could avail their resolution; I went out of Town, not to be in a place where so great a mischief was to be acted."[137] Charles I was executed on January 30, 1649. Dury's next efforts in behalf of Christian reunion were to be conducted under the auspices of the Commonwealth and the Protectorate.

[136] Dury, *Declaration of John Durie*, pp. 11, 12. An outline of the argument which Dury prepared in his attempt to secure a stay of execution is given in the same pamphlet (pp. 12–15). It seems probable that the brief which Dury furnished was used by Charles I in framing his argument that the court had no jurisdiction in his case. Compare the summary of the arguments contained in this brief as they are listed in the *Declaration of John Durie* with the account of the trial of Charles I as given by C. W. Coit, *The Life of Charles I*, pp. 340 ff.; see also the account of the trial and execution of Charles I as presented by W. C. Abbott, *Writings and Speeches of Oliver Cromwell*, I, 705 ff.

[137] *Declaration of John Durie*, p. 16.

CHAPTER VII

IN THE SERVICE OF THE COMMONWEALTH AND THE PROTECTORATE

DURY'S protest against the execution of Charles I naturally aroused the suspicions of the leaders of the dominant party in England, but he was soon able to gain their confidence. He secured an interview with John Bradshaw, who had presided at the trial of Charles I, and gave an explanation of his efforts to save the King which was accepted as satisfactory. The Council of State passed an order to the effect that Dury was "to have liberty to abide within the Commonwealth."[1] By the middle of March, 1649, he was busily engaged in preparing pamphlets in defense of the new government. "The Council," says Masson, "had their eye specially on the celebrated Durie, as a man who might be of use, both by his abilities, and by the multiplicity of his European connections."[2]

In less than a year the Council was employing Dury to prepare tracts for "satisfying the people" concerning the new program for the regulation of the affairs of the churches.[3] On August 14, 1650, Dury was appointed to serve with a number of Independent leaders on a commission which was intrusted with the duty of taking over the records of the Westminster Assembly and preserving these documents for the use of the Commonwealth.[4] From 1649 to 1654 there was an increasing disposition on the part of the Independent leaders to favor Dury and to make use of his services.

Dury has been severely criticized by contemporary and later writers because he accepted appointments under the Commonwealth and defended the new government.[5] By championing the cause of

---

[1] *Calendar of State Papers, Domestic Series, 1650*, p. 272.

[2] *Life of Milton*, IV, 228.

[3] *Calendar of State Papers, Domestic Series, 1649–1650*, p. 448.

[4] Masson, *op. cit.*, IV, 228, quotes from the Council Order Book as follows: "Ordered: That Mr. Thomas Goodwin, Mr. Byfield, Mr. Bond, Mr. Nye, Mr. Durie, Mr. Frost, Mr. Milton, or any three of them, of which Mr. Frost or Mr. Milton to be one, to be appointed to view and to inventory all records, writings, and papers whatsoever, belonging to the Assembly of the Synod, to the end that they may not be embezzled, and may be forthcoming for the use of the Commonwealth."

[5] E.g., see the criticism by William Prynne as presented in Dury's *Unchanged Peacemaker*, p. 12.

the King and then receiving favors from the party which was responsible for the death of the King, he obviously invited accusations of inconsistency. However, Dury maintained that his actions were thoroughly consistent. The prime motive of his life, he claimed, was to advance the cause of peace and unity.[6] He had attempted to live *extra partes* and to interest all parties in the cause of peace. He had feared that the execution of the King would produce anarchy.[7] After the execution of Charles I the only existing government was in the hands of the Independent leaders who had the new Commonwealth government in full operation by March, 1649.[8] Dury then believed that anarchy could be avoided and peace could be established only by the general recognition of the *de facto* government. He therefore recognized the new government, entered its service, and soon gained prominence as one of its most vigorous proponents in the pamphlet literature of the period.

The execution of the King was most severely criticized by the Presbyterian ministers. In sermons and pamphlets they sought to arouse opposition to the new government. These ministers, said Dury, "seemed to make it a main design to incense the people to a tumultuous and inconsiderable rising . . . . [and] to heighten the animosities of the discontented parties to an utter confusion."[9] The dangers arising in this quarter prompted Dury to prepare two pamphlets, which were designed to protest against "ministers meddling in politics" and to "shew that it did not belong to the Ministeriall work of the Gospell to handle such state matters in their sermons or to inform the people concerning the same as they were wont to do."[10] The first of these pamphlets, entitled *A Case of Conscience Resolved: Concerning ministers meddling with State Matters in their Sermons,* was issued on March 15, 1649. It was the first of Dury's many pamphlets designed to settle "cases of conscience"—writings which

---

[6] Newman Smyth ("John Dury: A Peacemaker among the Churches," *Constructive Quarterly,* IV, 418) says: "Dury was a man of one idea, but it was a great one; and it is noteworthy how in the light of one luminous Christian idea he was enabled to follow a steady and consistent course through the revolutionary changes of those troublous times."

[7] Dury, *Declaration of John Durie,* p. 16.

[8] W. C. Abbott, *Writings and Speeches of Oliver Cromwell,* II, 32 ff.

[9] *Declaration of John Durie,* p. 16.

[10] *Ibid.,* p. 17. Here, in further explanation of his objectives in preparing these pamphlets, Dury adds: "To obviat this danger, which was occasioned by the inconsiderateness of some Ministers; I conceived it answerable to the aims of my employment, and necessary to preserve the moderate party, to bear witness against that way and manner of preaching, which some followed by directing their sermons to meddle with affairs of state."

indicate his interest in the application of casuistical morality toward the solution of contemporary problems of duty.[11] Here Dury compares the political sermons and activities of the preachers who were opposed to the new government with the methods used by the Anglican ministers under the Laudian regime; criticizes their policy of obstruction as motivated by bitter partisan spirit; and pleads for the co-operation of all factions in the establishment of civil and ecclesiastical peace under the auspices of the *de facto* government.[12]

This pamphlet provoked considerable discussion. The opponents of the new government charged that Dury prepared it "for a private end and to gain . . . . by preferment."[13] This accusation caused Dury to prepare a second pamphlet on the subject, which was published in 1650 under the title *A Case of Conscience Concerning Ministers medling with state matters in or out of their Sermons resolved more satisfactorily then heretofore.* He stated that it was his purpose "not to increase any breaches, confusions and animosities amongst us; but rather [to] heale, redresse and allay the same."[14] In the opening sections of the pamphlet suggestions are offered regarding rules which should be observed in Christian debate.[15] Mere scholastic disputes are harmful. Only subjects useful for edification are worthy of debate. Christian debates must be prefaced by a careful definition of terms, conducted in the spirit of Christian charity, and argued by means of the right use of Scripture and reason. Applying these rules to the problem of ministerial participation in state affairs, Dury attempted to prove the thesis that it does not "belong to the ministers of the Gospel of Christ to declare concerning the affaires of state, which are the magistrates employment, their opinions in their sermons touching the Gospel."[16] Distinguishing between the duties of ministers and magistrates,[17] he argued that ministers "in their places are not properly *over* men as magistrates are in human affairs, to command and compel obedience to that which they injoyn; but only *towards* men in Divine affairs, to let them know the will of God, to intreat them to yeeld obedience thereunto for Christ's sake."[18]

---

[11] On the development of casuistry in the Puritan age see J. T. McNeill, "Casuistry in the Puritan Age," *Religion in Life*, XII (1942), 76–89.

[12] The full text of this pamphlet is presented in the *Harleian Miscellany*, VI, 196–212.

[13] See Dury, *Concerning Ministers medling with state matters in or out of their Sermons*, p. 3.

[14] *Ibid.*, p. 4.   [15] *Ibid.*, pp. 5 ff.   [16] *Ibid.*, pp. 24 ff.

[17] *Ibid.*, pp. 50 ff.   [18] *Ibid.*, p. 52.

Ministers are under obligation to recognize the *de facto* government of the Commonwealth because it is the only existing government, and "God hath given to those that are now over us in places of Rule a conquest of all that hath hitherto opposed them in their designes."[19] Anarchy, he asserts, is inevitable unless the Commonwealth leaders are given an opportunity to save the nation.[20] The salvation of society is conditioned upon the more perfect co-ordination of the activities of ministers and magistrates.

> For seeing the magistracy and the ministery are the two great and Master-wheels of all the public States of the Christian world, therefore we see, that by the motions thereof, if regular upon their Axletrees, and duly correspondent one with another, all the affaires of human societies are carried on successfully, for the attainment of their eternall and temporall felicity, both towards God and man: But if their motions be either irregular within themselves, or inconsistent with each other, it is evident in all Ages, that from thence the affaires of all societies become unsuccessful, and tend onely to the misery and desolation of mankind.[21]

If the ministers and magistrates of England were to offer "their joynt strength and cooperation in this way of God, we may confidently hope that the work of our Reformation may be speedy, safe, full, and permanent." If co-operation could take the place of conflict in the relationships of ministers and magistrates, they could work out the solution of vital problems confronting the nation, such as the following:

> 1. How the Knowledge, Practice, and Power of Godlinesse may be most effectually advanced throughout the nation, either by an impartiall settlement and regulating of Catecheticall Exercises, or Propheticall Conferences, and of a preaching ministery. . . . .
>
> 2. What the scandals and disorders are, which may fundamentally destroy this designe, and how they may be prevented.
>
> 3. How without prejudice to good order on the one hand, and to true Christian liberty on the other, the causes of our present breaches and offences may be remedied. . . . .
>
> 4. How throughout the Nation, the Schools of Learning, and the education of youth therein, may be rectified, and reduced to a more compendious, profitable and uniform way of teaching tongues, morall vertues, Industry and Sciences then now it is.[22]

[19] *Ibid.*, p. 162.

[20] *Ibid.*, pp. 12, 20, and *passim*.

[21] *Ibid.*, p. 25. Dury's arguments in this pamphlet were probably influenced by the work of Hugo Grotius entitled *De imperio summarum potestatum circa sacra* (1647). An analysis of the Grotian arguments on the relationship of church and state is presented by Douglas Nobbs, *Theocracy and Toleration*, pp. 62 ff.

[22] *Concerning Ministers medling* . . . . , p. 174.

It was soon evident that this co-operation of ministers and magistrates would not be secured. Cromwell and the Independents had full control of the new government. Their proposed policy for the regulation of church affairs was outlined in the *Agreement of the People*. This document, as issued in 1649, announced that a reformed profession of Christianity should be the national religion; that penalties should not be used to enforce public confession; and that persons of differing judgment should be protected in the exercise of their religion and the confession of their faith, with the reservation that this liberty must not be permitted to disturb the public peace and that it must not "extend to popery and prelacy."[23] Anglicans, of course, protested against such a settlement. The Presbyterians were alarmed over the indications that the new government would reject their polity which had been established by law. Consequently, Anglicans and Presbyterians united in opposing the new regime.

Thus threatened, the new government drew up the Engagement in 1649 for the purpose of using it as a test oath. The Engagement read as follows: "I do declare and promise that I will be true and faithful to the commonwealth of England, as it is now established without a king or House of Lords."[24] In 1650 Parliament abolished the obligation of subscribing to the Solemn League and Covenant and substituted the requirement that all Englishmen over eighteen years of age should subscribe to the Engagement. The imposition of this test oath served to bring the opposition to the new government into the open. Many Anglican and Presbyterian ministers and laymen refused to take the Engagement. Their opposition was voiced in numerous pamphlets. Dury was one of the most prolific pamphleteers among the many who sought to answer the criticisms of the Engagement.

Dury regarded the Engagement as a harmless pledge, which, if taken by all, would form a bond of union under a government that would advance the cause of peace among the churches at home and abroad. He interpreted the Engagement as a recognition of the *de facto* government and a pledge "to be true and faithfull to the Nation, notwithstanding the absence of the King and House of Lords from the government."[25] He prepared a written interpretation of the meaning of the Engagement, which he presented to the Council

[23] H. Gee and W. J. Hardy, *Documents Illustrative of English Church History*, pp. 574, 575.

[24] *Ibid.*, p. 575.   [25] Dury, *Declaration of John Durie*, p. 18.

and various leaders of the new government.[26] When he was assured that his interpretation was satisfactory, he was convinced that it was his duty to subscribe and to persuade others to take the Engagement.[27] During the years 1649–51 Dury prepared at least nine pamphlets urging subscription to the Engagement.[28] He thought these pamphlets would advance the interest of civil as well as ecclesiastical peace. Although the literary advocacy of the establishment of civil peace was a new field for Dury, he regarded such activity as well worth the effort and as thoroughly consistent with his self-appointed duties as a peacemaker. He records his reactions as he assumed this new role as follows:

It is my right, to live as well under the one Government as the other, walking in Peace and Truth towards all men inoffensively. In effect by scanning of matters relating to this subject, I find that I am fallen upon a branch of the studie of Peace which heretofore, in the Pursuit thereof I never did reflect upon so directly: for in former times my direct aim was to minde onely the Rules of religious Peace and unitie amongst the professors of the Gospel, in reference to Christianitie; but now have been carried on to minde also the Rules, by which a Christian is obliged to behave himself peaceably, in civil and outward relations; which is, and will be a necessarie point of knowledg, as wee are in the flesh, and as long as Babylon is not fallen, and the New Jerusalem, the mother of us all, is not come down from above. I have therefore caus to thank God, that I have not been led forth by any worldlie end in meddling with this Subject; So I have learned thereby, somewhat more of the waies of peace, then I ever knew before.[29]

In his pamphlets on the Engagement, Dury attempted to prove that it was the duty of all Englishmen to subscribe. He insisted that the Engagement should be interpreted simply as a form of acknowledging the validity of the *de facto* government.[30] Subscription to the Engagement, he maintained, did not conflict with the previous acceptance of the Oath of Allegiance and the Solemn League and Covenant.[31] The King had been unfaithful to his trust, and this infidelity absolved his subjects from their allegiance to him, his heirs,

[26] For the text of this paper see Dury, *Considerations Concerning the Present Engagement* (3d ed., 1650), p. 26.

[27] *Ibid.*, pp. 23, 24.

[28] See the titles of these pamphlets as listed in the "Trial List of the Printed Writings of John Dury," pp. 217–19.

[29] Dury, *A Second Parcel of Objections Against the taking of the Engagement Answered*, p. 73.

[30] Dury, *Conscience Eased*, pp. 2 ff.; and *Considerations Concerning the Engagement* (1649), pp. 24 ff.

[31] Dury, *Just Re-Proposals*, pp. 10 ff.; *Disingaged Survey*, pp. 2–6; *Two Treatises Concerning the Engagement*, pp. 3 ff.; and *Objections Against the Engagement Answered*, pp. 2 ff.

and his counselors.[32] The Solemn League and Covenant pledged
men to the preservation and defense of the true religion, and under
the existing circumstances this could be secured only by loyalty to
the new government.[33] In the passing of the old order the cause
of freedom and religion had made significant gains, but the new
liberty must not be permitted to degenerate into license and divisive
quarrels about religion.[34] The spread of anarchy and the further
disruption of the churches must be avoided by a general recognition
of the existing government.[35] The gains which had been made in the
course of years of struggle could be conserved, if the narrow, selfish, and
partisan spirit could be supplanted by a spirit of co-operation among
all factions. The new government afforded protection, and it should
receive support from all those whom it protected.[36] It was the only
government which was then properly accredited by the representatives of the people.[37] It afforded advantages which could not be
secured by the restoration of the crown to the Stuarts or by the
recognition of any pretender to the throne.[38] Furthermore, private
citizens have no right to pass judgment on the validity of the existing government, as the powers that be are ordained of God and all
citizens are under obligation to obey them.[39]

Dury's pamphlets in defense of the Engagement often evidence
hasty preparation and faulty logic, but they soon attracted the attention of the leaders of the new government. As early as December 21, 1649, the Council of State expressed the opinion that his
writings would be "of great use for better carrying on the Test" and
ordered that a reward should be given to him for his efforts.[40] Dury

---

[32] Dury, *Considerations Concerning the Engagement* (1649), p. 3: "If the King should set
himself wilfully above this Reason of the Nation, which is the onely Originall of the Law, and
refuse obstinately the Lawes, which they shall chuse to be settled: he puts himself ipso facto
out of the capacity of being a King any more unto them. . . . . It is evident, that so far as he
[the late king] did by that means actually un-king himself as to this nation: so far also, they
that assisted him in that design, [the Lords] did un-Lord themselves in the State."

[33] *Ibid.*, pp. 4–7.

[34] Dury, *Objections Against the Engagement Answered*, p. 17.

[35] Dury, *Considerations Concerning the Engagement* (1649), p. 23.

[36] *Ibid.*, pp. 16, 17.

[37] Dury, *Considerations Concerning the Engagement* (3d ed.), p. 25.

[38] Dury, *Considerations Concerning the Engagement* (1649), pp. 21, 22.

[39] Dury, *Objections Against the Engagement Answered*, p. 12; *Disengaged Survey*, p. 10; and
Declaration of John Durie, pp. 18, 19.

[40] *Calendar of State Papers, Domestic Series, 1649–1650*, p. 448.

cultivated the friendship and co-operation of these leaders in the hope that they would be willing to indorse and support a new effort in the interest of the union of the Protestant churches. When the Commonwealth government had demonstrated its military strength at home, there was little necessity for further literary effort in support of the Engagement. However, public opinion on the Continent was disposed to regard the new regime in England with distrust. The execution of Charles I had aroused vigorous protests from Continental writers, especially in Holland and Germany.[41]

The Commonwealth leaders wished to counteract this criticism by the circulation of literature defending their policies. They used Dury's services in this work. *Eikon Basilike* was being widely circulated by friends of the Stuarts in Europe. Milton had prepared his *Eikonoklastes* as an answer to this work. On May 20, 1651, the Council of State ordered Dury to translate *Eikonoklastes* into French.[42] His translation was printed by the government and given a wide circulation on the Continent.[43] Dury also sought to defend the policies of the Commonwealth in his extensive correspondence. In a letter to John Bergius, court preacher of Brandenburg, he attempted to answer the criticisms of the Cromwellian regime which were current in Brandenburg.[44] He also sent his friend Peter du Moulin a letter, in which he gave a somewhat extravagant description of the flourishing condition of the English, Irish, and Scottish churches under the Commonwealth.[45]

Dury's services in behalf of the Commonwealth government cost him many friends and subjected him to criticism and abuse. The

[41] See C. Mitsukuri, *Englisch-niederländische Unionsbestrebungen im Zeitalter Cromwells*, pp. 26 ff.; H. Wätjen, *Die erste englische Revolution und die öffentliche Meinung in Deutschland*, pp. 18 ff.; and S. von Bischoffshausen, *Die Politik des Protectors Oliver Cromwell in der Auffassung und Thätigkeit seines Ministers des Staatssecretärs John Thurloe*, pp. 3 ff.

[42] *Calendar of State Papers, Domestic Series, 1651*, p. 208.

[43] *Calendar . . . ., 1651–1652*, Introd., p. xxxii. Charles Bastide (*The Anglo-French Entente in the Seventeenth Century*, p. 153) states that Dury's translation was issued under the following title: "Εἰκονοκλάστης ou réponse au livre intitulé Εἰκὼν βασιλική ou le pourtrait de sa sacreé majesté durant sa solitude et ses souffrances. Par le Sr. Jean Milton. Traduite de l'Anglois sur le seconde et plus ample édition. A Londres. Par Guill. Du Gard, imprimeur du Conseil d'Etat. 1652"; see also D. M. Wolfe, *Milton in the Puritan Revolution*, pp. 219 ff. and *passim*.

[44] For the text of this letter see T. Hasaeus, *Biblotheca Bremensis historico-philologica-theologica*, IV, 683–716.

[45] H. G. N. Tollin, *Geschichts-Blätter für Stadt und Land Magdeburg*, XXXII, 254. This letter was published at London in 1658 under the following title: *Epistola ad Petr. Molinaeum de statu ecclesiae Anglicae, Scotiae et Hibernae sub Cromwello* (see Pierre Bayle, *Dictionnaire historique et critique*, II, 1044).

Scottish Presbyterians now distrusted him because he had advocated the substitution of the Engagement in place of the Solemn League and Covenant.[46] Many of the English Puritans, unwilling to reconcile themselves to the rule of the Independents, were caustic in their comments on Dury's compliant attitude toward the new order. In 1650 an anonymous pamphlet, appearing under the title *A Pack of Old Puritans*, accused Dury of attempting "to varnish over that complicated piety of subscribing the new Engagement with the Orient colours of an indispensable duty, necessary, just and equall." After listing a number of Dury's pamphlets, the statement is made that

we have found them so full of contradictions, absurdities, and irrationall reasonings, vented with such heighths of Majesterial confidence, or impudence, as makes us fear, that if ever he had any ministeriall gifts or abilities, they are, by the just judgement of God, blasted, for undertaking a service so sinful, as to render him accessary to the perjury of all those persons who have subscribed to the new Engagement by his perswasion.[47]

Such criticism caused Dury to complain that he received worse treatment from his brethren in England than from the "stiffest Lutherans."[48] A more severe criticism came from the pen of William Prynne, who attacked Dury in an anonymous pamphlet which was entitled *The Time Serving Proteus, and Ambidexter Divine Uncased to the World* (London, 1650).[49] Prefacing his pamphlet with copies of Dury's letters to Hall and Laud, Prynne charged that Dury, prompted by the desire to advance his own interests, had shifted his allegiance from the Presbyterian to the Anglican party, then from the Anglican to the Presbyterian party, and, finally, from the Presbyterian to the Independent party. Dury issued an extended reply, which was published under the title *The Unchanged, Constant and Single-hearted Peacemaker drawn forth unto the World* (London, 1650). In this book he explained his relationships with Anglican, Presby-

---

[46] Tollin, *op. cit.*, XXXII, 255.

[47] *A Pack of Old Puritans*, p. iv. John Westby-Gibson ("John Durie," *Dictionary of National Biography*) makes the careless mistake of listing this bitter diatribe against Dury as one of Dury's own writings.

[48] Dury, *Two Treatises Concerning the Engagement*, pp. 60, 61: "It hath been my earnest work to intreate men to say in a Christian way that which they had to say, and I have used all the industry I could to bring them without partiality to it, that by the things wherein we agree, we might come to a further light in that wherein we agree not; but I have reaped nothing almost but jealousies, reproaches and slanders for my pains; and have been worse rejected here, even by men otherwise Godly, then I have in Forrain parts amongst the stiffest Lutherans."

[49] *Catalogue of the Printed Books in the British Museum*, Vol. "Dru–Dyz," p. 191.

terian, and Independent leaders;[50] presented proofs that he had not advanced his private interests in any way by the activities which Prynne described;[51] and professed that he had constantly maintained a position *extra partes* in the hope that he might be an instrument under God to lead all parties to think in terms of peace and union.[52] Of the consistency of his "wayes in the midst of all these changes," he said:

I can rejoyce that God doth give me occasion and hath drawn me forth by vindicating myself, to let all men who shall read this, see the constant tenour of orderliness, wherein I have endeavored to walk first and last by a known rule, to be without offence towards everyone; for my conscience doth bear me record, as in the presence of God, that my study hath been to walk without any privat or partial designes, sincerely by the grace which I have received; framing my whole course by one and the same main Rule of Gospel-principles towards all, which is to walk in love and holiness for universal serviceableness in that which is good, holding forth the Word of life as the ground of this walking, by the particular directions which the Scriptures testify to be the will of God.[53]

On October 28, 1650, Dury was appointed to serve under Bulstrode Whitelocke as library keeper of St. James's Library. He held this position until the Restoration.[54] Although he was serving as a deputy under Whitelocke, he was intrusted with the responsibility of caring for the valuable collections of books and jewels.[55] He found the books in a confused jumble and, with characteristic energy, set to work to prepare a catalogue and inventory.[56] After he had performed this service, his duties were almost nominal, as few visitors came to the library. A letter written by Christopher Arnold, later professor of history at Nuremberg, preserves an impressive account of Dury's methodical care in the conduct of his office as librarian.[57] Not content with the performance of routine duties, Dury at-

[50] Dury, *Unchanged Peacemaker*, pp. 2 ff.

[51] *Ibid.*, pp. 6 ff., 9 ff.

[52] *Ibid.*, pp. 8 ff.

[53] *Ibid.*, p. 10.

[54] *Calendar of State Papers, Domestic Series, 1650*, p. 401; John Worthington, *Diary and Correspondence*, I, 199.

[55] Bulstrode Whitelocke (*Memorials of English Affairs*, III, 74) refers to the circumstances of Dury's appointment as follows: "I know the greatness of the charge, and considered the prejudice that might fall out by being responsible for those rich jewels. . . . . I did accept the trouble of being library-keeper at St. James . . . . and recommended Mr. Durey, a German by birth, a good scholar, and a great friend to Parliament, to be my deputy."

[56] *Calendar of State Papers, Domestic Series, 1651*, p. 468.

[57] See the text of Arnold's letter describing his visit to Dury at the library of St. James, as quoted by Masson, *op. cit.*, IV, 350.

tempted to work out practical suggestions that would place library work on a more scientific and efficient basis. His conclusions were stated in a book entitled *The Reformed Librarie-Keeper* (London, 1650).[58] Here Dury suggests that a librarian should be chosen by a type of civil service examination which would thoroughly test his fitness for the work. The librarian should regard himself as a "Factor and Trader for helps to learning, ... a treasurer to keep them, and a dispenser to apply them to use." He also presents practical suggestions regarding the purchasing and cataloguing of books and a discussion of the proper relationships between the librarian and the patrons and directors of his library.[59] A detailed description is given of the Wolfenbüttel Library, which Dury regarded as "one of the chiefest libraries in Germany."[60] Library work provided Dury with ample support, comfortable lodgings, and full control of his time. Such employment enabled him to devote much of his energy to the tasks in which he had a primary interest.

His first efforts were directed to the promotion of a new movement in the interest of the peace of the churches at home. He regarded the existing conditions as extremely unstable. In his "Epistolical Discours," which was printed in 1651 as a Preface to the *Clavis apocalyptica*,[61] he expressed his concern over the situation in England. Sharing to a large degree the interests of Andreae and Comenius in apocalyptic speculation, Dury recorded his agreement with the opinion of the author of the *Clavis apocalyptica* to the effect that the commotions of the times indicated an impending fulfilment of the apocalyptical promises and subscribed to the belief that "the Propheticall numbers [might] com to an end in the year of our Lord 1655."[62]

Dury was convinced that the danger which threatened England was not Roman Catholicism, but the alternative of either a highly

---

[58] The importance of this book in the history of the development of library methods is indicated by the fact that it has been twice reprinted in comparatively recent times. For the text of the first reprint see "John Durie's Reformed Librarie-Keeper and the Author's Career as a Librarian," *Library*, IV (1892), 81 ff. A new edition, with an excellent Introduction by Ruth Grannis, was issued at Chicago in 1908.

[59] Ruth Grannis, Introduction to Dury's *Reformed Librarie-Keeper*, p. 30.

[60] See "John Durie's Reformed Librarie-Keeper and the Author's Career as a Librarian," *loc. cit.*, pp. 84 ff.

[61] Dury's "Epistolical Discours" was printed as a Preface (pp. 1–79) of the *Clavis apocalyptica: Or A Propheticall Key: By Which the Great Mysteries in the Revelations of St. John and the Prophet Daniel are opened*. The manuscript of the *Clavis apocalyptica* was sent to England by Comenius. It was published at London in 1651.

[62] Dury, "Epistolical Discours," *Clavis apocalyptica*, pp. 1, 2, 4 ff.

centralized absolutism or a destructive anarchy.[63] The failure of the Christians of England to reconcile their differences would tend, he argues, to advance the establishment of an oppressive absolutism or a destructive anarchy. Both dangers might be avoided if Christians would adjust their differences and insist on the co-operation of ministers and magistrates in uniting the churches on a basis of comprehension. He urged his readers to co-operate in labors designed to inaugurate an era "when the banner of the spirit of love without partialitie, shall be lifted up in the beautie of Holiness, as the Ensign of the unitie of the Faith, and the badg of the common profession of Christianitie amongst Professors, and when Magistrates and ministers shall understand their true conjunction in the waie of their testimony."[64]

Dury sincerely believed that the immediate settlement of religious differences on a basis of comprehension was the imperative need of the English nation. In a further effort to promote such a settlement, he published his pamphlet entitled *A Demonstration of the Necessity of Settling some Gospel-Government Amongst the Churches in this Nation* (London, 1654). In this work he presented a forceful argument to prove that delay in settling a comprehensive type of church government would produce further disunion and additional excuses for governmental interference in church affairs.[65] He proposed that the first step toward healing the divisions among the English churches should take the form of an accommodation between the Presbyterians and the Independents. He says:

> I thought it sutable .... for me to represent .... some reasons for which I conceived them obliged in conscience to mind the interest of Religion amongst Protestants, and to give some countenance to the endeavors whereby their differences might be reconciled..... [These] reasons were also imparted unto the leading ministers of the Congregationall and Presbyteriall Churches in London; who by my sollicitation were brought together, and upon this occasion met several times for a special conference held at Blackfryers to compose their own differences first, and so to joyne with me in the designe of my negotiation towards the Churches.[66]

In the groups with which Dury conferred at this time there were leaders of various parties, including John Owen, who stood in close relationship to Cromwell; four Independent leaders who had taken a prominent part in the Westminster Assembly, Thomas Goodwin,

---

[63] *Ibid.*, pp. 73, 74.

[64] *Ibid.*, p. 76.

[65] See Dury, *Necessity of Settling some Gospel-Government*, pp. v, 1 ff., 18, 19 ff., 53 ff.

[66] *Declaration of John Durie*, pp. 23, 24.

Nye, Simpson, and Bridges; three Presbyterian members of the West-minster Assembly, Greenhill, Carter, and Adoniram Byfield; and John Goodwin, who had been an outspoken advocate of toleration and a vigorous opponent of any type of established church.[67] After numerous conferences these leaders were persuaded to approach Parliament in an effort to secure legislation establishing a state church on the basis of a compromise agreement. On February 10, 1652, John Owen, acting as spokesman for the group, presented to the Rump Parliament a petition, together with a "printed book."[68] This printed book was a copy of an English translation of the Raco-vian Catechism, which was presented as evidence that dangerous theological opinions would continue to spread unless some effort was made to save the churches and the nation by the settlement of reli-gious differences.[69]

Parliament then appointed a committee of fourteen, Cromwell included, to confer with the petitioning ministers in the preparation of a plan for "Better Propagation of the Gospel." On March 31, 1652, the petitioning ministers presented to this committee a paper entitled *The Humble Proposals of Mr. Owen and Other Ministers who presented the Petition to Parliament.*[70] Masson says:

> Altogether the proposals were thought to be a considerable stretch of liberality; and indeed the proposers professed to have framed them with "equal respects to all persons fearing God, though of differing judgments." Evidently, however, they were a kind of half-way scheme of a state-church much less formal than that of the Presbyterians, and with a Toleration sound about it, but still a scheme of a distinct state-church and of a Toleration within fixed limits.[71]

In the *Proposals* Dury and his associates listed fifteen fundamen-tals of Christianity, which were so worded as to exclude Quakers and Unitarians as well as Anglicans and Roman Catholics from the pro-posed establishment.[72] In 1652 Dury sought to enlist public interest in this new movement by collaborating with Hartlib in the prepara-tion and publication of a pamphlet entitled *The Reformed Spirituall Husbandman.* Cromwell was inclined to oppose a settlement based on the *Proposals* on the ground that they granted too limited a type

---

[67] Masson, *op. cit.*, IV, 392.

[68] *Ibid.*, p. 390.

[69] *Ibid.*, p. 438.

[70] *Ibid.*, p. 391; cf. Dury, *Reformed Spirituall Husbandman*, pp. 25-29.

[71] Masson, *op. cit.*, IV, 392; cf. Abbott, *op. cit.*, II, 519 ff., 537, 612.

[72] Masson, *op. cit.*, IV, 393.

of toleration. Richard Baxter, who participated in some of the conferences of the ministers who drew up the *Proposals*, wished to replace the list of fifteen fundamentals with the simple requirement of
the acceptance of the Apostles' Creed, the Lord's Prayer, and the
Ten Commandments.[73] The Rump Parliament was disposed to regard the *Proposals* with favor, but this Parliament was ejected before
it had opportunity to legislate on standards of conformity and toleration. Thus the control of church affairs continued in the hands of
Cromwell, who granted a wide degree of toleration to all groups except the Anglicans and Roman Catholics.[74]

After the failure of the effort to promote the organic unity of the
English churches, Dury turned his attention to other measures designed to develop a unity of spirit among Christians. He attempted
to prepare the way for a new advance in his irenic program by renewing his efforts to enlist the interest of his contemporaries in practical theology or, as he called it, "practical divinity"—a term which
he applied to doctrines of faith and morals, which were of practical
rather than scholastic importance. Dury's emphasis upon practical
theology was regarded by Charles A. Briggs as one of his most noteworthy contributions to the progress of Christian irenics and as an
important step in the promotion of a new type of syncretism, which
stressed Christian ethics rather than Christian dogma.[75]

Although this viewpoint had been suggested in the writings of
Andreae,[76] Boehme,[77] Comenius,[78] Ames of Franeker,[79] and others,
Dury and Calixtus were the most zealous advocates of this idea in
the middle period of the seventeenth century. In their championship
of this view they stressed ideas which were later advocated by the
German Pietists and also sounded a distinctly modern note in their
insistence upon the recognition of the social and ethical import of the
Christian message. Newman Smyth has expressed the opinion that

[73] W. H. Hutton, *The English Church from the Accession of Charles I to the Death of Anne*,
p. 168.

[74] Thomas Carlyle, *Oliver Cromwell's Letters and Speeches*, pp. 269, 270; and W. K. Jordan,
Development of Religious Toleration in England, III, 138 ff.

[75] C. A. Briggs, *Theological Symbolics*, pp. 21, 22.

[76] F. E. Held, *Christianopolis*, pp. 12 ff.

[77] M. L. Bailey, *Milton and Jacob Boehme*, pp. 20 ff., 28 ff.

[78] Matthew Spinka, *John Amos Comenius, That Incomparable Moravian*, pp. 57 ff., 115 ff.,
146 ff.

[79] See Hartlib's Preface to Dury's *Earnest Plea for Gospel Communion*, p. iii.

Dury and Calixtus opened a new epoch in the history of Christian ethics. They attempted to construct a moral philosophy based on the direct appeal to the moral consciousness. They insisted that the primary ethical elements of the Christian religion should not be "allowed to become lost or confounded, in any system of divinity which may be built up philosophically, or taught with authority in the creeds of the Church."[80] Dury had maintained this view from the very beginning of his union activities, but now he had more time which could be given to the development of this interpretation of the Christian message. His views on the subject were finally presented in the form of an appeal to the English churches to promote the study of practical divinity. This appeal was published at London in 1654 under the title, *An Earnest Plea for Gospel Communion in the Way of Godliness.*

In this pamphlet Dury defines practical divinity "as the revealed truths of God, concerning the obedience of the faith which is to be yielded unto his will."[81] He points out the fact that the churches have thus far valued scholastic divinity more than practical divinity because their leaders have failed to recognize the fact that "theoretical truths notionally apprehended bring the soul to no perfection except they become fruitful in actions of virtue." Religion is essentially the life of God in the soul of the believer, and

Godliness, therefore, which is the practice of divine Truth is the measure of all intellectual truths; for whatever matter of knowledge is not proportionate, subordinate, and subservient unto the production of the life of God in the soul of the believer is not to be received as a divine truth. . . . . From all which we shall inferre this Conclusion: That the studie of Practical Divinitie, is of far greater concernment unto all, and far more to [be] heeded, esteemed, and entertained in the Schools of the Prophets, then the studie of contemplative mysteries and notions of Divinitie; whereupon Controversial matters are ordinarily attendants. And seeing there are so many bodies and Systemes of Theoreticall and Controversal matters, that it would be no easie task to any man to reckon them all up; and yet there is not so much as one compleat bodie or Systeme of Practicall Divinitie found in all the Churches. . . . . This then is the compleat end of Practical Divinitie, to teach men the wisdom which is profitable unto the salvation of their souls, and the direction of the whole conversation to God's will; that they may be enabled whatever they do, to do all in God by walking in his light.[82]

[80] Newman Smyth, *Christian Ethics*, pp. 10 ff.

[81] Dury, *Earnest Plea for Gospel Communion*, p. 1.

[82] *Ibid.*, pp. 6, 7. Like the followers of Jacob Boehme and Conrad Weigle in Germany and the Quakers in England, Dury put much stress upon the idea of the "inner light" and sometimes exalted the voice of the Holy Spirit above the authority of churches and creeds. Thus, in his *Seasonable Discourse*, p. 5, he says: "The sufficient qualification of ministers is the gift of God's spirit in them."

Here Dury also renewed his appeal for the co-operation of English churchmen in the preparation of a "Compleat Body of Practical Divinity," which would incorporate the best English thought on the subject and prepare the way for further developments in this field. His appeal was reinforced by the citation of a letter signed by eighteen German divines, who had requested the publication of such a work and also letters from Archbishop Ussher and others who advocated co-operation in the project.[83] Dury proposed an outline for use in the preparation of the book. In the first place, it must contain a statement of those basic facts of the Christian religion which must be taken for granted in building a system of Christian ethics;[84] secondly, a careful attempt to define those "principles of the life of Godliness" which are involved in the Covenant of Grace;[85] and, finally, a detailed study of the ethical obligations of the individual *per se* and the duties which devolve through membership and responsibility in the various groupings of society, such as the family, the state, and the church.[86] Roman Catholic criticisms of Protestantism could be effectively answered by constructing a well-developed system of ethical standards and by encouraging obedience to these standards.[87] English churchmen should co-operate in this work, as it would serve both to strengthen their own churches and to promote the common cause of Protestants.[88] Dury was unable to secure the preparation of a Body of Practical Divinity by means of the co-operative effort of a group of English clergymen, but many individuals attempted to prepare works in the field of practical divinity at this time, and it is probable that Dury's pamphlet served to increase the interest in the subject.[89]

In the years 1649–54 Dury also devoted considerable time and effort to the advocacy of the long-delayed project for the reform of the English educational system. In the background of his thinking on the problem of educational reform there was the humanistic idea of world reform which he shared with Boehme,[90] Andreae,[91] and Comenius.[92] These advocates of the humanistic idea of world reform

[83] For the full text of this letter see Dury, *Earnest Plea for Gospel Communion*, pp. ix–xvii, 81–85.

[84] *Ibid.*, p. 13.

[85] *Ibid.*, pp. 18 ff.

[86] *Ibid.*, pp. 33–47.

[87] *Ibid.*, p. 57.

[88] *Ibid.*, pp. 58, 59, 66.

[89] See McNeill, *op. cit.*, pp. 80 ff.

[90] Bailey, *op. cit.*, pp. 71 ff.

[91] Held, *op. cit.*, pp. 79 ff.

[92] Matthew Spinka, *The Irenic Program and Activity of John Amos Comenius*, pp. 37 ff., 54 ff.

had been strongly influenced by survivals of the Neo-Platonic philosophy which had gained wide acceptance during the Renaissance
period. As a rule the German leaders who attempted to follow these
currents of thought were inclined to emphasize mysticism in their
interpretation of the Christian religion; to exalt piety above scholastic dogmatism; to foster the organization of national and international societies of learned men for the purpose of exchanging ideas
and advancing the progress of science; to promote the union of the
churches; and to advocate the reform of existing educational systems.
As indicated above,[93] Dury had become interested in each of these
objectives during his stay at Elbing, and throughout his career he
lost no opportunity to promote all these causes. He deserves a more
prominent place in the history of English thought because of his
varied efforts to transmit to England the views of Continental Neo-
Platonists of the seventeenth century.

In the period of his activity under the Commonwealth, Dury renewed his efforts to form an association of learned men to promote
these objectives. Acting in co-operation with Hartlib, he now succeeded in bringing together a group of distinguished men in meetings
which were somewhat similar to the Platonic "academies" of the
Renaissance period. The circle of friends who gathered informally
in these meetings was frequently referred to as the "Invisible College."[94] Keller has presented definite proof that the Invisible College
was a part of a larger scheme for the establishment of an "International Academy of Natural Philosophers," which was to foster the
exchange of scientific ideas, the establishment of a uniform system
of education, and the movement toward the reunion of the churches.[95] In the informal meetings which were held at London during the
Commonwealth the leaders were Dury, Hartlib, Robert Boyle, Henry Oldenburg, John Milton, John Pell, and Theodore Haak. This
group prepared the way for the organization of the Royal Society.[96]

[93] See above, pp. 16 ff.

[94] Bailey, *op. cit.*, pp. 76, 89, 122.

[95] L. Keller, "Comenius und die Akademien der Naturphilosophen des 17. Jahrhunderts,"
Monatshefte der Comenius Gesellschaft, IV, 133–84.

[96] On the interests and activities of this group see F. Althaus, "Samuel Hartlib, ein deutsch-
englisches Charakterbild," *Historisches Taschenbuch*, 6th ser., III, 238 ff.; Held, *op. cit.*,
p. 124; Robert Boyle, *Works*, VI, 76–136; Masson, *op. cit.*, V, 229–36; R. H. Quick, *Essays on
Educational Reformers*, pp. 203 ff.; and Spinka, *John Amos Comenius, That Incomparable
Moravian*, pp. 87 ff. However, F. R. Johnson ("Gresham College, Precursor of the Royal
Society," *Journal of the History of Ideas*, I [1940], pp. 413–38) presents convincing evidence
to prove that the original impetus toward the founding of the Royal Society dates from the

When the Long Parliament ceased to be the controlling factor in the government, Dury and Hartlib attempted to secure the favor of the Commonwealth officials in behalf of their scheme for educational reform. They received some encouragement, as is indicated by the fact that the Council ordered them to draft and present their proposals concerning the "Reforming of Schools."[97] This new interest prompted Dury to prepare several additional works on educational reform, which won further recognition for him as a pioneer in this movement. In 1649 he published his *Seasonable Discourse* in response to requests from citizens of Lincolnshire who wished to secure a manual which would present his views on educational reform.[98] The book reflects his indebtedness to the educational programs of Bacon and Comenius and also presents Dury's own views on the subject, which had been tested out in practical experiments while he was serving as tutor to the royal children and while he was teaching in the schools of Winchester.[99]

The first part of the book is given over to arguments in proof of his favorite thesis that educational reform was the most important means of advancing the public good.[100] The objectives of education, he continues, must be the development of piety and the advancement of knowledge, because individuals and the social order could advance only as they make progress in piety and knowledge. Keeping in mind his central interest in peace and unity, he maintains that a universal and uniform system of public instruction would develop a sense of unity in civil and religious interests which would gradually curb the prevailing tendencies toward strife and disunion.[101] The new system of education must prepare men for life in all ranks of the social order. To accomplish this there must be a fourfold classification of schools: the lower or popular schools; schools for the education of the

opening of Gresham College, 1598. He thinks the meetings held by Haak and his associates should be regarded as a continuation of the movement originating at Gresham College. This younger generation of scholars, he argues, co-operated in the further advancement of the interests which had been initiated by the Gresham College group.

[97] Masson (*op. cit.*, IV, 229) quotes a Council Order of September 7, 1650, as follows: "That when propositions shall be presented to the Council concerning the Reforming of Schools the Council doth declare that they will receive them and give them all possible furtherance."

[98] On this pamphlet see T. Klahr, "Johannes Duraeus: sein Leben und seine Schriften über Erziehungslehre," *Monatshefte der Comenius Gesellschaft*, VI, 72 ff.; and H. J. Scougal, *Die pädagogischen Schriften John Durys*, pp. 29–33.

[99] Scougal, *op. cit.*, p. 29.

[100] Klahr, *op. cit.*, p. 72.   [101] Scougal, *op. cit.*, p. 30.

children of the gentry and nobility; a school for masters of worldly and
natural knowledge, which would serve as a training school for teachers; and a school of the prophets, which would train men as masters
of the knowledge of the spiritual and supernatural.[102] The change of
objectives and proper reorganization of schools would necessitate
the training of teachers who would be willing to discard old practices
and experiment in developing a more practical type of educational
method.[103] The government should establish an "Agency of Universal Learning," which should co-operate with similar agencies in
European countries in the exchange of information regarding experiments and discoveries.[104]

The Reformed School, prepared by Dury in 1649 and published at
London in 1650, presents his ideas on educational reform more fully.[105] It is Dury's most important pedagogical treatise. In a Preface
to the work, Hartlib expressed the conviction that a thorough reformation of the adult population in England was hopeless. Consequently, attention must be centered upon children, who could be
effectively trained in reformed schools by reformed schoolmasters.[106]
In this book Dury proposed that there should be an "Association"
of persons who, supported by the government, should devote their
lives to the conduct of a new type of educational experiment. While
this association was not to be monastic or "religious" in the technical sense, it is obvious that Dury's proposals for such an organization were prompted by his acquaintance with the methods in use in
the Jesuit and other monastic schools on the Continent.

This association should seek to train teachers for service in schools
that would provide the best type of education for a good commonwealth's man. In his discussion of the training which should be offered in these schools, he lists the educational objectives in order of
importance as follows: "their advancement in piety; the preservation of their health; the forming of their manners; [and] their proficiency in learning." Proficiency in learning is to be regarded as the
last and least part of education, since "godliness and bodily health
are absolutely necessary, the one for spiritual and the other for their

[102] *Ibid.*, pp. 30, 31.

[103] *Ibid.*, p. 32.   [104] Klahr, *op. cit.*, pp. 72, 73.

[105] On the contents of this pamphlet see *ibid.*, pp. 73–76, 191–98; J. W. Adamson, *Pioneers
of Modern Education*, pp. 138–55; Scougal, *op. cit.*, pp. 33–41; and Quick, *op. cit.*, pp. 203–6.

[106] Adamson, *op. cit.*, p. 142.

temporal felicitie."[107] In contrast to the prevailing system, he suggests that "nothing must be made tedious and grievous to the children, but all the toilsomeness of their business the Governors and Ushers are to take upon themselves; that by dilligence and industry all things may be so prepared, methodized and ordered for their apprehension, that this work may unto them be as a delightful recreation by the variety and easiness thereof."[108]

Dury is the outstanding advocate of realism among the English educational reformers of the seventeenth century.[109] In the *Reformed School* he insists that the emphasis in educational method must be shifted from "words" to things. "Tongues," he said, "without their subordination unto arts and sciences are worth nothing towards the establishment of our happiness."[110] Children must be taught to deal with concrete life-situations, because "the true end of all human learning is to supply in ourselves and others the defects which proceed from our ignorance of the nature and use of creatures [created things], and the disorderliness of our natural faculties in using them and reflecting upon them."[111] Emphasis should, therefore, be placed upon the development of the use of the natural faculties. Sense, tradition, and reason are the three sources of knowledge, and the natural faculties more readily apprehend knowledge that is imparted through the senses.[112] In the remainder of the treatise Dury discusses the methods which should be used in applying these basic principles in the operation of a model reformed school of fifty or sixty pupils. Contemporary critics of the *Reformed School* charged that Dury's program would make the existing colleges and universities useless. In answer Dury published his *Supplement to the Reformed School* (1651), in which he discussed types of learning which should be made available to all the people and the specialized types of learning which should be furnished by the colleges and universities.[113] In this brief pamphlet he was making an attempt to solve the complicated problem of the proper correlation of higher and lower institutions of learn-

[107] Dury, as quoted by Quick, *op. cit.*, p. 204.

[108] *Ibid.*

[109] See the critical evaluation of Dury's contribution to English educational reform as given by Scougal, *op. cit.*, pp. 42–46.

[110] Paul Munroe, "John Dury," *Cyclopedia of Education.*

[111] Quick, *op. cit.*, pp. 204, 205.

[112] Adamson, *op. cit.*, p. 145.   [113] *Ibid.*, pp. 152 ff.

ing. Dury and Hartlib continued to advocate educational reform
throughout the period of the Commonwealth.

In this period Dury also devoted much of his time to projects designed to arouse interest and activity in Christian missions. In the
earlier stages of his union activity, he had reached the conclusion
that the co-operation of the Christian churches in the proclamation
of the Christian message among unbelievers and among those who
had fallen away from the true faith would serve to advance the realization of a unity of spirit among Christians, which would prepare the
way for organic union of the churches. With this in mind he drafted
an elaborate plan for a series of missionary enterprises which indicates a breadth of missionary statesmanship that was unusual in
Protestantism of the seventeenth century.[114] As early as 1636, he had
interested himself in a project for co-operative Protestant mission
work in Russia and among the adherents of the Greek Orthodox
Church.[115] He later advocated the inauguration of Protestant missionary activity among the Mohammedans and among the North
American Indians. Convinced that the first step in Christian missionary work should be directed toward furnishing the non-Christian
peoples with translations of the Scriptures in their own languages, he
co-operated in a number of enterprises which foreshadowed the activities of the modern Bible societies. He was one of the group which
secured the publication of a Lithuanian Bible as a useful aid in the
conduct of missions among the Slavic peoples of eastern Europe.[116]
He also promoted plans for the translation of the Bible into the
Turkish language.[117] The difficulties encountered in securing these
translations prompted him to advocate the teaching of more of the
oriental languages in the English universities as a preparatory step
for the training of missionaries for work among the Jews and the
peoples of the East.[118]

This emphasis upon the obligation of the churches to evangelize
the world was an integral part of Dury's plan for co-operation and
unity among the Protestant churches. In his *Memoriall Concerning
Peace Ecclesiasticall* (1641), he urged the churches to stop their strife

[114] For a summary of this missionary program for a united Protestant Church as presented
by Dury in his paper, *De mediis ad scopum evangelicae unionis obtinendum requisitis*, see
K. Brauer, *Die Unionstätigkeit John Duries unter dem Protecktorat Cromwells*, pp. 208, 209.

[115] J. Kvačala, *Korrespondence Jana Amosa Komenského*, pp. 10, 11.

[116] B. Brook, *Lives of the Puritans*, III, 373.

[117] Worthington, *op. cit.*, I, 160.   [118] Klahr, *op. cit.*, p. 72.

and establish a "correspondency" in order that they might co-oper-ate in this work.[119] In his *Letter to Lord Forbes*, as published in 1643, he pleaded for the preparation of a "Fundamental Confession of Faith" in order that the churches might be in agreement on the basic truths of the Christian message, which they were under obligation to impart to the heathen.[120] Dury believed that the contemporary un-rest among the Roman Catholics, especially in France, indicated that the time was opportune for the inauguration of a Protestant mission to Roman Catholics on the Continent.[121] He suggested that Protes-tants should unite in organizing a "Société pour le propagation de la vérité" to offset the work of the "Congregatio de propaganda fide." He anticipated the program of some modern mission boards by sug-gesting that the Waldenses should be used as co-agents in the con-duct of Protestant missionary activities among the Roman Catholics on the Continent.[122] Living in an age of colonization and trade ex-pansion, Dury advocated a program of missions which would spread the gospel throughout the ever extending frontiers which were touched by the trade movements of his day.[123]

In 1649 news of John Eliot's successful missionary work among the American Indians reached England. Projects for arranging adequate support for the continuation and extension of this work were popular among the English Puritans. Dury co-operated with a group of these Puritans in securing the passage of an act of Parliament in 1649 pro-viding for the incorporation of "The Society for the Propagation of the Gospel in New England," which was to have as its object the dif-fusion of Christianity and education among the American Indians.[124] In an effort to advance the interests of this society, Dury persuaded his friend, Thomas Thorowgood, to publish his pamphlet, *The Jewes in America*, in which Thorowgood advanced the theory that the American Indians were descendants of members of the Lost Tribes of Israel and that their conversion should be sought as a means for the fulfilment of the prophecies concerning the conversion of the Jews. The idea that the American Indians were descendants of members of the Lost Tribes was widely current in the seventeenth century.[125]

[119] P. 8.

[120] P. 3.

[121] Brauer, *op. cit.*, p. 209.   [123] Kvačala, *op. cit.*, p. 11.

[122] *Ibid.*, pp. 230, 231.   [124] Masson, *op. cit.*, IV, 387.

[125] Lucian Wolf (*Menasseh ben Israel's Mission to Oliver Cromwell*, p. 152) presents a bibliography of the seventeenth-century literature on this subject.

Dury accepted this theory and prepared an "Epistolicall Discourse," which was printed in 1650 as a Preface to Thorowgood's *Jewes in America*. In this work Dury indorsed the theory presented by Thorowgood and appealed to his readers to support the mission work among the Indians.[126] He also stated that he had secured from Menasseh ben Israel, a distinguished Jewish rabbi at Amsterdam, a copy of a *Relation* by Antonio Montezinios, a Portuguese traveler who had found evidence in South America that seemed to prove a Jewish ancestry for the American Indians.[127] At Dury's suggestion, the *Relation* of Montezinios was printed as an appendix to Thorowgood's *Jewes in America*.

Dury was intensely interested in mission work designed to secure the conversion of Jews to the Christian faith. He believed that mission work among the Jews was a part of God's plan for the Christians of his age; that it was a necessary preliminary to the coming of the millennium; and that the successful outcome of such effort would inaugurate a new era in the fulfilment of Bible prophecies.[128] This interest in the conversion of the Jews, together with an abiding curiosity about rabbinic teaching, prompted him to cultivate the friendship of a number of rabbis on the Continent. His correspondence with Menasseh ben Israel set in motion a series of developments that culminated in a major effort to secure the readmission of the Jews to England. Lucian Wolf, the best-informed historian who has dealt with this incident in English history, states that Dury "practically started the first agitation" in favor of the readmission of the Jews.[129] The Jews had been expelled from England, in 1290, during the reign of Edward I. Although some Jews were residing in England in the seventeenth century, the laws of Edward I were still in effect.

Under the Commonwealth conditions seemed more favorable for obtaining a modification of these laws. Numerous writers, including Edward Nicholas, Robert Rich, and Roger Williams, had publicly advocated the readmission of the Jews.[130] Dury's letters to Menasseh ben Israel in regard to the *Relation* of Montezinios made frequent references to the indications of a more sympathetic English attitude

[126] Dury, "Epistolicall Discourse" in Thorowgood's *Jewes in America*, pp. 1–9.

[127] *Ibid.*, pp. 9–12.

[128] *Ibid.*, pp. 7, 8, 12–16.

[129] *Op. cit.*, p. xliii.

[130] Alfred Stern, "Menasseh ben Israel et Cromwell," *Revue des études juives*, VI (1882), 98–100.

toward the Jews. This correspondence encouraged the distinguished rabbi to look to England as a place where a friendly interest in Judaism might be cultivated to the end that England might furnish a place of refuge for Jews, who were encountering widespread disabilities and persecution on the Continent.[131] Menasseh ben Israel hoped to secure from Cromwell a cancellation of the old statutes against the Jews and a recognition of the right of Jews to reside in England with the full enjoyment of liberty of trade, freedom of worship, and permission to acquire property for synagogues, cemeteries, and other purposes. He prepared several pamphlets for circulation in England. The most important of these pamphlets was entitled *The Hope of Israel*.[132] As soon as this work was published in a Latin edition, Dury began to distribute copies among the leading Puritans.[133] Two English editions were published by Moses Wall, and Dury's friendship with Menasseh ben Israel occasioned the erroneous supposition that he was the translator of the pamphlet.[134]

Menasseh ben Israel was persistent in the advocacy of his cause. In 1655 he came to England and presented a number of his books to the Council, requesting a hearing on his petition for the readmission of the Jews. Cromwell was inclined to favor the Jews and ordered that a conference, composed of the Council and twenty-eight additional appointees, should meet to hear the arguments and then recommend a policy in this matter. Four sessions of this Conference were held in December, 1655.[135] Despite the fact that Cromwell openly supported Menasseh ben Israel, the members of the Conference opposed readmission. Their opposition prompted Cromwell to forego the abrogation of the old laws against the Jews, but he admitted small groups of Jews and allowed them to form a colony and possess their own synagogue and cemetery. He also indicated his favor toward Menasseh ben Israel by granting him a pension of £100.[136]

Dury's views on the proposed policy of readmitting the Jews have been misrepresented by many writers. Neal states that Dury wrote

[131] A. M. Hyamson, *A History of the Jews in England*, pp. 189, 190.

[132] Wolf, *op. cit.*, p. lxxviii.

[133] *Ibid.*, p. xxvii; cf. A. M. Hyamson, "The Lost Tribes and the Return of the Jews to England," *Transactions of the Jewish Historical Society*, V (1903), 132 ff.

[134] Wolf, *op. cit.*, p. 67.

[135] See Worthington, *op. cit.*, I, 78. A contemporary narrative of the proceedings in these Conferences is reprinted in the *Harleian Miscellany*, VI, 445–55, under the title: "Narrative of the Late Proceedings at Whitehall Concerning the Jews (London, 1656)."

[136] Stern, *op. cit.*, VI, 103–5.

"fiercely against the Jews."[137] And Stoughton maintains that "even
Durie, with all his zeal for union amongst Protestants as fellow-co-
religionists, contended earnestly against the participation of the
Jews in the social rights which were enjoyed by Christians. Men of
that class contended that to tolerate Israelites was a sin."[138] These
statements are based upon hazy and incorrect ideas about a pamphlet which was issued by Dury in 1656 under the title, *A Case of
Conscience, Whether it be lawful to admit Jews into a Christian Commonwealth?*[139] In his solution of this "Case of Conscience," Dury
outlined the policies of the Continental countries in dealing with the
Jews and expressed himself as favoring their readmission into England. However, he suggested that considerations of expediency
should be given due weight and proposed that it would be advisable
to impose certain disabilities upon the Jews in order to guarantee the
preservation of Christian interests. He takes the position that the
Jews

must be restrained from certain things, ... chiefly these: 1. Not to blaspheme the
person of Jesus Christ, or if any doth, that he shall be liable to the law, which Moses
hath given, in case of blasphemy in the name of God. 2. Not to seduce any, or go
about making proselytes; or, if any doth, he shall ipso facto, forfeit his liberty, or
undergo some other heavier punishment. 3. Not to blaspheme the Christian
sabbath; and not to dishonor any of the ordinances of Christianity, under some
punishment to be inflicted suitable to the offence.[140]

He further suggested that steps should be taken to secure a hearing
for the Christian message among the Jews. They must be restrained
from covetous practices and from all attempts to undermine the
state. Dury's views certainly fell far short of present-day principles
of toleration, but there is nothing in the pamphlet to justify the as-
sertion that he "wrote fiercely against the Jews."[141] On the contrary,
he said: "I conceive matters may be so ordered toward them, that
they may be made to understand that the intention of the state in
admitting them, is not to have profit or temporal advantages by

[137] D. Neal, *History of the Puritans*, I, 159.

[138] John Stoughton, *History of Religion in England*, II, 428.

[139] This pamphlet was reprinted in the *Harleian Miscellany* (1810 ed.), VI, 438–44.

[140] Dury, "Case of Conscience, Whether it be lawful to admit Jews," *Harleian Miscellany*,
VI, 441.

[141] *Ibid.*, VI, 439: "It is not only lawful, but, if rightly ordered towards them, expedient
to admit of them; nay to invite and encourage them to live in reformed Christian Common-
wealths."

them . . . . but rather out of Christian love and compassion towards them."[142]

Throughout the years of his service in the employ of the Commonwealth and the Protectorate, Dury sought an opportunity to renew his peace negotiations on the Continent. It was necessary for him to secure the sanction and support of Cromwell if such negotiations were to be successful. In the earlier years of the Commonwealth, Cromwell's foreign policy was wavering and uncertain. It was motivated chiefly by the desire to win recognition for the new government and guaranties for the security of English trade. From 1654 onward the championship of the Protestant Interest became the dominant factor in his foreign policy.[143] Early indications of this shift in interest may be seen in the attempt to secure an alliance between England and Sweden in 1653 and also in Cromwell's efforts to provide a refuge for persecuted Polish Protestants in Ireland and a refuge for exiled Bohemian Brethren in England.[144] The championship of the Protestant Interest involved the protection of Protestants on the Continent, the preservation of peace among the Protestant nations, and the union of the Protestant powers in a confederation which should be designed to oppose aggression on the part of the Roman Catholic powers. After the conclusion of the war with Holland in 1654, Cromwell regarded these objectives as of major importance.

It is probable that the influence of Dury had considerable weight in the molding of this new foreign policy of the Protectorate. His ready knowledge of Continental affairs would naturally gain a hearing for his suggestions. There is ample evidence that he had risen, within the short period of five years, from a place as a literary hack in government service to a position as a trusted adviser and aid to the Council in shaping its foreign policy.[145] Since the death of Gustavus Adolphus he had been the most outspoken advocate of the English championship of the Protestant Interest. The foreign policy

[142] *Ibid.*, p. 442.

[143] J. N. Bowman, *The Protestant Interest in Cromwell's Foreign Relations*, pp. 2 ff.; cf. Bischoffshausen, *op. cit.*, pp. 25 ff.

[144] S. Hubler, "Unionsbestrebungen des John Durie," *Berner Beiträge zur Geschichte der schweizerischen Reformationskirchen* (1884), p. 291.

[145] *Calendar of State Papers, Domestic Series, 1652–1653*, pp. 130, 221, 245, 254. In addition to his salary as library keeper, Dury was now receiving a yearly allowance of £200 from the Council (see *ibid.*, p. 487; *Calendar . . . . , 1653–1654*, p. 164; and *Calendar . . . . , 1654*, p. 281).

adopted by Cromwell in 1654 is substantially identical with the policy which Dury had proposed in three pamphlets which he had issued in 1641.[146] It is certain that foreign observers thought that Dury was partly responsible for the formulation of this new policy. Early in the year 1654 Austrian officials were linking his name with rumors of a new scheme to oppose the Roman Catholic hegemony under the leadership of Austria.[147] Likewise a French agent, Lamilletière, reported to Mazarin that Cromwell had adopted a design to unite all Protestant communions in order to pave the way for the establishment of a formidable confederation of Protestant powers and that Dury had been placed in charge of propaganda in the interest of this new program.[148] Similar reports were made by the observers of other European powers.[149]

In advocating the English championship of the Protestant Interest, Dury steadily maintained the thesis that the formation of an effective civil confederation of the Protestant powers must be preceded by an effort to promote peace, co-operation, and union among the divided and contending Protestant churches. This need of the establishment of a "correspondency" between the Protestant churches had been emphasized in his pamphlets of 1641. It was advocated with the support of more detailed arguments by Dury and Hartlib in a pamphlet published at London in 1652 under the title, *The Reformed Spiritual Husbandman*.[150] The *Calendar of State Papers* furnishes documentary evidence that Dury was frequently urging Cromwell and the Council to make a new effort to secure more effective co-operation on the part of the Protestant churches. He submit-

---

[146] The titles of these pamphlets were as follows: *Motives to Induce the Protestant Princes to Mind the worke of Peace Ecclesiasticall; A Memoriall Concerning Peace Ecclesiasticall Amongst Protestants;* and *A Summary Discourse concerning the work of Peace Ecclesiasticall, How it may concurre with the aim of a civill Confederation amongst Protestants.* For an analysis of the contents of these pamphlets see above, pp. 85 ff.

[147] It was discovered that Dury was in correspondence with Comenius and other Continental leaders regarding a secret Evangelical association designed to overthrow the House of Austria. A Hungarian official reported: "Tres esse audimus Caesaris juratos hostes, Duraeum quendam et J. A. Comenium; tertii nomen nondum scire possumus" (see Matthew Spinka, *The Irenic Program and Activity of John Amos Comenius,* p. 59; A. Patera, *Jana Amosa Komenského Korrespondence,* pp. 176, 177; and D. Angyal, *Geschichte der politischen Beziehungen Siebenbürgens zu England,* pp. 47–49).

[148] See J. Lindeboom, "Johannes Duraeus en Zigne werkzaamheid in Dienst van Cromwell's Politiek," *Nederlandsch Archief voor Kerkgeschiedenis,* XVI (1921), 248, 249. For the text of this report see F. Guizot, *Histoire de la République d'Angleterre et de Cromwell,* II, 426–36.

[149] Bischoffshausen, *op. cit.,* p. 36.

[150] See *Calendar of State Papers, Domestic Series, 1654,* p. 431.

ted copies of his own irenic writings to the Council and also furnished copies of pamphlets written by Continental authors in advocacy of new union efforts. Dury has left a record of some of his efforts to persuade Cromwell and the Council to advance the Protestant Interest. In his *Declaration of John Durie*, written in 1660 to explain his activity under Cromwell to the satisfaction of Charles II and his advisers, he says:

When he was made Protector, and the Treaty of Peace was drawing towards a conclusion between England and the Low-Countries; and all that were in publick places did own him as the Chief Magistrate of the Nations: I thought it sutable to the end for which I was come to England; and every way seasonable and fit for me to represent to him and to his Councel, some Reasons for which I conceived them obliged in conscience to mind the interest of Religion amongst Protestants, and to give some countenance to the endeavors whereby their differences might be reconciled. . . . . I desired nothing further from the Protector but his countenance and support; that he would only own me, as a Gospel minister, setting myself apart for the work of Peace and Unity amongst Protestants, I might have a letter of recommendation from him to the Churches of Switzerland . . . . that they might know that I being approved by the chief of the Ministery of England for such a work, and moved of mine own accord to go about it, he could not refuse to recommend it unto them to be taken into consideration, promising also thereunto his own concurrence.[151]

It is evident that Dury was able to win Cromwell's cordial support for his design of establishing a correspondency between the Protestant churches. Dury was appointed by the Council of State to accompany Bulstrode Whitelocke on his mission to Sweden in 1653.[152] When Whitelocke left England, Cromwell instructed him "to bring back a Protestant alliance" and to provide for a nearer "union and correspondence then heretofore; whereby commerce may be preserved and provided for, with respect to the common interest and concernment of the true Protestant religion."[153] Burnet, basing his account on information furnished by Stoupe, indicates that Cromwell had planned a scheme for a definite organization to promote the co-operation between the various Protestant churches. The plan which he describes as approved by Cromwell is essentially the same scheme for the establishment of "correspondency" between the Protestant churches which Dury had advocated.[154] Cromwell's employment of Dury as his messenger to the churches of the Continent

---

[151] Pp. 23, 24.   [152] *Calendar of State Papers, Domestic Series, 1653–1654*, pp. xv, 164.

[153] Bowman, *op. cit.*, p. 15. Cf. S. R. Gardiner, *History of the Commonwealth and Protectorate*, II, 377.

[154] Gilbert Burnet's description of this plan, as presented in his *History of My Own Times* (1766 ed.), I, 106, 107, is as follows: "Stoupe told me of a great design Cromwell had intended to begin his kingship with, if he had affirmed it: He resolved to set up a Council for the

from 1654 onward indicates that Burnet's account is substantially correct.

Meanwhile Dury made numerous attempts to prepare the way for the inauguration of a new mission on the Continent. The Swiss Protestant cantons were now threatened by the Roman Catholic cantons, supported by neighboring Roman Catholic powers. The leaders of the Protestant cantons were interested in negotiations favoring peace, co-operation, and unity among Protestants. The formation of a strong Protestant alliance might prove their salvation in the event of more aggressive measures on the part of the Roman Catholics.[155] In 1653 the Protestant cantons sent John Jacob Stockar to England to offer his services as mediator between the English and the Dutch. Dury approached Stockar shortly after his arrival in London and described his plans. Stockar was enthusiastic in his indorsement of Dury's scheme and promised to open the way for negotiations between Dury and the Swiss churches.[156] Dury also interviewed the Dutch statesmen who came to London to negotiate the treaty of peace and requested their co-operation. He renewed his correspondence with Continental leaders who had previously indicated an interest in his reunion efforts.[157] While in Sweden on the Whitelocke mission of 1653, he made good use of the opportunity to urge Matthiae and other irenic leaders to renew their advocacy of the cause of Christian reunion.[158]

Protestant Religion in opposition to the Congregation de Propaganda fide at Rome. He intended it should consist of seven councellours, and four secretaries for different provinces. These were the first, France, Switzerland, and the Valleys: The Palatinate and the other Calvinists were the second: Germany, the North, and Turkey were the third: And the East and West Indies were the fourth. The secretaries were to have 500£ apiece, and to keep correspondence everywhere, to know the state of religion all over the world, that so all good designs might be by their means protected and assisted. Stoupe was to have the first Province. They were to have a fund of 10,000£ a year at their disposal for ordinary emergencies, but to be farther supplied as occasions should require it. Chelsea college was to be made up for them, which was then an old decayed building, that had been at first raised to be a college for writers of controversy. I thought it not fit to let such a project as this be quite lost: It was certainly a noble one: But how far he would have pursued it must be left to conjecture."

[155] See Alfred Stern, "Oliver Cromwell und die evangelischen Kantone der Schweiz," *Historische Zeitschrift*, XL (1878), 61–65; and E. Bloesch, *Geschichte der schweizerisch-reformierten Kirchen*, I, 445 ff.

[156] Brauer, *op. cit.*, pp. 14, 15, 17, 22, 29, 54 ff.

[157] He was especially anxious to secure the support of John Bergius, court preacher of Brandenburg (see the text of the letter from Dury to Bergius as quoted by Hasaeus, *op. cit.*, IV, 683–710).

[158] Matthiae's writings on Christian reunion were given wide publicity by Dury. Two of Matthiae's pamphlets were reprinted by Dury in his *Irenicorum tractatuum prodromus*, pp. 322–31, 332–78.

As the prospects became brighter for a renewal of reunion negotiations with the Continental churches, Dury again resorted to the printed page as a useful medium of union propaganda. In the year 1654 he published his *Irenicum: In quo casus conscientiae praecipui, de viis quaerendae et constituendae inter ecclesias evangelicas pacis, breviter proponuntur et deciduntur.*[159] In this interesting tract Dury listed and classified the various problems which had arisen during a quarter of a century of union effort; invited suggestions for the solution of these problems from his readers; and proposed his own solution as a basis for further discussion. Copies of this tract were widely distributed on the Continent in the hope that its message would enlist the support of church leaders.

Dury also sought the indorsement of the Congregational divines of New England. In a series of letters he communicated his union plans to the ministers of Massachusetts and Connecticut. Cotton Mather has preserved a part of a letter to Dury which was prepared by John Norton and signed by more than forty ministers of the colony of Massachusetts.[160] John Davenport prepared a similar indorsement, which was signed by all the ministers of the colony of Connecticut.[161]

While thus soliciting support for his union projects throughout the Protestant world, Dury continued to make constant appeals to the people of England. He was especially desirous of securing the united

[159] This pamphlet was reprinted by Dury in *ibid.*, pp. 28-50.

[160] *Magnalia Christi Americana*, I, 299-301. Norton's letter read, in part, as follows: "We give thanks to Mr. Dury . . . . who hath by his letter exhorting to such an agreement given us an occasion to bring this testimony, such as it is, for our 'brotherly communion' with the whole company of Protestants professing the faith of Jesus Christ. . . . . We chose rather to depart unto the remote and unknown parts of the earth, for the sake of a purer worship, than to lie down under the Hierarchy in abundance of all things, but with prejudice of conscience. But that in flying from our country we should renounce communion with such churches as profess the gospel, is a thing which we confidently and solemnly deny. . . . . In whatever assemblies amongst the whole company of those that profess the gospel, the fundamentals of doctrine, and the essentials of order, are maintained, though in many niceties of controversial divinity they are at less agreement with us, we do hereby make it manifest, that we do acknowledge them all and everyone for brethren, and that we shall be ready to give unto them the right hand of fellowship in the Lord, if in other things they be peaceable and walk orderly."

[161] *Ibid.*, pp. 326, 327. Davenport's letter read, in part, as follows: "While the fire of schism has been raging, the hateful fury has miserably torn to pieces the churches that should have been held together in the strictest bonds of love and unity. . . . . Behold! the minds of all good men do with a raised hope expect an happy close of these mischiefs; and with most hearty prayers do beseech the Father of Mercies, that he would, by the grace of his Spirit, according to his Word, please to direct the counsels and actions of his servants, for the glory of his own holy name. You have done right well, reverend brother, in that you have, after a brotherly manner, unto the promoting of this affair, in the communion of the saints, invited us, who belong to the same mystical body with yourselves, under one head, our Lord Jesus Christ."

support of the Presbyterian and Independent parties and the in-dorsement of the English universities. In his Declaration he describes his tireless efforts to secure the co-operation of these groups before he left England to undertake his mission to the Continent. He states that he drafted a list of

Reasons for which I conceived them obliged in conscience to mind the interest of Religion amongst Protestants, and to give some countenance to the endeavors whereby their differences might be reconciled. . . . . The same reasons were also im-parted unto the leading ministers of the Congregationall and Presbyteriall Churches in London; who by my sollicitation were brought together, and upon this occasion met several times for a special conference . . . . to compose their own differences first, and so to joyne with me in the design of my negotiation towards the Churches: the chief heads of the Universities also were acquainted with the same reasons; which took this effect with them all, that they did approve of the work as very expedient and reasonable to be undertaken: and to inable me to go about it, a Declaration was penned which the heads of both the Universities and the ministers of London, as well Congregational as Presbyterial did subscribe; authorizing me to Act that business amongst the Churches in their name.[162]

These manifestations of interest in union projects at home and abroad once more encouraged Dury to hope for the success of his program. It is probable that conditions were more favorable for un-ion effort than at any previous period in his long career as an advo-cate of Christian reunion. The patronage and support of Cromwell might enable him to succeed where he had so often failed. He was eager to renew his negotiations with the leaders of the Continental churches.

[162] Declaration of John Durie, pp. 23, 24.

CHAPTER VIII

CROMWELL'S MESSENGER TO THE CHURCHES OF THE CONTINENT

THE war between England and Holland was the chief obstacle in the way of the renewal of Dury's union efforts on the Continent after he had secured the support of Cromwell. This war was brought to a close by a treaty of peace, which was signed on April 5, 1654. On the same day Dury left England for the Continent. It was his purpose to inaugurate a series of negotiations similar to those which he had conducted prior to 1641. However, as he had thus far succeeded in enlisting more sympathetic co-operation from Calvinists than from Lutherans, he decided to begin this mission by treating with leaders of the Reformed Churches.[1] He planned to begin his work among the Reformed Churches of Switzerland, as this was a field to which he had thus far devoted little effort except through correspondence and personal interviews with Swiss leaders like John Jacob Breitinger and John Jacob Stockar.[2]

After 1648 the political position of the Protestant cantons of Switzerland was very insecure,[3] as they were threatened by the Roman Catholic cantons within the confederacy. From without they were threatened by the Spaniards, then powerful in Italy, by the Austrians, and by the Savoyards.[4] Prevailing conditions caused uncertainty and confusion on the part of the Swiss Protestant leaders in their efforts to shape a foreign policy. Some thought that protection should be sought from the *Corpus Evangelicorum* of the empire. Some would look to France for help against impending dangers. Others looked to England for effective aid. The latter group stressed the fact that Cromwell wished to establish a closer alliance between Eng-

[1] F. H. Brandes, "John Dury and His Work for Germany," *Catholic Presbyterian Review*, VIII, 94.

[2] See E. Bloesch, *Geschichte der schweizerisch-reformierten Kirchen*, I, 443–46.

[3] D. Masson, *Life of Milton*, V, 41; cf. also Robert Vaughan, *The Protectorate of Oliver Cromwell and the State of Europe during the Early Part of the Reign of Louis XIV*, Introd., I, cvii.

[4] S. Cheetham, *A History of the Christian Church since the Reformation*, p. 11.

land and Switzerland.[5] Since 1653 there had developed an increasing
interest in the prospect of an English alliance. Under these favorable
auspices, Dury hoped that by visiting the various cantons he would
be able to secure the support of the Swiss Protestants in his union
negotiations. This might prove to be the first step toward a larger
program of establishing a civil confederation of Protestants.[6]

There was, indeed, some justification for Dury's high hopes for the
success of his mission. This time the English government provided
him with ample financial support. He enjoyed the confidence of
Cromwell, who provided him with a passport and numerous letters
of introduction to leaders of the Swiss Protestant cantons.[7] He possessed an imposing collection of documents indorsing his union program, which had been furnished by the authorities of the English
universities and by influential groups of Presbyterian and Congregational ministers.[8] Furthermore, Dury now took every precaution
to guard his mission from all appearance of political motivation.[9] On
this account Dury's friend, John Pell, was sent to Switzerland at the
same time to negotiate for the closer co-operation of the Swiss and
the English in political matters.[10]

On the journey to the Continent Dury was accompanied by his
wife. They traveled with Pell from London to The Hague. Leaving
Pell at The Hague, Dury visited Amsterdam in order to confer with
Godefroy Hutton, pastor of the French congregation in Amsterdam,
who had already attempted to interest the leaders of the Swiss Reformed Churches in efforts to unite the evangelical churches of Europe.[11] Dury arranged for his wife to make her home in Amsterdam
while he was on his mission. After conferring with Hutton and other

---

[5] A. Stern, "Oliver Cromwell und die evangelischen Kantone der Schweiz," *Historische Zeitschrift*, XL, 56 ff.; cf. also S. von Bischoffshausen, *Die Politik des Protectors Oliver Cromwell in der Auffassung und Thätigkeit seines Ministers John Thurloe*, p. 26.

[6] Dury, *Consultationum Irenicarum Prodiorthosis*, p. 125.

[7] See K. Brauer, *Die Unionstätigkeit John Duries unter dem Protektorat Cromwells*, pp. 232–35.

[8] These documents are listed by Dury in his *Syllabus Documentorum*, p. i.

[9] *Declaration of John Durie*, p. 24: "I desired (and that as discreetly as I could) that if he [Cromwell] had any State affairs to propose to forrainers, he would make use of somebody else for that end."

[10] See extracts from Pell's *Diary* as quoted by Vaughan, *op. cit.*, II, 485, 486. J. N. Bow-man, in his *Protestant Interest in Cromwell's Foreign Relations*, pp. 26, 27, incorrectly states that Pell was sent as ambassador to Switzerland in the autumn of 1654. Pell's *Diary*, as cited above, clearly indicates that he left England in company with Dury in April, 1654.

[11] On Hutton's irenic activity see C. Sepp, *Polemische en irenische Theologie*, p. 136.

friends in Amsterdam, he went to Utrecht and prepared to accompany Pell on the journey to Switzerland. They left Utrecht on April 25, 1654, and, traveling by way of Cologne, Heidelberg, Strassburg, and Basel, arrived in Zurich on May 18.[12] On the following day they were officially welcomed to the city by the Antistes John Jacob Ulrich. In the somewhat elaborate exchange of compliments on this occasion there were numerous expressions of the desire for an alliance of both the churches and the governments of England and Switzerland.[13] Later Dury presented his credentials to the Little Council, and that body proposed the call of an assembly of delegates from all the Reformed cantons to meet at Aarau on June 13 in order to hear the proposals of Dury and Pell.

Meanwhile, the Zurich Council appointed a committee of three ministers and three theological professors to examine Dury's proposals. Dury stated the purpose of his mission to this committee and asked that its members discuss his proposals and offer advice concerning the scope, means, and methods of union negotiations which might prove most effective.[14] His suggestions were favorably received, and two of the members of the committee—Ulrich and John Rudolf Stucki—began to advocate the inauguration of a new effort to secure the union of the evangelical churches.[15] The written report of the Zurich committee indicated a genuine interest in the reunion movement, and Dury was confident that he would now be able to secure the co-operation of the Swiss churches.[16]

On June 13, 1654, a general assembly of deputies from the Reformed cantons met at Aarau. Both Dury and Pell were given a hearing. Pell stressed Cromwell's earnest desire to advance the Protestant Interest and his willingness to promote brotherly co-operation and unity among the Reformed Churches.[17] Dury explained that it was his mission to serve as Cromwell's messenger, charged with the duty of promoting peace and unity among the churches. He made

---

[12] The itinerary of the journey from England to Zurich as listed in Pell's *Diary* and cited by Vaughan (*op. cit.*, II, 485, 486) concludes with the words: "So from Westminster to Zurich, forty-three days; our way was crooked, and at least 700 miles long."

[13] Brauer, *op. cit.*, pp. 21 ff.

[14] *Ibid.*, pp. 23 ff.

[15] *Ibid.*, pp. 25, 26.

[16] Dury, *Syllabus Documentorum*, p. i; Bloesch, *op. cit.*, I, 447; and Brauer, *op. cit.*, pp. 33, 34.

[17] S. Hubler, "Unionsbestrebungen des John Durie," *Berner Beiträge zur Geschichte der schweizerischen Reformationskirchen*, p. 306.

suggestions regarding the scope and the possible means and methods of union activity, using the same arguments which he had presented in his *Irenicum*. The deputies promised to refer his proposals to the various cantons and then report their decision to him. On July 27 the "General Resolutions of the Cantons" were delivered by the Senate of Zurich. Dury summarizes these resolutions as follows:

That the Cantons rejoiced much to find his Highnesse favourable affection expressed unto them; and acknowledged it a great honour, that hee had acquainted them before others, with his purpose to advance the Union of Protestants of Europe.

That to Master Dury's proposall and scope, they gave their full assent as to a work most commendable and necessary.

That they would not onely commend it to all their Churches and Academies, but would concurre to further it with their advice and authority.

That to find the effect of this their inclination, they invited him to visit their chief Cities and Academies,

Intreating him withall to testifie unto his Highness, their reciprocall love and affection; and that his recommendatory letters have with them a great weight.[18]

Dury at once accepted this invitation to communicate his proposals to the leaders of the different cantons. He had already prepared the way for a visit to Bern by correspondence and personal interviews with the Bernese theologian, Christoph Lüthard, and the Burgomaster Anton von Grafenried.[19] At the suggestion of these friends, the Council invited Dury to Bern for a conference. On arrival—August 5, 1654—he was met and escorted into the city by a number of the city officials.[20] At Dury's request a commission was appointed to examine his proposals. This commission cordially indorsed his union activity.[21] Two members of the commission, Christoph Lüthard and John Heinrich Hummel, were so much interested in Dury's proposals that they later traveled extensively with him in an effort to win the indorsement and support of other cantons.[22] After the commission had investigated Dury's project, a meeting of all the ministers and theological professors of the city was called. This assembly presented Dury with a written declaration, expressing cordial indorsement of the movement toward Christian reunion.[23]

[18] *Summarie Account of Mr. John Dury's Former and Latter Negotiation*, p. 25.

[19] Brauer, *op. cit.*, p. 35.

[20] Vaughan, *op. cit.*, I, 48.

[21] Brauer, *op. cit.*, pp. 36 ff.; cf. also Hubler, *op. cit.*, pp. 305, 306.

[22] Hubler, *op. cit.*, p. 306.

[23] Dury, *Summarie Account*, p. 25. Hubler (*op. cit.*, p. 308) presents the text of the Bernese indorsement of Dury's program.

Leaving Bern on August 31, 1654, Dury proceeded to Basel. Prior to his arrival the authorities of the churches in that city had made an investigation of the purposes of his mission. The Antistes Theodor Zwinger, after corresponding with Stucki in regard to Dury's schemes, had reached the conclusion that Cromwell could scarcely be interested in efforts to unite all Protestants, as he had made little effort to secure order and unity among the churches of England.[24] On August 2, 1654, Zwinger had written Dury a letter in which he expressed the conviction that Dury's program was impracticable.[25] The two most influential church leaders of Basel—Zwinger and John Buxtorf—regarded Dury as an advocate of a dangerous type of syncretism. Moreover, the political leaders of Basel supported the theory that the Swiss Confederation should seek a close alliance with France instead of accepting Cromwell's proposals for an alliance of all Protestant powers. They feared that the indorsement of Dury's plan by Zurich and Bern might serve as the first steps toward the adoption of a new foreign policy, which would provide no adequate safeguards against the dangers of an alliance between the Roman Catholic cantons and France.[26] This suspicious attitude on the part of the Basel leaders marked the beginning of an opposition to Dury's union plans and the English alliance which was to increase until it effectively thwarted the program of the Dury-Pell mission to Switzerland.

Upon arrival at Basel, Dury proceeded with his negotiation in the same manner as at Zurich and Bern. After an exchange of greetings, a commission of six deputies was appointed to treat with him. One member of this commission—the distinguished scholar, John Rudolf Wettstein—was inclined to favor Dury's proposals, but he could not induce his colleagues to join him in advocating Dury's program.[27] Throughout Dury's stay in Basel he was treated as an honored guest and lavishly entertained,[28] but in the discussions with the commission he was constantly on the defensive and was forced to devote much of his time to explanations of Cromwell's failure to unite the churches of England. He patiently labored to explain and support his own program, but it was opposed and severely criticized. Owing to his buoyant optimism, it is probable that he was not fully aware of the extent and bitterness of this opposition.

[24] Brauer, *op. cit.*, pp. 38 ff.

[25] *Ibid.*, pp. 41, 42.

[26] *Cambridge Modern History*, VI, 612, 613.

[27] Brauer, *op. cit.*, pp. 42, 43.

[28] Stern, *op. cit.*, p. 77.

Certainly, Dury failed to realize that his own proposals and the offer of an English alliance had now occasioned further division and strife among the Swiss leaders. In his *Summarie Account* he says: "He dealt with them to the same effect as he had done with those of Zurich and Bern, onely they varied a little in their declaration concerning the way of proceeding; adding some advices and limitations to the work which the others had not yet expressed; although they had not been unmindful of them."[29] The Basel officials furnished Dury with a paper in which they professed an interest in the cause of unity and the establishment of more friendly relations between the English and the Swiss, but this paper failed to present a cordial indorsement of Dury's union program such as had been expressed in the documents furnished by the authorities of Zurich and Bern.[30]

From Basel, Dury proceeded to Schaffhausen, where Stockar's advocacy of the English alliance had already prepared the way for the favorable reception of his plans.[31] He arrived in Schaffhausen on October 20, and the Senate promptly ordered the call of an assembly of all the ministers and theological professors of the city, together with a number of senators. After a series of conferences the assembly approved a written declaration in which they indorsed Dury's union plans and promised their co-operation in the union movement.[32] Similar visits were made with favorable results to St. Gall and Appenzell.[33] The Reformed congregations among the Grisons asked Dury to negotiate with them in secret, as they were unwilling to arouse the suspicions of their powerful Roman Catholic neighbors.[34]

At the close of the year 1654 the leaders of the Reformed cantons were still undecided as to whether they should seek an alliance with England or with France.[35] This uncertainty prompted Dury to new

[29] P. 26.

[30] Dury, *Syllabus Documentorum*, pp. i, ii; see also Hubler, *op. cit.*, pp. 308, 309.

[31] Brauer, *op. cit.*, pp. 54 ff.

[32] Dury, *Syllabus Documentorum*, p. ii.

[33] Dury, *Summarie Account*, pp. 26, 27; cf. also *Syllabus Documentorum*, p. ii.

[34] *Summarie Account*, p. 27.

[35] Vaughan, *op. cit.*, I, 104. Dury furnished Pell with a memorandum in which he refers to the political conditions as follows: "There is, in many of the chief leading men, a good inclination to do really that thing which tends to a correspondency with us, and for the common cause, though they cannot yet own such a design in a way of a treaty; because many of them look to France with a hope of gaining their ends by it, especially Bern, which is entangled in a kind of particular treaty. Yet Bern hath promised that they will not renew the League without Zurich. . . . . I believe, also, that things here tend to a greater distance with France, and that they will ripen."

zeal and haste in his negotiations. He resolved to extend his efforts into West Switzerland, where French agents were active in attempts to thwart the proposed alliance with England. Dury visited Lausanne and conferred with church leaders, assuring them of Cromwell's intention to champion the Protestant Interest and asking them to prepare a declaration of their views regarding his union proposals.[36] From Lausanne he went to Geneva. He had looked forward to an opportunity to plead the cause of Christian reunion in this city, which had exercised so much influence on the Reformed Churches of many lands. Cromwell was also interested in gaining the support of the Genevans. He had prepared a special letter, which Dury was ordered to deliver to the magistrates of Geneva. Able leaders of the Genevan churches, including the ministers, Theodor Tronchin and Jeremias Pictet, and the theological professors, Antoine Leger, Philippe Mestrezat, and François Turretin, had already indicated an interest in his reunion proposals.[37] But the French agents were especially active in Geneva. Observers were of the opinion that Dury would not dare to visit the city.[38]

Dury arrived in Geneva on January 20, 1655, and remained there for ten days.[39] He received a cordial welcome and was assigned quarters in the building which had formerly served as the home of Calvin and Beza. After delivering the letter which Cromwell had addressed to the magistrates, he was allowed to present his plans before an assembly composed of the ministers of the city and the surrounding districts, together with the professors of the academy. On January 23, a commission was appointed to make a detailed examination of his proposals.[40] In conferences with this commission he proposed measures designed to promote union among the Reformed

---

[36] Vaughan, *op. cit.*, I, 117.

[37] Brauer, *op. cit.*, p. 68.

[38] Vaughan, *op. cit.*, I, 122, 123. Pell to Thurloe, January 27, 1655: "By a letter written at Geneva, Jan. 23rd, by old Mr. Tronchin .... I perceive that he [Dury] was then come thither, and lodged in his house. ..... Some of Zurich began to say that he durst not go to Geneva, because the magistrates of that city would not bid him welcome, nor take him into their protection for fear of displeasing the French king, who is the Protector of Geneva. But now M. D. is there, and the forecast of those considerate persons is not a little thereby disparaged."

[39] Dury, in his *Summarie Account*, p. 28, states that he "thought it not fit to make any long stay there, lest being much observed, his Negotiation at the Court of France (whence many spies are upon Geneva) might become suspected, and so prejudiciall unto their good correspondency there, for this cause hee made hast to bee gone."

[40] Brauer, *op. cit.*, p. 73.

Churches, projects for securing a correspondency between the Lutheran and Reformed Churches, and a request that the Genevan theologians should take upon themselves the task of preparing a new "Harmonia Confessionum."[41] Dury believed that the preparation of such a work, stressing points of agreement in essential doctrines, would serve as a useful means of promoting irenic activity. Regardless of the danger from France, the Genevan authorities professed an interest in Cromwell's offer of friendship and Dury's union proposals. The City Council forwarded a letter to Cromwell in which they indorsed Dury's union efforts.[42] The Venerable Company also drew up a declaration, which gave such cordial indorsement to Dury's plans that he had the document printed for wide distribution.[43]

From Geneva Dury went to Bern. Here he "stayed to print something which was to bee sent to Geneva, that it might bee by them dispersed amongst the Churches of France, to cure them of some prejudices which were taken up against his work in that kingdom."[44] He was forced to deal with the French Huguenots through indirect channels, as the French authorities would not allow him to enter their country. However, many of the reports from France indicated

[41] Dury had already secured the publication of a *Harmonia Confessionum* at Geneva in 1654 (see H. G. N. Tollin, "Johann Duraeus," *Geschichts-Blätter für Stadt und Land Magdeburg*, XXXIII, 78). But this was only a new edition of the *Harmonia Confessionum* of 1581, with additions from the doctrinal statements issued by the Synod of Dort, together with the Confession of Cyril, Patriarch of Constantinople, and the General Confession of the Reformed Churches of Poland (see G. J. Slosser, *Christian Unity—Its History and Challenge in All Communions and in All Lands*, p. 362). The *Harmonia Confessionum* of 1654 was concerned chiefly with the effort to harmonize the confessional statements issued by the Reformed Churches. Dury was now urging the theologians of Geneva to undertake the preparation of a *Harmonia Confessionum Protestantium*, which would show the essential harmony of the doctrinal statements issued by all the Protestant churches. Dury had presented a draft of the plan for such a work in his *Consultatio Theologica* (1641), pp. 21–24. Here he suggested that one of the less rigid doctrinal statements accepted in each Protestant country should be selected for use in preparing the *Harmonia*. He expressed the belief that "ex hisce confessionibus inter se collatis, Consensus Evangelica veritate dignosci potest." Dury further ventured the advice that attention should be given primarily to harmonizing the following confessions of faith: the Augsburg Confession (1530); the Tetrapolitan Confession (1530); the Basel Confession (1534); the First Helvetic Confession (1536); the Saxon Confession (1551); the Württemberg Confession (1551); the Gallican Confession (1559); the Thirty-nine Articles of the Anglican Church as adopted by Parliament in 1571; the Heidelberg Catechism (1563); the Belgic Confession (1561); the Consensus of Sendomir (1570); and the Scottish Confession of 1560. It should be noted that Dury omitted from this list three Confessions which had been involved in current theological strife, viz., the Formula of Concord, the Decrees of the Synod of Dort, and the Westminster Confession of Faith.

[42] The letter is quoted in part by Brauer, *op. cit.*, p. 75.

[43] *Syllabus Documentorum*, p. iii.

[44] Dury, *Summarie Account*, p. 27.

that the Huguenots were interested in the success of his mission.[45]
Meanwhile, Comenius, in an effort to promote a pan-Protestant
alliance as a measure of protection against Roman Catholic aggression, was again urging George Rákóczy II, prince of Transylvania,
to ally himself with Cromwell and take a position of leadership in
championing the Protestant cause in Eastern Europe in defiance of
Austria.[46] At Pell's suggestion, Dury renewed his correspondence
with Bisterfield, who was then serving as advisor to Rákóczy.[47] This
correspondence of Dury, although it was discovered and aroused the
suspicions of the Austrian authorities,[48] prompted Rákóczy to look
to England for help as he formulated his plans for a revolt against
Austria and an attempt to gain the Polish crown. In April, 1655,
Rákóczy sent Konstantin Schaum to London to enlist the support of
Cromwell. It is probable, as Angyal suggests, that Cromwell wished
to furnish moral and material support to Rákóczy in his revolt
against Austria, but the pressure of other political problems made it
impossible for him to give effective support.[49] Sweden, instead of
England, was the ally of Rákóczy when finally, in 1657, he made his
unsuccessful attempt to gain the Polish crown, and all the schemes
of the Transylvanian prince collapsed when Charles X withdrew his
support.[50]

In February, 1655, Dury again attended a meeting of deputies
from all the Protestant cantons at Aarau. He presented an account
of the progress of his negotiations, thanked the deputies for their
assistance, and asked them "to move their Churches to give him their
common Declaration to be made use of in the name of all, to adde a

[45] Vaughan (*op. cit.*, I, 48) quotes a letter of a French Huguenot, dated September, 1654,
as follows: "I have understood that M. D. has gone from Zurich, to continue his conferences
with other churches, about the accommodation, etc. God bless his intentions with happy
success. Monsieur Mestrezat .... hath been in this city these two days. .... In our discourse
I gave him occasion to speak of Mr. Dury's design. He approved it very much, and said that
our Churches [in France] and that of Geneva shall do well to assist M. D. with their good
counsells and advice; but that he would not encourage him to come into France to treat with
the reformed churches there, because he would be personally suspected at court, the cardinal
having already conceived an ill suspicion. .... He said, that as for them, they should be able
to do nothing in Mr. Dury's good work but accompany it with their good wishes and prayers."

[46] A. Patera, *Jana Amosa Komenského Korrespondence*, pp. 176 ff.

[47] Vaughan, *op. cit.*, I, 38.

[48] Brauer, *op. cit.*, p. 96.

[49] See D. Angyal, *Geschichte der politischen Beziehungen Siebenbürgens zu England*, pp. 47 ff.

[50] *Cambridge Modern History*, IV, 429, 580, 583; V, 344 ff.

Declaration in their own name thereunto as a State, and to write to
the German Princes of the reformed Religion, to preinform them of
this negotiation, and to prepare them to Concurrance in the work."[51]
But the opposition of Basel to Dury's program and the tense political
situation in the Piedmont prompted the Swiss leaders to be extremely cautious. They were willing to give general indorsement to measures in the interest of the peace and unity of the churches and to bestow liberal praise and generous presents upon Dury, but they were
unwilling to make any definite proposals for union.[52] They would
go no further than to make professions of a readiness to enter a closer
alliance with England and to negotiate for unity with the churches
of England and with the Lutherans, providing that it was possible to
do this without the sacrifice of their own convictions. Dury was now
anxious to conclude his negotiations in Switzerland in order that he
might begin to plead his cause in Germany. During March, April,
and a part of May he spent most of his time at Zurich in order that he
might have opportunity "to write letters to all parts; to expect the
promised Declarations of the Church and State; to print some preliminary informations to bee sent before hand into Germany; to
settle the course of a Theologicall Correspondency; and to receive
the answer of the Protestant Cantons to his Highness Letter."[53]

While attending the assembly at Aarau, Dury received information
of the hostile edict against the Piedmontese Protestants, which had
been issued on January 25, 1655, by the Duke of Savoy. He immediately sent a letter to Pell to inform him of the danger threatening
the Vaudois. He urged Pell to persuade Cromwell to use his influence
in an effort to avert the impending disaster. This letter, dated from
Aarau, February 24, 1655, was forwarded by Pell to England. It
furnished the government and the people of England with the first
definite news of the plans for the persecution of the Vaudois.[54] In
reporting this news to Pell, Dury wrote as follows:

SIR,—I am spoken to by the Lords of Zurich who are here, to entreat you to help,
by your letters to his highness, to second their request unto the Duke of Savoy, in
behalf of the poor distressed Protestants of the Piedmont, who are commanded to be

[51] Dury, *Summarie Account*, p. 28.

[52] On the general character of the declarations given to Dury by the leaders of the Swiss
churches see Brauer, *op. cit.*, pp. 79–92; and Hubler, *op. cit.*, pp. 310, 311.

[53] Dury, *Summarie Account*, p. 29.

[54] J. Stoughton, *History of Religion in England from the Opening of the Long Parliament
to the End of the 18th Century*, II, 462.

supporter of the men who were responsible for the death of his uncle, Charles I.[63] He warned Pell that Dury must not approach his territory.[64] After this failure to secure a hearing from the Elector, Dury attempted to present his plans through correspondence with the Heidelberg theologian, Daniel Tossanus. But Tossanus, following the lead of his prince, manifested only slight interest in Dury's schemes.[65]

Dury finally opened his negotiations with the Reformed Churches of Germany by making a visit to Hanau, the chief city of the Wetterau. Traveling from Switzerland by way of Württemberg, he reached Hanau on June 14, 1655. He renewed his acquaintance with the clergymen of Hanau and explained the scope of his union plans. The churches of the city furnished him with papers pledging their co-operation in union effort.[66] He decided to make Hanau his headquarters for several months. Stopping in the city long enough "to deal with the ministry of that place and to print such papers as were necessary to be sent abroad to the reformed Churches of Germany and to their Princes for information," he continued his travels and spent the months from June to September in visiting the churches of the Wetterau, Nassau, and surrounding districts.[67] The declarations furnished by the leaders of the churches which he visited were uniformly favorable. Count Wilhelm of Sohms and Count Wilhelm Otto of Isenburg also indorsed his union proposals.[68]

Meanwhile, Dury had addressed a number of letters to leaders of the churches of Cassel, but the replies to these letters were unfavorable, and he decided to visit that principality. He arrived at Marburg on October 19 and spent some time "in conference with the Professors of Divinity of that University."[69] His earnest efforts to win the support of the two leading theologians of Marburg, John Crocius and Sebastian Curtius, proved unavailing.[70] The Marburg

[63] *Ibid.*, pp. 106 ff.; cf. also Dury, *Summarie Account*, p. 29.

[64] Vaughan, *op. cit.*, I, 190.

[65] Brauer, *op. cit.*, p. 105.

[66] Dury, *Syllabus Documentorum*, p. iv.

[67] The course of Dury's travels during this period may be traced in his *Summarie Account*, p. 29; see also Dury, *Syllabus Documentorum*, p. iii.

[68] Tollin, *op. cit.*, XXXII, 259.

[69] *Summarie Account*, p. 30.

[70] Brauer, *op. cit.*, pp. 128 ff. Brandes (*op. cit.*, p. 96) states that "Crocius at Marburg, one of the interlocutors at Leipsic in 1631, advised him [Dury] to sweep before his own door, and reconcile the parties in Great Britain, instead of meddling with foreign affairs—all this merely because of the suspicion he had incurred by having consented to the regicide." Johann

teachers and ministers professed a genuine interest in the peace and
unity of the churches, but they obviously regarded Dury's proposals
as both indefinite and impractical. They held that the Reformed
Churches should not take the initiative in union efforts until the
Lutherans manifested a willingness to negotiate.[71] The papers which
they furnished to Dury abound in expressions of good will toward
Dury and his work, but it is evident that they had neither an expectation of a successful issue for his negotiations nor an inclination
to co-operate in an effective manner.[72]

From Marburg, Dury proceeded to Cassel, arriving in that city on
November 3, 1655. He was able to secure an audience with the Landgrave William VI. He made a favorable impression during this interview, and the Landgrave soon became his most consistent supporter and patron among the German princes.[73] Dury was asked to
explain his program to the Superintendent Theophilus Neuberger
and other ministers who were appointed by the Landgrave to examine his proposals. These commissioners, though recognizing the
many difficulties which stood in the way of union, approved Dury's
plans and promised to co-operate with him in the conduct of union
negotiations.[74] Dury was elated over the promises of support which
he received from the Landgrave and the clergy of Cassel.[75]

The Landgrave gave Dury one of the most cordial letters of indorsement which he received during the whole course of his irenic
activity.[76] He also ordered the theological faculty at Marburg to prepare a new declaration of their opinion regarding Dury's proposals.
This time, though using guarded terms, they expressed a more favorable judgment.[77] The Landgrave's support was of great service to

---

Heinrich Heidegger was a student under Crocius at Marburg when Dury visited the university
in 1654. It is probable that Dury enlisted his support at this time. F. W. J. H. Gass ("Johann
Heinrich Heidegger," *Allgemeine deutsche Biographie*, XI, 295, 296) states that Heidegger befriended Dury. Heidegger located in Zurich in 1665. He attained recognition as an outstanding Reformed theologian. In 1675 he prepared the *Formula consensus Helvetica*, which
was accepted by most of the Swiss cantons.

[71] Tollin, *op. cit.*, XXXII, 259.

[72] Brauer, *op. cit.*, pp. 129 ff.

[73] *Ibid.*, pp. 131 ff. Landgrave William VI belonged to a line of princes who had distinguished themselves as supporters of irenic movements. Philip of Hesse and William V had
made special efforts to reconcile Lutheran and Reformed Churches.

[74] Dury, *Syllabus Documentorum*, p. v.

[75] *Summarie Account*, pp. 30, 31.

[76] For the text of this letter see Brauer, *op. cit.*, pp. 243 ff.

[77] For text of this paper see *ibid.*, pp. 241–43.

Dury in his negotiations in Lower Saxony and Westphalia. In December, 1655, he was able to secure letters from the Heidelberg professor, Frederick Spanheim, and the celebrated church historian, John Heinrich Hottinger, in which they also professed a more favorable attitude toward his union program.[78] The Elector Karl Ludwig likewise expressed an interest in union projects at this time.[79]

The Landgrave William VI had married Hedwig Sophia, the daughter of George William, Elector of Brandenburg. The interest in reunion manifested by William VI encouraged Dury to seek the support of Frederick William, the Great Elector. This prince had labored for years in an effort to reconcile the Lutheran and Reformed parties within his territories.[80] In 1648, during the course of the negotiations at Münster and Osnabrück, he had used his influence to secure equal rights for the Lutheran and Reformed Churches within the empire.[81] Thus the policies of Frederick William and Cromwell were similarly designed to produce peace and unity among the Protestant churches within their territories, but the Elector's distrust of Cromwell prevented their co-operation in a movement for the union of all Protestant churches.[82] It was Dury's purpose to approach the Great Elector through his court chaplain, John Bergius, who had manifested a conciliatory attitude in the Leipzig Colloquy and had supported Dury's earlier union efforts. While at Frankfort, Dury had asked the Elector's ambassador, Fortmann, to forward a number of his union pamphlets to Bergius.[83] This paved the way for an extended interchange of letters between Dury and Bergius.

In this correspondence Bergius, prompted by orders from the Great Elector, expressed his readiness to support union effort but professed his distrust of the leadership of England in the reunion movement. He also stated that he was unwilling to co-operate with Dury, because of his frequent change of party allegiance and his association with men who were responsible for the execution of the king and the consequent prevalence of anarchy in both the church and the

[78] See the calendar of these letters as given by Dury, *Syllabus Documentorum*, p. v.

[79] Tollin, *op. cit.*, XXXII, 260. The Elector appeared in the assembly summoned to discuss union proposals and declared his interest in the union of Protestants of all lands, especially the union of the churches of Germany.

[80] Müller, *op. cit.*, II, Part II, 591, 592.

[81] Brandes, *op. cit.*, p. 95.

[82] See Hugo Landwehr, "Johannes Duraeus' Unionsverhandlung mit Kurbrandenburg," *Zeitschrift für Kirchengeschichte*, X (1889), 468 ff.

[83] Tollin, *op. cit.*, XXXII, 261.

state affairs of England.[84] These charges were made in a letter to Dury, dated October 17, 1655. Dury prepared a lengthy reply in which he maintained that his apparent changes in party allegiance were due to the fact that, in his efforts to advance the peace and unity of the churches, he had remained aloof from all party connections and had served all parties alike. He also defended his service under Cromwell by advancing the thesis that only the Cromwellian regime could save England from the type of anarchy which Bergius had deplored.[85]

The correspondence with Bergius convinced Dury that it was useless for him to visit Berlin at this time. Although the Great Elector was unwilling to treat with Dury, he ordered Schlezer, his ambassador in England, to investigate the union plans of Cromwell and to indicate his readiness to deal directly with Cromwell regarding measures to promote the peace of the Protestant churches.[86] Schlezer was interested in the success of Dury's plans, but he was unable to secure the effective co-operation of Cromwell and Frederick William in the union movement.[87] Six years later the Great Elector made a new effort to advance the cause of Christian reunion within his own territories, but he again refused to use Dury's services and advice in promoting the union movement.[88]

In January, 1656, Dury attempted to win the support of the clergy and princes of Anhalt in behalf of his program. He had every reason to expect a favorable reception in this section, as many of the Anhalt theologians, including Christian Beckmann, had cordially supported his union efforts during the course of his earlier negotiations in Germany.[89] He visited Dessau on February 10 and secured an interview with John Casimir, the Senior Prince of the House of Anhalt. The Prince and the Lutheran superintendents of Anhalt furnished cautiously worded indorsements of his union proposals.[90] The Lutheran superintendents of Köthen and Dessau, Daniel Sachs and George Raumer, urged Dury to secure the call of a general Lutheran convention by the King of Sweden and the Elector of Saxony. Such

[84] C. J. Benzelius, *Dissertatio de Johanne Duraeo pacificatore celeberrimo maxime de actis eius Suecanis*, p. 46.

[85] T. Hasaeus, *Bibliotheca Bremensis historico-philologica-theologica*, IV, 683–710.

[86] Tollin, *op. cit.*, XXXII, 261.

[87] Brauer, *op. cit.*, p. 141.

[88] Landwehr, *op. cit.*, pp. 463–89.

[89] Brauer, *op cit.*, pp. 145 ff.   [90] Dury, *Summarie Account*, p. 30.

a meeting, they held, would give representatives of all the Lutheran
Churches an opportunity to deliberate on the drafting of a Harmony
of Confessions which might be acceptable to both the Lutheran and
the Reformed Churches.[91]

In March, Dury visited Weimar for the purpose of interviewing the
Dukes of Weimar "to the end that hee might by those two Lutheran
princes seek some overture towards the rest; and by cleer information
given to them of his design, prevent the false reports which might bee
raised, and remove the prejudices which were conceived by some concerning his work."[92] He interviewed Duke Wilhelm at Weimar.
Equipped with letters of introduction from Duke Wilhelm, he traveled from Weimar to Gotha, where he secured an interview with
Duke Ernest the Pious. He recorded the results of this visit as follows:

> In effect two whole days were spent together in a serious proposall and disquirie
> of the means and ways, by which true Christian Unity and Gospel moderation of
> affections should be advanced amongst Protestants; and the result was, that the
> Prince would contribute all that lay in his power to further the designes whereof
> they had conferred together; and that Master Dury was desired in time to come to
> entertain a correspondency about the same with the Prince.[93]

Dury's ceaseless round of travel brought him to the Academy at
Rintelen in the County of Schaumburg on May 11, 1656. This school
was under Lutheran control, but its theologians were "so moderate
that Master Dury thought fit to make acquaintance with them to
prepare them to co-operate with him in the work of peace towards the
Churches and Universities of their own side."[94] After a stay of nine
days at Rintelen, he was able to secure a promise of co-operation from
its theologians. Then, with the permission of the Count of Schaumburg and the Count of Lippe, he made extensive journeys in the
territories of these princes in an effort to enlist the support of their
clergy.[95] In June he visited Emden and the surrounding districts. In
July he reached Wesel and went from there to Duisburg, where a
general synod of deputies from the dukedoms of Jülich, Cleves, and
the Mark was in session. After he had explained his objectives, this
synod resolved that "a Declaration should be penned in the name of
all their Churches, to bee given to Master Dury in approbation of
his work."[96]

[91] Benzelius, *op. cit.*, p. 48; and Tollin, *op. cit.*, XXXII, 262.

[92] Dury, *Summarie Account*, p. 31.

[93] *Ibid.*, p. 32.　　[94] *Ibid.*, p. 34.　　[95] *Ibid.*　　[96] *Ibid.*, p. 36.

On a visit to Cleves, Dury secured an interview with Prince
Maurice of Nassau, who referred his proposals to the theologians of
the Academy at Duisburg and also to Martin Hundius, the court
preacher. Hundius, with the consent of the state authorities and in
collaboration with his son, prepared a paper supporting the union
program and pointing out the fundamental principles in which all
Protestants were in agreement.[97] The Academy at Duisburg had
been established by the Great Elector to counteract the influence of
the Jesuits, who were especially active in the district about Düssel-
dorf. With the exception of Hundius and his son, the Duisburg
theologians were unwilling to give cordial indorsement to Dury's
proposals.[98]

The visit to Cleves brought Dury's negotiations in Germany to a
close. During his stay, from June, 1655, to July, 1656, he had made
constant efforts to interest the Lutheran and Reformed leaders in a
new movement toward Christian reunion. His *Syllabus Documentorum* cites papers which indicate the extent of his activities during this
period of his work as Cromwell's messenger to the churches of the
Continent.[99] In Germany Dury was forced to rely upon his own re-
sources in order to get a hearing, as the indorsements of Cromwell
had little weight with most of the German princes. He had failed to
win the effective support of Karl Ludwig and the Great Elector—the
two princes who could most effectively advance his cause—but he
had gained the cordial support of the Landgrave William VI and a
number of minor princes. He had also secured an imposing array of
indorsements of the reunion movement from ministers and theologians of both the Lutheran and the Reformed Churches. Moreover,
the subject of Christian reunion had been brought to the attention
of the public in a challenging manner in many of the German principalities.

Dury next began the advocacy of reunion plans in the Netherlands.

[97] This paper, entitled *Instrumentum Catholicae pacis cum deo et piis hominibus*, was given
wide publicity by Dury. He presents the full text in his *Irenicorum Tractatuum Prodromus*,
pp. 201–67.

[98] Benzelius, *op. cit.*, p. 49.

[99] In the *Syllabus Documentorum*, pp. iii ff., Dury calendars the papers which were furnished
to him as judgments concerning his union proposals by church leaders of the Wetterau, Nassau,
Hesse, the Palatinate, Anhalt, Lippe, Emden, Bremen, Tecklenberg, Bentheim, Steinfurt,
Jülich, Cleves, the Mark, and Gelders. He also calendars similar indorsements by princes
such as Wilhelm Otto, Count of Isenburg and Budingen; Wilhelm, Count of Sohms; the
Prince of Deuxpont; the Landgrave William VI of Hesse-Cassel; John Casimir; Christian,
Prince of Anhalt; Maurice of Nassau; and others.

The Dutch clergy had shown little interest in his proposals on the occasion of his previous visits. Now conditions were even more unfavorable for the successful promotion of union efforts. New handicaps had developed owing to the divisive tendencies which had been intensified in the course of the Arminian controversies, to the dominance of a rigid type of Calvinistic scholasticism, whose adherents regarded the Lutherans with distrust, and to the increasing interference of the civil powers in church affairs.[100] Despite these handicaps, Dury remained in the Netherlands from July, 1656, to February, 1657. Crossing the frontier at Nymwegen, he consulted a deputy of the Synod of Gelderland "concerning the way of furthering his work in the United Provinces." He was advised to visit the various synods and present his cause in person. He resolved to follow this advice, and for months he traveled constantly, visiting the synods and conferring with ministers and statesmen who were in position to aid his cause.[101]

From Nymwegen Dury proceeded to Utrecht, where he met with the chief preachers of the city and the professors of the university and informed them of the progress of his union negotiations. After a brief visit to Amsterdam, he went to Dort where the Synod of South Holland was in session. Here he was refused a hearing, as the lay commissioners interfered and encouraged the Synod to give him "a dilatorie answer which made him perceive their unwillingness to take the business into consideration."[102] He then went to Harderwick, where, by solicitation of influential friends, he was granted a public hearing before the Synod of Gelderland on July 23. This Synod, he says,

Declared by the mouth of their President, That they thanked him for imparting his businesse unto them; that they highly approved the work, that they would join with their correspondent Synods to further it; that they would take the advice of their severall Classes about it, and if need were would also confer with their supreme magistrate concerning it.[103]

Encouraged by this declaration, Dury again visited The Hague and Leyden. At Leyden he conferred with John Hoornbeck, one of

---

[100] See the excellent study of the relations of church and state in the Netherlands, 1600–1650, by Douglas Nobbs, *Theocracy and Toleration* (1938).

[101] Dury, *Summarie Account*, p. 37; cf. also Brauer, *op. cit.*, pp. 173 ff.

[102] Dury, *Summarie Account*, p. 37.

[103] *Ibid.*, p. 38; cf. J. Lindeboom, "Johannes Duraeus en zijne werkzaamheid in dienst van Cromwell's politiek," *Nederlandsch Archief voor Kerkgeschiedenis* (N.S.), XVI, 259.

the three divinity professors of the university. He soon found that
Hoornbeck was primarily interested in polemics rather than irenics,
but he was able to secure the support of the other divinity professors
of Leyden.[104] He next visited Utrecht and conferred with the local
deputy of the Synod and discussed his union plans with three members of the theological faculty, Voetius, Essenius, and Nethenus, who
professed a friendly interest in his proposals.[105] In August he attended the Synod of North Holland at Alkmaar, but he was refused
a hearing on the ground that "the business ought first to bee brought
to the cognisance of the States before the Churches should meddle
therewith."[106] This rebuff caused Dury to change his methods and
seek the support of the secular power in order to gain a hearing before the synods. Accordingly, he went to The Hague and made an
appeal to the States General. He succeeded in securing a resolution
whereby the States General officially referred his proposals to each
province for consideration by the churches and universities.[107]

With customary patient determination, Dury set out to plead his
cause once more in each province. On September 2 he visited the
Synod of Utrecht, "where his business being examined by the Deputies, a resolution was Declared to approve his work and to concur in
it."[108] After a hurried journey, Dury reached Middleburg on September 4, in time to present his cause in the closing sessions of the
French Synod of Middleburg and in the Classis of Walcheren. He
secured an indorsement of his union proposals in each of these meetings.[109] He also visited the Classes of Bergen-op-Zoom and Zieriksee,
securing similar indorsements.[110]

Dury next resumed his negotiations in the central provinces of the
Netherlands. He visited Utrecht again and secured an indorsement
from the professors of divinity in the university.[111] Thence he went to
The Hague and asked for the approval of his proposal by the States
of Holland. But the Grand Pensionary John de Witt, who controlled

---

[104] *Summarie Account*, pp. 38, 39.

[105] Brauer, *op. cit.*, p. 175.

[106] Dury, *Summarie Account*, p. 39.

[107] *Ibid.*; cf. J. Thurloe, *A Collection of the State Papers of John Thurloe*, V, 306.

[108] *Summarie Account*, p. 39. This resolution is calendared by Dury in his *Syllabus Documentorum, Supplementum*, p. ix.

[109] *Syllabus Documentorum, Supplementum*, p. ix.

[110] *Summarie Account*, pp. 40, 41.

[111] *Syllabus Documentorum, Supplementum*, p. x.

the civil government of the province, was inclined to regard Dury's proposals as impracticable.[112] Under his direction the States of Holland answered Dury's appeal by issuing a declaration to the effect that they would take no action regarding reunion negotiations until the Lutherans had declared themselves in favor of the movement.[113] Recognizing the dominant influence of the Province of Holland, Dury attempted to satisfy the objections offered by printing indorsements of his reunion proposals which he had received from Lutheran groups.[114] But this was without effect, and he failed to secure the support of the civil authorities of the Province of Holland.

Dury then returned to Leyden and renewed his negotiations with the divinity professors of the University of Leyden. Through the influence of Abraham Heidanus, "an old acquaintance of 30 years or more," and John Cocceius, who was the leader of a protest movement directed against the narrow confessional interest of the Dutch churches,[115] he was able to secure a declaration "commending his endeavors, approving fully the designe; giving their advice on it, and promising freely their concurrence to advance the effect thereof."[116] He also visited Friesland and secured the indorsement of the University of Franeker. Here he had opportunity to explain his union proposals to Frederick William of Orange, who promised a "ready willingness to help in the advancement of it."[117] He next visited Groningen, where he secured favorable judgments from the deputies of the states, the deputy of the synod, and the theological professors of the university.[118] In November, 1656, Dury also made visits to Oberijssel, Zwolle, Deventer, and Campen.[119] He then returned to Amsterdam, where he spent the months of December and January, giving much of his time to the preparation of letters which were designed to furnish information regarding his negotiations in Holland "to all his Correspondents in foreign Churches where he had been Negotiating

---

[112] Brauer, *op. cit.*, p. 182.

[113] Dury, *Summarie Account*, p. 41.

[114] *Ibid.*, pp. 41, 42.

[115] Brauer, *op. cit.*, p. 184.

[116] Dury, *Summarie Account*, p. 43. See the calendar of this declaration in Dury's *Syllabus Documentorum, Supplementum*, pp. x, xi.

[117] *Summarie Account*, p. 42.

[118] The text of the judgment of the theological professors of the University of Groningen, dated November 13, 1656, is given by Lindeboom, *op. cit.*, pp. 267, 268.

[119] W. P. C. Knuttel, *Acta der particuliere Synoden van Zuid-Holland, 1621–1700*, IV, 117–20.

before."[120] Comenius was residing at Amsterdam at this time. Dury and Comenius once more had opportunity to collaborate in the preparation of plans for further union efforts.[121] While at Amsterdam, Dury secured an audience with Prince Adolf of Sweden, the brother of Charles X. The Prince expressed himself as favoring the union movement.[122]

Dury now had opportunity to survey the results of his mission to the Continent under Cromwell. He believed that he had prepared the way for a new advance in the reunion movement. In the course of his negotiations he had encountered many difficulties, such as the prejudices of the German princes against the Commonwealth leaders, whom they regarded as the murderers of Charles I; the outbreak of the Swedish-Danish War, which had seriously hindered the efforts to secure co-operation among the Protestants of the North;[123] and the conclusion of a defensive alliance of England, France, and Spain, which, though guaranteeing the preservation of the rights of the Swiss Protestants and the Huguenots, was regarded in Switzerland as prejudicial to the Protestant Interest.[124] Dury was especially anxious to secure more hearty support for his union plans in the Netherlands. He had obtained many indorsements during his stay in the country, but the powerful Synods of North and South Holland still remained aloof from the projected union movement; the Grand Pensionary John de Witt had refused to co-operate; and the States General had repeatedly refused to indorse his proposals. Dury was convinced that his work would be more successful in the Netherlands if he could return to England and secure additional supporting papers from Cromwell for use in dealing with the next meeting of the States General. With this idea in mind, he sailed from Flushing on February 14, 1657, and landed at Margate the following day. He hastened to London to give an account of his stewardship and to enlist support for a new effort in behalf of the union of the Protestant churches.

It seemed to Dury that he had arrived in England at an opportune time. Cromwell, now securely entrenched in power at home, was

---

[120] Dury, *Summarie Account*, p. 43.

[121] Comenius had moved to Amsterdam after the destruction of Lesna in 1656 (see S. S. Laurie, *John Amos Comenius, Bishop of the Moravians: His Life and Educational Works*, pp. 51, 58, 59).

[122] *Summarie Account*, pp. 44, 45.

[123] Bowman, *op. cit.*, pp. 46 ff.

[124] *Ibid.*, p. 60; see also Stern, *op. cit.*, p. 93.

gradually developing a more vigorous foreign policy. This new policy was to be anti-Spanish and anti-Hapsburg. His interest in a pan-Protestant union was stronger than ever before, as is clearly evidenced in the State Papers prepared by Milton at this time. Cromwell was shaping plans for the formation of a new alliance of England, Holland, Switzerland, Denmark, and the Protestant princes of Germany and Transylvania. He also planned to send John Bradshaw to Russia to enlist the co-operation of the Russians with the new alliance.[125] Dury's knowledge of Continental affairs might prove of service in drafting the plans for this new alignment of powers, and it was decided that, for the time being, he would be of most "service in behalf of his life-long idea of a Pan-Protestant union" by remaining in England.[126] At no time had Cromwell manifested more interest in political co-operation among the Protestant powers. The Protestant Interest had become the dominant factor in the formation of his foreign policy.

However, the situation demanded cautious procedure. Cromwell wished to continue the alliance with France. He regarded France as the only Roman Catholic power with which there could be safe dealing. This Anglo-French alliance stood in the way of the formation of the proposed new pan-Protestant alliance. The war between Denmark and Sweden also delayed the realization of the proposed plans, but Cromwell was steadily negotiating to secure peace in northern Europe.[127] It was obviously unwise to make church-union projects loom too large at the time. The agitation of such projects might seriously handicap political objectives. Therefore, Cromwell, in a letter prepared by Milton, advised the zealous Landgrave William VI that he was thoroughly sympathetic with Dury's idea and willing to co-operate in the movement which Dury was promoting, but he considered the present moment unfavorable for any new efforts other than those which might be designed to establish a general peace between contending churches.[128]

---

[125] Bradshaw wished to secure the services of Dury as his assistant on this mission. Thurloe (*op. cit.*, VI, 138) quotes a letter of Bradshaw to Thurloe as follows: "The Council of State was pleased to send Mr. Dury with Mr. Lisle to Sweden: I should be glad of such a friend and companion, if he would undertake it, beinge now in London as I heare he is. He is one whom I love and honour for his eminent parts and good affections."

[126] Masson, *op. cit.*, V, 295.

[127] *Ibid.*, V, 312, 313; and Bischoffshausen, *op. cit.*, pp. 213, 214.

[128] Masson (*op. cit.*, V, 291, 292) presents this letter, in part, as follows: "We have particularly desired the same peace for the Churches of all Germany, where dissension has been

Dury, anxious to renew his negotiations on the Continent, was obviously impatient at this delay. At the time of the Restoration he asserted that Cromwell's seeming unwillingness to make new advances in union effort at this time caused him to doubt the Protector's intention of championing the cause of Christian reunion in an effective manner. Writing in 1660, in his *Declaration of John Durie*, he refers to his disillusionment in the following words:

> It was no difficult matter to conceive; that the whole aime which Oliver might have in countenancing me and my business; was to gaine some Reputation amongst the Protestant Churches to be a Zelot for their Interest; and thereby wipe off the odium of his incroachment of power. . . . . For although I could suspect at first some such thing might be possibly, yet I cannot say that I could conclude it probably; but when I was come home, and had shewed how all things were laid for a Religious correspondency, and prepared to carry on the work as it relates to the Gospell; then I could see plainly and demonstratively, that his aim was not that which at first he had pretended; because when all was ready to hand; and the Ministers here in England of different parties were disposed to act further in the work he did not at all mind the business further.[129]

These words were written by Dury when he was seeking the support of Charles II. They are manifestly unfair to Cromwell, who had supported his union project for years and had made the formation of a pan-Protestant union one of the major objectives of his foreign policy. It is evident that Dury sought to induce Cromwell to adopt a less cautious attitude at this time. He had influential friends interview the Protector in an attempt to secure at once the inauguration of a new movement in the interest of the union of the churches. It is probable that he pursuaded Milton to make an effort to enlist the support of the Protector.[130] When it was certain that Cromwell would not take immediate action, Dury renewed his correspondence with Continental irenic leaders and urged them to continue their propaganda in behalf of the reunion movement. Matthiae now sug-

---

too sharp and of too long continuance; and through our Durie, laboring at the same fruitlessly now for many years, we have heartily offered any possible service of ours that might contribute thereto. We remain still in the same mind; we desire to see the same brotherly love to each other among these Churches: but how hard a business this is of settling a peace among those sons of peace as they pretend themselves, we understand, to our great grief, only too abundantly. For it is hardly to be hoped that those of the Reformed and those of the Augustan confession will ever coalesce into the communion of one Church; they cannot without force be prevented from severally, by word and writings, defending their own beliefs; and force cannot consist with ecclesiastical tranquillity. This at least, however, they might allow one to entreat —that, as they do differ, they would differ more humanely and moderately, and love each other nevertheless."

[129] Pp. 26, 27.

[130] See Masson, *op. cit.*, V, 295, 296.

gested that Dury should make another attempt to win the favor of the Great Elector.[131] Following his advice, Dury renewed his correspondence with John Hundius with the hope that, through him, he might be able to persuade Frederick William to promote the union movement in Germany.[132]

Dury wished to secure new assurances of the support of the English churches as a means of preparing the way for further union negotiations. In the year 1657 he attempted to inform the English public in regard to his previous union efforts by the publication of two pamphlets entitled: *The Effect of Master Dury's Negotiations for Uniting of Protestants in a Gospel Interest* and *A Summarie Account of Mr. John Dury's Former and Latter Negotiation For the procuring of true Gospel Peace, with Christian Moderation and Charitable Unity amongst the Protestant Churches, and Academies.* Numerous attempts were made to secure the support of clergymen of the various parties. Richard Baxter was genuinely interested in Dury's union plans at this time and promised to prepare a work designed to advance the peace of the churches. In 1658 Dury published a tract by Baxter indorsing the movement toward reunion under the title, *The Judgment and Advice of the Associated Ministers of Worcestershire, concerning Mr. John Dury's Endeavors After Ecclesiastical Peace.*[133]

Dury also sought a new indorsement of his union program from the English Parliament.[134] Finally, a committee was appointed by Par-

---

[131] For the text of the letter from Matthiae to Dury see J. Kvačala, *Korrespondence Jana Amosa Komenského*, p. 115.

[132] Landwehr, *op. cit.*, p. 469. The text of the Dury-Hundius correspondence was published by Dury in his *Irenicorum Tractatuum Prodromus*, pp. 201 ff.

[133] William Orme, *Life and Times of Richard Baxter*, II, 223, 224. Orme gives Baxter's account of this publication as follows: "Mr. Dury having spent thirty years in endeavors to reconcile the Lutherans and the Calvinists, was now going over sea again in that work, and desired the judgment of our association, how it should be successfully expedited; which at their desire I drew up more largely in Latin and more briefly in English. The English letter he printed." Baxter produced a number of books dealing with the subject of Christian reunion. Among his other writings in the interest of unity and comprehension, the following are of special importance: *Catholic Unity, or the Only Way to Bring us all to be of One Religion* (London, 1660); *Universal Concord* (London, 1660); *The Cure of Church Divisions* (3d ed.; London, 1670); *Church Concord* (written, 1667; published, 1691); and *The True and Only Way of Concord of All the Christian Churches* (London, 1680). An appreciative estimate of Baxter's union ideas is presented by Slosser, *op. cit.*, pp. 50–57.

[134] Vaughan, *op. cit.*, II, 195. Dury to Pell, June 24, 1657: "I have endeavored to bring my business to be considered by them [the members of Parliament] and approved of and recommended to his highness. Whether their pressing affairs for money matters will suffer them to take it into consideration, I know not; but I have the chief of the leading men engaged to watch an opportunity to offer it; and all promise to further it; and if it receive countenance from Parliament, I may begin to act again."

liament to examine the reports of his union negotiations on the Continent. On recommendation of this committee, the House of Commons passed a resolution on June 26, 1657, which read, in part, as follows: "Ordered, that it be recommended to his highness the Lord Protector, as the desire of the Parliament, that his Highness will be pleased to encourage Christian endeavors for uniting the Protestant Churches abroad; and that the Lord Deputy . . . . be desired to present this note to his Highness the Lord Protector."[135] Dury hoped that this recommendation would "open a door of action" for him.[136] Just as public opinion in England was becoming more inclined to favor the inauguration of new union efforts Cromwell died, and all hope of immediate advance was lost. The death of Cromwell, September 3, 1658, was a most serious blow to Dury's irenic program.

After the death of Cromwell no further progress was made in the formation of the pan-Protestant political alliance which he had planned. Under the weak administration of Richard Cromwell the English government lost much of the prestige which it had won as the champion of the Protestant Interest on the Continent. Dury remained in England until after the Restoration, as he was now without a patron to support his cause. Since the peace of the churches in England was disturbed anew after the death of Cromwell, England seemed to provide a most needy field for Dury's work of "ecclesiastical pacification." For two years he concerned himself with efforts "to treat with the churches, and chiefly with the associations of churches of this nation, and with the Universities, and with the Churches in New England."[137] In dealing with the "associations of churches," Dury co-operated with Baxter in his attempts to promote agreement and union between the English Presbyterians and Independents. Baxter's plans to provide connectional bonds between the churches through the organization of associations, his proposals regarding the ordination of ministers, and his suggestions as to the guaranties of rights for each individual congregation are identical with the propositions which Dury had advanced in his *Model of Church Government* (1647) and *Peacemaker Without Partiality* (1648).[138]

---

[135] Thomas Burton, *Diary of Thomas Burton, Esq.*, II, 312, 313.

[136] Dury to Pell, July 9, 1657, as quoted by Vaughan, *op. cit.*, II, 209.

[137] Dury, as quoted by Thurloe, *op. cit.*, VII, 648.

[138] The similarity of the proposals for accommodation as offered by Dury and Baxter may be seen by the comparison of Dury's *Model of Church Government*, pp. xxviii, 17-19, and his *Peacemaker Without Partiality*, pp. 47, 48, with Baxter's *Universal Concord*, pp. 70-84.

Under the leadership of Baxter, satisfactory terms of agreement were drafted by the Presbyterians and Independents of Manchester.[139] At Dury's request, Baxter and the Associated Ministers of Worcester prepared a "Form of Agreement for the Pastors of such Churches as are left to Voluntary Associations and Communion."[140] Dury advocated the adoption of similar terms of agreement by groups of Presbyterian and Independent ministers throughout the nation. He approached the London Provincial Synod and other groups with proposals for an accommodation between Presbyterians and Independents on a basis of comprehension such as Baxter had suggested. He also asked these groups to unite in supporting new attempts to promote peace and unity among the Continental churches, but little interest was aroused by these efforts.

As the confusion of the churches tended to increase, Dury reached the conclusion that peace and unity could be established only by the action of Parliament. On April 9, 1659, he addressed a petition to Parliament which was printed under the title, *The Humble Petition . . . . Concerning the Parliament's Consulting about Matters of Religion.*[141] In this paper, after announcing a series of basic maxims "concerning the undoubted way of Christianity free from all human interests," he asked for the inauguration by Parliament of a new effort "to hold forth a testimony of the national profession of Christianity and to advance thereby the unity of spirit among professors" both at home and abroad.

But Parliament was too busy with other problems to consider Dury's proposals. It soon became evident that Charles II would be restored to the throne. Thereafter, Dury's efforts during the remainder of his stay in England were devoted to attempts to enlist the support of the incoming government in behalf of his union schemes. In the year 1660 he published two pamphlets which were designed to interest the authorities who would be in charge of the new government. The first of these, entitled *The Plain Way of Peace and Unity*, was devoted to the proof of the thesis that the moment was propitious for England to take the lead in the promotion of the union of all Protestants. The second pamphlet, entitled *A Declaration of John Durie*, was concerned chiefly with an attempt to justify

[139] W. A. Shaw, *History of the English Church during the Civil Wars and under the Commonwealth, 1640–1660*, II, 170.

[140] See Baxter, *Universal Concord*, p. 2.

[141] The full text of this petition is given by Thurloe, *op. cit.*, VII, 647–51.

his activities in the service of the Commonwealth and the Protectorate. Here he sought "to make known the Truth of his way and comportment in all these times of trouble; And how he hath endeavored
to follow Peace and Righteousness therein innocently towards all:
That the offences taken against him, through the mis-construction
of some of his actions may be removed; and the work of Peace and
Unity amongst the Protestant Churches at home and abroad advanced in due time."[142] Special emphasis was given to his services
under the reign of Charles I and his attempts to save the king from
the scaffold.[143] He insisted that his willingness to serve under the *de
facto* governments of the Commonwealth and the Protectorate was
prompted solely by his interest in the cause of peace and unity among
the churches—a cause to which he had pledged his life.[144] The pamphlet closes with a petition for the pardon of past offenses and an
urgent plea that Charles II should now sanction and support a new
effort in behalf of the union of the churches at home and abroad.[145]

On June 6, 1660, Dury sent a letter to Charles II, proposing
methods which should be used for "treating about peace and unity
in matters of Religion between the Episcopal and Presbyterian
parties."[146] No answer was made to this letter, and Dury was refused a hearing when he applied for the privilege of an interview with
the King and Archbishop Juxon. He then sent a memorandum account of his union negotiations to Juxon.[147] Finally, the Archbishop
informed Dury by letter that he desired the union of all Christians,
but the work of reunion must begin at home, and there was no occasion for consulting with the King in regard to Dury's project until
the foreign princes should express a desire for the mediation of the
Anglican Church.[148]

Dury also made unavailing efforts to secure the support of the Earl

[142] *Declaration of John Durie*, title-page.

[143] *Ibid.*, pp. 4 ff., 11 ff.

[144] *Ibid.*, pp. 2 ff.

[145] *Ibid.*, pp. 22 ff.

[146] *Calendar of State Papers, Domestic Series, 1660–1661*, p. 112.

[147] The text of this paper is presented by Eekhof, *De theologische Faculteit te Leiden in de
17de Eeuw*, pp. 352–55.

[148] Benzelius, *op. cit.*, pp. 52 ff.; cf. also "Dury, Calixtus, and the Peacemakers," *Christian
Intelligencer*, XXIX, 27.

of Manchester and Lord Chancellor Hyde.[149] Not content with refusing to sanction and support Dury's reunion negotiations, the authorities of the new government indicated their disfavor by removing
Dury from his office as library keeper of St. James, a position which
he had held since 1650.[150] Thus Dury was thrown upon his own re-
sources, and, recognizing the hostile attitude of the English authorities, he left England, never to return. In March, 1661, he was once
more on the Continent, busily engaged in drafting new plans for
union negotiations. These negotiations were conducted during the
closing period of his life without the slightest aid from the authorities
of the new government in England.

[149] The text of Dury's letter to Lord Chancellor Hyde, dated July, 1660, is quoted by J. Reid,
*Memoirs of the Lives and Writings of Those Eminent Divines Who Convened in the Famous
Assembly at Westminster*, I, 272, 273, as follows:

"MY LORD,

In the application which I made to your honor when you were at the Hague, I offered the
fruit of my thirty years labours towards healing the breaches of Protestants; and this I did
as one who never had served the turn of any party, or have been biassed by particular interests
for any advantage to myself; but walking in the light by rules and principles, have stood free
from all in matters of strife, to be able to serve through love. My way hath been, and is, to
solicit the means of peace and truth among dissenting parties, to do good offices, and to quiet
their discontents, and I must still continue in this way if I should be useful. But not being
rightly understood in my aims and principles, I have been constrained to give this brief account
thereof, as well to rectify the misconstructions of former actings, as to prevent farther mistakes concerning my way; that such as love not to foment prejudices may be clear in their
thoughts concerning me; and may know where to find me, if they would discern me or any of
my talents which God hath bestowed upon me for the public welfare of his churches, which is
my whole aim; and wherein I hope to persevere unto the end, as the Lord shall enable me, to
be without offence unto all, with a sincere purpose to approve myself to his Majesty in all
faithfulness.

Your Lordships' most humble servant in Christ,

JOHN DURY."

[150] J. Worthington, *The Diary and Correspondence of Dr. John Worthington*, I, 199.

CHAPTER IX

THE COMPLETION OF FIFTY-TWO YEARS OF REUNION EFFORT

WHEN Dury returned to the Continent in 1661 he was sixty-five years of age. He had devoted himself to union activity for a third of a century. At no time during the course of his long career were conditions more unfavorable for a successful issue of his reunion negotiations. His work was thoroughly discredited in England as the authorities of the new regime were unwilling to support him because he had been in the service of the Protector. The rejection of his proposals in England made it exceedingly difficult for him to gain a hearing on the Continent, where there was general rejoicing over the restoration of the Stuarts.[1] He soon discovered that he must constantly defend himself and clear his work from the odium incurred by the patronage of Cromwell.[2] At this time there was no powerful patron, such as Roe, Laud, Gustavus Adolphus, or Cromwell, upon whom he could rely for letters of recommendation and for assistance in financing his reunion propaganda. A less determined advocate would have abandoned the cause as hopeless, but Dury labored throughout the remaining nineteen years of his life, with all his accustomed zeal, to advance the cause to which he had pledged himself.

It is probable that Dury had planned to begin his new negotiations among the Lutherans of Sweden. The interest in union proposals manifested by Prince Adolf of Sweden had prompted him to look for support in that quarter.[3] Matthiae had been pleading the cause of Christian reunion in Sweden,[4] but his efforts had served only to

---

[1] See H. Wätjen, *Die erste englische Revolution und die öffentliche Meinung in Deutschland,* pp. 56–61.

[2] J. Lindeboom ("Johannes Duraeus en zijne werkzaamheid in dienst van Cromwell's politiek," *Nederlandsch Archief voor Kerkgeschiedenis,* XVI, 265) quotes from a letter of Dury to his Swiss friend, Hans Ulrich, dated January, 1661, as follows: "Si vous voulez toucher un mot de ma négotiation avec vous ... il ne faut nullement nommer le Protecteur ny de près ny de loin, aussi ne faut-il pas mentionner avec aucun tiltre odieux le Pape ny les Papistes." Cf. O. Ritschl, *Dogmengeschichte des Protestantismus,* IV, 267.

[3] K. Brauer, *Die Unionstätigkeit John Duries unter dem Protektorat Cromwells,* pp. 188, 226.

[4] C. J. Benzelius, *Dissertatio de Johanne Duraeo pacificatore celeberrimo maxime de actis eius Suecanis,* p. 54.

arouse the hostility of the strict Lutheran party.[5] This party succeeded in winning the favor of Charles X. Its adherents worked
steadily to counteract the efforts of Matthiae. In 1664 they were
able to persuade the authorities to deprive Matthiae of his see of
Strengnas, thus forcing him into retirement throughout the remainder of his life.[6] Under these circumstances Dury decided that it
was useless for him to visit Sweden.

The Lutheran principalities of Germany were unfavorable fields
for reunion negotiations at the time. The opponents of syncretism
were aroused to new activity in 1655 by the failure of their efforts to
secure confessional recognition for their *Consensus repetitus fidei vere
Lutheranae.*[7] The death of Calixtus, in 1656, brought a temporary
lull in the syncretistic controversy, but the opponents of syncretism
inaugurated a new campaign in 1660 in the interest of the preservation of strict Lutheran orthodoxy. The writings of Hülsemann,
Calovius, Dannhauer, and other opponents of syncretism were given
a wide circulation in an effort to thwart all proposals for compromise
or union with the Reformed Churches.

Dury voiced the opinion that these advocates of strict Lutheran
orthodoxy must experience a change of heart before the Lutheran
Churches would heed the call for the reunion of Protestantism.[8] He
did not give up hope of ultimately securing the co-operation of the
Lutherans in the movement toward reunion; but, recognizing the
difficulty of treating with the Lutheran party at this time, he decided
to begin the new phase of his union efforts by conducting further negotiations among the Reformed Churches of Holland, Germany, and
Switzerland. Such negotiations were to serve as preparatory measures for a larger program, involving both the Lutheran and the Reformed Churches, which was to be attempted as soon as sufficient
support could be gained.[9] Dury prepared carefully drafted plans for
his new campaign, and these plans were published in 1662. His book,
Irenicorum Tractatuum Prodromus, was given a wide circulation in

[5] K. Müller, *Kirchengeschichte*, II, Part II, 696, 697.

[6] M. Tabaraud, *De la réunion des communions chrétiennes*, p. 305.

[7] Müller, *op. cit.*, pp. 586 ff.

[8] J. Worthington, *The Diary and Correspondence of Dr. John Worthington*, I, 280. Dury to
Worthington, March 25, 1661: "Our friends' judgment of syncretism is true, for except the
hearts and lives of men be made soft and meek by grace, there will neither be any agreement
lasting, nor truly made upon any gospel grounds."

[9] See Dury, *Consultationum Irenicarum Prodiorthosis*, p. 127.

the hope that it would develop public interest in his proposed program.[10]

Dury renewed his union negotiations in Holland early in March, 1661. He arranged conferences with Cocceius and other influential leaders who had manifested an interest in his earlier efforts. He traveled constantly, pleading his cause with ministers and statesmen, circulating pamphlets on the subject of reunion, and seeking the support of the various Dutch synods. His visits to the synods were ineffective, since the leaders of the Dutch churches were now inclined to regard his schemes as altogether impractical. In June, 1661, Dury visited Leyden and made a new attempt to persuade the theological faculty of the university to undertake the championship of the cause of reunion.[11] Under the prevailing conditions they could do little to advance his cause, but during his stay in Leyden he gained some assurance of an increasing interest in union effort when he discovered that Timannus Gesselius had prepared and published an *Ecclesiastical History*, which gave major emphasis to irenic movements in history and quoted many of Dury's documents and papers. Dury hailed this work as a most favorable omen of an approaching shift in interest from polemics to irenics.[12] However, he was soon convinced that he could accomplish very little in Holland. "For here," he wrote to Hartlib, "the work of pacification is minded, but without any settled course to prosecute it constantly in a concurrence with others which makes the endeavors ineffectual."[13]

Dury was confident that his new program would ultimately succeed if he could win the active support of Frederick William, the Great Elector, and the Landgrave William VI of Hesse-Cassel. These rulers were the most prominent princes of the Reformed faith. They were united by dynastic interests, as the Landgrave had mar-

[10] In the Preface of the *Irenicorum Tractatuum Prodromus*, Dury lists the details of his proposed plans for a new campaign in the interest of Christian unity. On his negotiations with the Dutch synods from 1661 onward see W. P. C. Knuttel, *Acta der particuliere Synoden van Zuid-Holland, 1621–1700*, IV, 277, 305, 307, 336, 338–40, 367, 369, 428.

[11] See the letter of Dury to the theological faculty of the University of Leyden, dated June 10, 1661, as given by A. Eekhof, *De theologische Faculteit te Leiden in de 17de Eeuw*, pp. 355–57.

[12] Worthington, *op. cit.*, I, 305. Dury to Hartlib: "There is a doctor of Physick, one Timannus Gesselius of Utrecht who hath written an ecclesiastical history, whereunto he hath annexed very many of the Latin treatises of my negotiations. The title of the book is, *Historia sacra et Ecclesiastica ordine Chronologico ex optimis Scriptoribus compendiose digesta ab anno mundi ad annum Christi 1125, in qua ad Pacem Ecclesiae viam aperire pio conatu affectu Timannus Gesselius M. D.* Trajecti ad Rhenum, 1659."

[13] Worthington, *op. cit.*, I, 309.

ried Hedwig Sophia, the sister of the Great Elector. Both princes ruled over Lutheran and Reformed subjects, and they were interested in the union of these groups in their respective territories. While in Holland, Dury was informed that the Great Elector, through Prince Maurice, his ambassador to England, had suggested to Charles II that he should initiate a project for reconciling the Protestants of Germany. Dury received this information in May, 1661.[14] He went immediately to Cleves, where the Elector was residing. Frederick William, however, regarded Dury with distrust and refused to grant him an interview. With a display of somewhat glacial geniality, his subordinates suggested that Dury should put his propositions into writing.

Dury then drafted a memorial, which was forwarded to Frederick William on May 16, 1661.[15] In this paper he proposed that committees composed of theologians and statesmen should be constituted in each principality for the purpose of establishing Christian concord and maintaining correspondence in the interest of the peace of the churches. Suggestions were also offered as to the program and methods which should be used by these committees in their negotiations and in planning the preparation of literature for use in union propaganda. On May 19, 1661, Dury sent a petition to Frederick William, in which he repeated the requests which he had made in the memorial and also asked for permission to undertake reunion negotiations under the patronage of the Elector.[16] But no answer was made to these requests.

A more promising opportunity for union effort was presented in Hesse-Cassel. Here the Landgrave William VI was eager to unite the Lutheran and Reformed parties, especially those of his own dominions.[17] The Landgrave, his wife, and a majority of his subjects were members of the Reformed Church. However, there were many Lutherans among his subjects, particularly in northern Hesse and in the district about Rintelen, which had been inherited from the Count of Schaumburg. The Landgrave had manifested more interest in reunion projects after his conferences with Dury in 1656. He had recommended Dury's union proposals to a number of neighboring princes. Dury's suggestions for the settlement of ecclesiastical peace

[14] See Dury, *Consultationum Irenicarum Prodiorthosis*, pp. 127, 128.

[15] Eekhof, *op. cit.*, pp. 349–51.

[16] For the text of this petition see *ibid.*, pp. 351, 352.

[17] See Brauer, *op. cit.*, pp. 117 ff., 131, 234 ff., 243 ff.

through friendly negotiations between theologians of the contending parties appealed strongly to William VI. In the year 1661 he decided to experiment with such negotiations within his own principality. There were two important theological schools within his territories: the University of Marburg, where the orthodox Calvinistic theology was popular, and the University of Rintelen, which was dominated by Lutheran theologians of the conciliatory party founded by Calixtus. The Landgrave summoned the theologians of the two schools to a colloquy, which was held at Cassel, June 1–9, 1661.[18]

The principal participants in the Cassel Colloquy were the Rintelen theologians, Peter Musaeus and John Henichius, and the Marburg theologians, Sebastian Curtius and John Heinius. Each member of the group was a man of conciliatory spirit. The Rintelen theologians were pupils of Calixtus. All the participants, with the exception of Heinius, had been interviewed by Dury and were thoroughly familiar with his union proposals.[19] The efforts to arrange a settlement were conducted along the lines which Dury had advocated. Brandes is probably correct in his conclusion that the positive results attained in the Colloquy were possible "chiefly owing to Dury's endeavors";[20] but he is in error in stating that Dury was present at the Colloquy, as he was then in Holland negotiating with the theological faculty of the University of Leyden.[21]

Following the methods which Dury had advocated for years, the participants in the Cassel Colloquy accepted the consensus reached by the Leipzig Colloquy as a starting-point for their discussions and then attempted to reach further agreement on doctrines relating to the Lord's Supper, the person of Christ, predestination, and baptism. Agreement was reached on many details involved in these doctrines. Acknowledgment was made to the effect that the remaining points of dissent were concerned only with matters which were neither essential to salvation nor of sufficient importance to stand in the way of mutual toleration. Again following the principles advocated by Dury, the participants recommended that the theologians should not revile one another because of divergent opinions on the remaining

---

[18] On the call of the Cassel Colloquy see H. Leube, *Kalvinismus und Luthertum*, I, 305–15; and H. Schmid, *Geschichte der synkretistichen Streitigkeiten in der Zeit des Georg Calixt*, pp. 370 ff.

[19] Brauer, *op. cit.*, pp. 128 ff., 165.

[20] F. H. Brandes, "John Dury and His Work for Germany," *Catholic Presbyterian Review*, VIII, 97.

[21] Eekhof, *op. cit.*, p. 357; and Dury, *Consultationum Irenicarum Prodiorthosis*, p. 128.

points in dispute; ministers should free their sermons from confessional polemics; personal attacks on theological opponents must be avoided in the future; and ministers and theologians must keep the peace in civil matters. Though finally declining intercommunion the participants condemned the supposed privilege of attacking theological opponents personally and publicly in their sermons.[22]

Even this measure of agreement marked considerable progress in curbing the bitter confessional strife of the times. Irenic leaders, such as Dury, John Mellet, and Moses Amyraut, regarded the results of the Colloquy as a distinct gain.[23] But the news of the Cassel Colloquy aroused the ire of the leaders of the strict Lutheran party, especially the Wittenberg theologians, Abraham Calovius, J. A. Quenstedt, and John Deutschmann. This group issued a violent literary attack against the Lutherans who had participated in the Colloquy. This attack marked the opening of the second phase of the Syncretistic Controversy, which was to continue with unabated fury in the German Lutheran churches during the next quarter of a century. Thus the Cassel Colloquy, in spite of the good intentions of the Landgrave William VI and the conciliatory spirit of the participants, unquestionably served to arouse more discord than it settled. This new outbreak of the Syncretistic Controversy in the German churches made it more difficult for Dury to make further progress in union work among the Lutherans.[24]

However, Dury believed that the Cassel Colloquy had prepared the way for a new movement in the interest of the union of the churches. He hoped that the Landgrave would serve as the patron of the new movement and that he would be able to gain the support of the Great Elector. Shortly after the Colloquy, William VI, at Dury's suggestion, proposed that a similar colloquy should be arranged, in which Lutheran and Reformed theologians from a number of German principalities should be asked to participate.[25] It was

---

[22] Dury's summary of the conclusions reached at the Cassel Colloquy may be found in his *Irenicorum Tractatuum Prodromus*, pp. 520–39. On the Cassel Colloquy see also *Realencyklopädie für protestantische Theologie und Kirche* (3 Aufl.), III, 744 ff.; Leube, *op. cit.*, I, 315 ff.; F. H. Brandes, *Geschichte der evangelischen Union in Preussen*, I, 230 ff.; Schmid, *op. cit.*, pp. 370 ff.; W. Gass, *Georg Calixt und der Synkretismus*, pp. 103 ff.; and C. W. Hering, *Geschichte der kirchlichen Unionsversuche seit der Reformation bis auf unsere Zeit*, II, 128–48.

[23] Schmid, *op. cit.*, p. 375.

[24] On the later stages of the Syncretistic Controversy see *ibid.*, pp. 367 ff.; Leube, *op. cit.*, I, 323 ff.; Gass, *op. cit.*, pp. 104 ff.

[25] W. Friedensburg, "Kurfürst Friedrich Wilhelm von Brandenburg und die Wittenberger Theologen," in *Festgabe für Karl Müller* (1922), pp. 236, 237.

necessary to win the support of the Great Elector if this scheme was
to be fully realized. From June to November, 1661, Dury made this
his chief objective. As soon as he received an account of the proceedings of the Cassel Colloquy, he hastened to Cleves to present
this account to the Great Elector and to ask for his support in similar
negotiations on a larger scale.[26] John Hundius, court preacher of
Brandenburg, and other ministers of Brandenburg urged Frederick
William to co-operate in this movement.[27] It is certain that the Great
Elector manifested an increased interest in union efforts at this
time.[28] He declared that he favored more extensive union negotiations and announced his intention of adopting measures designed to
advance the peace of the churches within his own territories. But he
made it clear that he would negotiate for the union of the churches
through his own theologians and refused to give Dury patronage,
employment, and recognition in the work.[29]

Although Dury could secure no recognition from Frederick William, he decided to continue his efforts in Germany. On November
19, 1661, he wrote Hartlib from Frankfort as follows:

> As for my affairs, they are in a hopeful way of progress. For the Elector of
> Brandenburg and the Landgrave of Hesse are fallen upon a way to engage the Lu-
> theran princes to concur in the work, and I with the Divines of Cleves am fallen upon
> another way to deal with the Lutheran Divines. They have signed the Councils
> whereupon we are agreed, and give me authority in their name to propose them to
> others, which I am preparing to do, but before I begin I intend to take advice also at
> Cassel. The Princes will deal with the Princes of the Lutheran party, and those with
> their Universities, to bring them to some aimable conference, according to the exam-
> ple given this year between the Divines of Rintelen and Marpurg. And I suppose
> my way of dealing will be with the Divines who are not subordinate to the Univer-
> sities, but depend upon inferior magistrates, as in the free cities and countries, who
> have Superintendents, that with the permission of their superiors I may deal with
> them and oblige them to declare the sense of that which I (God willing) shall propose
> unto them.[30]

In accordance with these plans, Dury was busily engaged during the
closing weeks of the year 1661 in negotiations with William VI and
with the clergy and civil authorities of Hesse, Cleves, Hanover, the
Wetterau, and the Palatinate.[31]

[26] Dury, *Consultationum Irenicarum Prodiorthosis*, pp. 128–30.

[27] See Dury, *Irenicorum Tractatuum Prodromus*, pp. 515–20.

[28] H. Landwehr, "Johannes Duraeus' Unionsverhandlung mit Kurbrandenburg," *Zeitschrift
für Kirchengeschichte*, X, 470.

[29] Brandes, "John Dury and His Work for Germany," p. 97.

[30] Worthington, *op. cit.*, II, Part II, 80.

[31] Dury, *Consultationum Irenicarum Prodiorthosis*, p. 129.

During the five-year period 1662–67, Dury continued his efforts to lead a new movement in the interest of the peace of the churches. In 1662 he published his *Irenicorum Tractatuum Prodromus*. This volume contains 548 closely printed pages of quotations from the documents which Dury had gathered during the years of his irenic activity, together with Dury's comments on this material. The Preface of this work is of special interest, as it presents a draft of Dury's later plans for union effort, supplemented by suggestions as to the method and spirit in which these negotiations should be conducted.[32] At this time he renewed his emphasis upon the necessity of the Reformed Churches' agreeing upon a Harmony of Confessions. If such an agreement could be secured among all the Reformed Churches, the way would be opened for a new attempt to arrange a consensus with the Lutherans. Dury went to Switzerland and labored for months in an effort to secure from the Swiss churches a common recognition of the *Harmonia Confessionum*, which had been published at Geneva in 1654.[33] But the Swiss leaders again refused to co-operate with Dury.[34]

Dury also directed his attention to the French Huguenot churches. He had already conducted an extensive correspondence with leaders of these churches. He had won the sympathetic interest of Peter du Moulin of the Academy of Sedan.[35] For twenty-five years Dury had been in correspondence with Paul Ferry of Metz, the author of the *Catéchisme général de la Réformation* and a most zealous advocate of Christian reunion among the French Huguenots. In April, 1662, Dury visited Metz for the purpose of holding a conference with Ferry. Anxious to accommodate himself to the fashions of the place, Dury manifested an unaccustomed anxiety about his personal appearance which prompted Pierre Bayle and other writers to make merry at the expense of the two zealous union advocates.[36] Dury and

---

[32] Pp. iii–xxxvi.

[33] An excellent summary of Dury's later negotiations with the Swiss churches is presented by S. Hubler, "Unionsbestrebungen des John Durie," *Berner Beiträge zur Geschichte der schweizerischen Reformationskirchen*, pp. 317–25.

[34] Hubler, *op. cit.*, pp. 324, 325.

[35] Brauer, *op. cit.*, p. 101. Du Moulin to Paul Ferry of Metz: "Quant à Monsieur Duraeus son zele est sainct et louable et je suis de ceux qui prient Dieu pour le succes d'une si saincte entreprise."

[36] On this occasion Dury shaved off his long white square beard and dressed himself in French costume with meticulous care. Ferry, excited over the prospect of conferring with so noted a union advocate, dressed for the occasion but forgot to put on his trousers. On the Dury-Ferry interview, see Pierre Bayle, *Dictionnaire historique et critique*, I, 1145; and Robert Chambers, *A Biographical Dictionary of Eminent Scotsmen*, I, 522, 523.

Ferry discussed the prevailing conditions in the churches and encouraged each other to high hopes for the ultimate success of the union program. Dury's characteristic optimism is clearly reflected in contemporary accounts of this interview.[37]

From France, Dury went to Holland and renewed his efforts to secure the indorsement of his program by the Dutch synods. The records of the synods during the years 1662–66 abound in references to Dury's proposals and uniform expressions of judgments by the synods to the effect that Dury's schemes were altogether impractical.[38] Although these later negotiations in Holland were unsuccessful, Dury's Dutch friends remained loyal and assisted him on several occasions by defraying the cost of some of his more expensive publications.[39] In 1663 Dury made a new attempt to interest the Swedish Lutherans in his union program. Many of the Swedish clergymen who had formerly opposed him were now dead. John Kanut Lennaeus, a friend and patron of irenic activity, had become archbishop of Uppsala. Dury once more drafted papers urging the leaders of church and state in Sweden to sponsor a new movement designed to unite the Reformed and Lutheran Churches. Copies of these papers were sent to the Chancellor de la Gardie, to the Swedish Estates, and to the Archbishop of Uppsala.[40] But the strict Lutheran party remained in control in Sweden and opposed all efforts at compromise with the Reformed. Dury's urgent appeals to the Swedish leaders remained unanswered.[41]

The Landgrave William VI of Hesse-Cassel died in the year 1663. His death was a serious loss to Dury. The Landgrave had befriended him and had manifested an increasing interest in his union proposals. The loss of his patronage hindered the further progress of Dury's work in Germany. However, Hedwig Sophia, the widow of the Landgrave, proved to be a friend and supporter of Dury. She provided him with a home at Cassel, allowed him franking privileges for his extensive correspondence, and attempted to interest a number of German princes in the reunion movement. Cassel became Dury's headquarters after 1663. He traveled almost constantly until 1674, but after that date the most of his time was spent at Cassel.

[37] See H. G. N. Tollin, "Johann Duraeus," *Geschichts-Blätter für Stadt und Land Magdeburg*, XXXII, 267–69.

[38] See Knuttel, *op. cit.*, IV, 336, 338–40, 369, 428.   [39] Tollin, *op. cit.*, pp. 271, 272.

[40] The text of these papers is given by Benzelius, *op. cit.*, pp. 177 ff.

[41] Tollin, *op. cit.*, p. 269.

Dury's later reunion efforts in Germany merely served to arouse the strict Lutheran party to new polemical activity. In 1662 the Wittenberg theologians, Calovius, Quenstedt, and Deutschmann, issued a bitter polemical treatise under the title, *Epicrisis de colloquio Casselano Rintelio-Marpurgensium*. Repudiating all efforts to reach an agreement with the Reformed Churches, they asked that confessional recognition should be granted to the *Consensus repetitus fidei vere Lutheranae*, an expression of the theological opinion of uncompromising Lutheranism. It was inevitable that Dury would meet with censure from these vigorous opponents of syncretism. His negotiations with the Lutheran theologians of Strassburg gradually drew him into the maelstrom of this controversy.

In June, 1661, Dury had forwarded a letter to Conrad Dannhauer, the leader of the Strassburg theologians. In this letter he had called attention to the evils of a divided Christendom; announced his intention of continuing to work in the interest of ecclesiastical pacification; described the scope of his reunion negotiations and the means which he planned to use in the further advancement of his program; and asked Dannhauer's co-operation in the work.[42] In the correspondence which followed, Dannhauer professed a friendly interest in Dury's proposals but declined to co-operate in the effort because of weight of years, pressure of other duties, and the conviction that Dury's schemes were impractical and that his refusal to use the scholastic method in discussing differences of opinion in theological matters was altogether unreasonable.[43]

With the sharpening of the Lutheran polemic after the Cassel Colloquy, Dannhauer entered the lists against Dury. His attack was ably seconded by his assistant, Balthazar Bebel. The latter theologian claimed that Dury was the proponent of union with false teachers and a promoter of a dangerous type of syncretism.[44] He charged that Dury, in his zeal to make proselytes to syncretism, had misrepresented the true course of his reunion negotiations.[45] In a letter to Dury, dated April 27, 1663, Bebel presented a detailed list of his charges against Dury as the advocate of syncretism. Here he argued that Dury had failed to present any adequate measures for the establishment of ecclesiastical peace; he had prompted the civil

---

[42] For the text of this letter and a pamphlet, which was forwarded to Dannhauer with the letter, see Dury, *Consultationum Irenicarum Prodiorthosis*, pp. 7–14.

[43] The text of this correspondence is given in *ibid.*, pp. 15–44.

[44] *Ibid.*, pp. 48 ff.   [45] *Ibid.*, pp. 60 ff.

authorities to attempt undue interference in the affairs of the churches; and he had drafted union proposals which were ill-advised, dangerous, and impractical.[46] This attack was made public in 1664, when Dannhauer and Bebel published a work entitled *Nuntius nuntio—Britannico missus, cui accessit Hypomnema apologeticum B. Bebelii.* In this book Dury's program was severely criticized, and he was accused of stirring up new strife instead of settling existing quarrels.

At first Dury attempted to answer this attack by the publication of his *Consultationum Irenicarum Prodiorthosis* (Amsterdam, 1664). In this work he sought to win public approval by publishing his correspondence with the Strassburg theologians, together with a detailed answer to each of the charges which they had presented against him. When the attack on Dury became more violent, the kindly peacemaker, for once at least, lost patience. Refusing to participate in scholastic debate with Dannhauer and Bebel, he published his *Johannis Duraei Appellatio ad Tribunal Supremi Judicis Jesu Christi Domini* (Amsterdam, 1665), in which, after defending his own career as a union advocate, he summoned his opponents before the judgment seat of Christ to give an account of their calumny and blasphemy.

In the same year he published his *Exercitatio de Conatu suo Irenico* as a further answer to the criticism of Dannhauer and Bebel and as an effort to prove that the Strassburg theologians were contending for nonessentials, which were not of sufficient importance to keep the Lutheran and Reformed Churches apart.[47] Dannhauer replied in a bitter diatribe entitled *Repulsa Appellationis nullius contra Duraeum* (1666). This pamphlet was so violent that Dury announced his intention of leaving Switzerland, where he was conducting union negotiations, in order that he might go to Strassburg and debate with Dannhauer in person. Dannhauer died in 1666 before the debate could be held, but the attack which he had launched against Dury was continued with unabated zeal by Bebel.[48] Dury attempted to

---

[46] Dury presents the text of this letter and his lengthy but rather ineffective reply to its charges in *ibid.*, pp. 62–116.

[47] Pp. 65 ff.

[48] See C. M. Pfaff, *Introductio in historiam theologiae literariam*, III, 182–85. Among the pamphlets issued by Bebel in his attacks on Dury, the following are of special importance: *Manes Dannhaweriani vindicati Dureani* (1668); and *Repulsa appellationis, quam nuper edidit Jo. Duraeus ad tribunal judicis Christi adversus accusationes nuntii emissi a Dannhawero* (1666). In 1667, a new edition of a vigorous polemic treatise by Hülsemann was published under the title *Calvinismus irreconciliabilis*, with a Preface attacking Dury.

make a final answer in 1667 by publishing at Amsterdam his *Apologeticum Duraei pro suo tractatu de concordia Evangelica cum duobus Academiae Argentinensis.*[49] This pamphlet warfare obviously could not advance the cause of peace and unity.

After the death of the Landgrave William VI, Dury renewed his efforts to secure the patronage of Frederick William. He maintained an extensive correspondence with ministers and court officials of Brandenburg, including Hundius, Schwerin, and Stosch. The Great Elector, although he was an ardent Calvinist and an ecclesiastical despot, continued his efforts to establish peace and unity among the Calvinists and Lutherans of Germany. The bitter polemic attacks of the Wittenberg theologians prompted him to adopt new measures in the interest of the peace of the churches and the establishment of principles of toleration.[50] On June 2, 1662, he issued an edict in which he deplored the divisive spirit and consequent demoralization which prevailed in the churches and ordered that all candidates for the ministry should pledge themselves to avoid controversy and to preach sermons designed to edify their hearers rather than to provoke them to theological controversy.[51] When Calovius and his associates intensified the current strife by further attacks on the "syncretists," Frederick William issued a new edict, dated August 26, 1662, in which he prohibited theological students of his territory from attending the University of Wittenberg.[52] Finally, following the advice offered by the Landgrave William VI and Dury, he summoned a number of Lutheran and Reformed leaders to a colloquy at Berlin and charged them with the responsibility of conducting negotiations in the interest of more peaceful relations between the churches.

The Berlin Colloquy (September, 1662—May, 1663) was conducted along the lines which Dury had advocated for years as suitable means for adjusting disputes between churches. Although Dury was not present, his friend, Otto von Schwerin, presided at the Colloquy. He attempted to shape the course of the discussions so that proof would be provided in support of the thesis that the questions at issue did not concern doctrines essential to salvation and that the dissensus between the parties should not interfere with the mutual

[49] Benzelius, *op. cit.*, p. 58.

[50] Landwehr, *op. cit.*, p. 324.

[51] See the summary of this edict by Hering, *op. cit.*, II, 137, 138.

[52] *Ibid.*, pp. 148–50.

recognition of members of each party as Christians.[53] But the two leading Lutheran participants, Paul Gerhardt and George Reinhardt, urged to constancy by the Wittenberg theologians, refused participation in all efforts looking toward compromise, agreement, and comprehension. They explained their attitude by the statement that they were unwilling to participate in any movement which tended toward syncretism.[54]

The failure of the Berlin Colloquy convinced Frederick William that it was useless to hope that the theologians would establish peace and unity among themselves. On September 16, 1664, he issued a Toleration Edict, prepared by the court preacher Stosch, which forbade the use of abusive epithets in theological discussions and outlawed the practice of attributing doctrines to theological opponents when such doctrines were not publicly acknowledged.[55] This edict and similar measures designed to promote toleration and ecclesiastical peace were without effect. When Paul Gerhardt and other influential Lutheran ministers declined to obey the edict, they were removed from clerical office.[56] After such vigorous measures had failed to produce an improvement in conditions, Dury once more attempted to secure permission for the conduct of union negotiations in Brandenburg.[57] He sought recommendations from friends far and near in a new effort to win the favor of the Great Elector. In 1667 he secured an indorsement from Prince Frederick of Anhalt.[58] In July, 1668, the Landgravine Hedwig Sophia furnished Dury with letters of recommendation to her brother, the Great Elector, and instructed him to go to Berlin and offer his services as a mediator in the settlement of religious differences in Brandenburg.[59]

On arrival at Berlin in August, 1668, Dury found that Frederick William was at Königsberg. He applied at once to the Elector's representative, Prince George of Anhalt, and to the privy councillors and court preachers, with the request that his proposals might be given a

---

[53] On the Berlin Colloquy see Tollin, *op. cit.*, pp. 273 ff.; Landwehr, *op. cit.*, pp. 208 ff.; Hering, *op. cit.*, II, 148 ff.; and Brandes, *Evangelischen Union in Preussen*, I, 238 ff.

[54] Tollin (*op. cit.*, pp. 273, 274) calls attention to the fact that Reinhardt refused to recognize the Reformed as "brethren" and Gerhardt refused to recognize them as "Christian."

[55] See the summary of this edict as given by Brandes, *Evangelischen Union in Preussen*, I, 253 ff.

[56] Müller, *op. cit.*, II, Part II, 593.

[57] Landwehr, *op. cit.*, p. 325.

[58] See the extracts from this indorsement in Hering, *op. cit.*, II, 125, 126.

[59] Tollin, *op. cit.*, p. 275; and Landwehr, *op. cit.*, pp. 326 ff.

hearing. The fact that Dury had been sent by Hedwig Sophia prompted the court officials to treat him with respect, but they did not expect a successful issue of his negotiations. On August 21, 1668, he was given a hearing before the Privy Council. He was ordered to present a written draft of the method of procedure which he proposed to use in promoting the preparation of a new Harmony of the Lutheran and Reformed Confessions.

The members of the Council, disillusioned by the failure of previous union efforts, forwarded to the Great Elector a report in which they expressed the opinion that Dury should be given a further hearing out of respect to the Landgravine, although they were convinced that his proposals were impractical.[60] The court preachers reported to the Elector their judgment that it was hopeless to undertake the preparation of an acceptable Harmony of Confessions such as Dury had proposed.[61] Among the court preachers, Stosch was especially active in opposing Dury's scheme for the preparation of a new Harmony of Confessions. He expressed the view that Dury was misrepresenting the teaching of the Reformed Confessions on predestination and that his proposals, if tested out, would serve to provoke more factional strife instead of tending toward reconciliation and peace.[62] Von Schwerin attempted to aid Dury, but no progress could be made in enlisting support for his cause at Berlin.

The Elector had reached the conclusion that it was useless to attempt further negotiations for the union of the churches. He had adopted a policy designed to establish religious toleration and freedom of conscience rather than organic union of all the churches within his realm. On September 20, 1668, he sent orders to his court officials at Berlin to treat Dury as a private man and refrain from granting him any kind of official recognition which might be interpreted as governmental sanction for his union activity.[63] When Dury persisted in his efforts, Frederick William, following the advice of George Conrad Bergius, forwarded to the Berlin officials a paper in which he further warned against giving Dury any official recognition and suggested that the peacemaker should be granted a gift of 100 thalers and then dismissed.[64]

[60] Brandes, *Evangelischen Union in Preussen*, I, 295.

[61] *Ibid.*, pp. 295, 296.

[62] See Landwehr, *op. cit.*, p. 474.   [63] *Ibid.*, p. 475.

[64] *Ibid.*, p. 476; cf. Brandes, *Evangelischen Union in Preussen*, I, 298 ff.

Humiliated by this new failure in a field where he had expected
success, Dury returned to Cassel. He later made additional attempts
to win the co-operation of the Great Elector, but all his proposals
were rejected.[65] During the years 1668–70 he devoted much of his
time to literary activity in the interest of the movement toward reunion. Letters, treatises, and memorials came from his pen with
astonishing rapidity at this time. This literary activity was inter-
rupted by numerous visits to German princes. Efforts were made to
secure active co-operation from Prince Frederick of Anhalt, Duke
Ernest the Pious of Gotha, the Elector Karl Ludwig of the Palatinate, and Duke Frederick Ludwig of Zweibrücken.[66] Duke Ernest
the Pious indicated a willingness to champion Dury's proposals and
advocated the call of a council of all the Lutheran churches to treat
on the subject of Christian reunion,[67] but the reunion movement had
been so thoroughly discredited by the recent attacks of the strict
Lutheran party that no heed was paid to this proposal. Dury also
revived his efforts to establish peace and union between the Lutheran
and Reformed Churches in local districts, especially in Lübeck and at
Magdeburg.[68] These efforts also failed, due chiefly to the effective
opposition of Jerome Sievert of Magdeburg.[69]

The continued opposition of the leaders of the strict Lutheran
party prompted Dury to decide that he must begin his work anew
and interest the Lutheran principalities in his schemes by approaching them one by one.[70] From 1670 onward, he centered his efforts
upon an attempt to persuade the Lutheran theologians of each principality to accept a common confession of faith, which was to contain
the essential teaching of both the Lutheran and the Reformed confessions.[71] To arouse public interest in this project, he gave wide circulation at this time to the Latin, French, and German editions of
the *Harmonia Confessionum Protestantium*, which he had prepared in
1654 in collaboration with Theodor Tronchin of Geneva.[72] He also

[65] Tollin, *op. cit.*, p. 277; and Landwehr, *op. cit.*, p. 479.

[66] Tollin, *op. cit.*, pp. 277–80.

[67] Brandes, *Evangelischen Union in Preussen*, I, 299, 300.

[68] Tollin, *op. cit.*, pp. 277, 279 ff.

[69] *Ibid.*, pp. 32–71.

[70] Benzelius, *op. cit.*, p. 64.

[71] See Brauer, *Unionstätigkeit John Duries*, pp. 69, 115, 140, 142, 162, 195 ff., 204 ff., 217
220 ff.

[72] Tollin, *op. cit.*, XXXIII, 78.

published three additional pamphlets on this subject, viz., *Axiomata communia quae procurandae et conservandae paci inter Evangelicos judicata sunt observatu necessaria* (Cassel, 1670); *Une Information touchant le jugement qu'on doit faire de l'harmonie des Confessions et comment on s'en peut servir, pour moyenner la paix des églises protestantes* (Cassel, 1670); and *Extractus ex Harmonia Confessionum, oblatum ecclesiis Reformatis, ut examinetur antequam opus ipsum Lutheranis offeratur* (1671).[73]

Copies of these pamphlets were widely distributed. Some were sent to the Archbishop of Uppsala and the Swedish Chancellor de la Gardie.[74] When these pamphlets were distributed in Germany, they immediately provoked opposition from leaders of the strict Lutheran party. Dury's critics now charged that he had overlooked the essential teachings of both the Lutheran and the Reformed Churches in his efforts to prove their consensus on fundamental doctrines. Philip Jacob Spener, a man of conciliatory spirit, examined a copy of Dury's *Extractus ex Harmonia Confessionum* in 1672. He then prepared his *Judicium de Scripto Duraeo* for circulation among his friends.[75] In this paper Spener expressed the opinion that Dury's labors were in vain because he minimized or disregarded the vital points at issue between the Lutheran and Reformed branches of Protestantism. He refused to recognize the agreement which Dury had asserted; pointed out the lack of consensus between the parties within both the Lutheran and the Reformed Churches; and charged Dury with attempting to prove a verbal agreement between the confessions while neglecting the existing dissensus over the interpretation of the words involved.[76] Spener professed high regard for Dury, but he thought that there was no chance for the success of his union plans in Germany under the prevailing conditions.[77] The times were not ripe, he maintained, for union negotiations of the type proposed by Dury.[78] John Ludovicus Fabricius, court preacher at Heidelberg, also regarded Dury's proposals as futile.[79]

Finding that there was little disposition on the part of his con-

[73] *Ibid.*, pp. 77–80.

[74] See Benzelius, *op. cit.*, pp. 64, 181.

[75] The text of this paper is quoted by Spener in his *Consilia et judicia theologica*, Part III, pp. 49–52.

[76] *Ibid.*, pp. 49, 50.

[77] *Ibid.*, p. 101.

[78] *Ibid.*, pp. 183 ff.   [79] Benzelius, *op. cit.*, p. 61.

temporaries to agree upon a harmony of all the existing confessions of faith, Dury next attempted to suggest a broader basis of agreement. In 1672 he published at Cassel his *Brevis disquisitio de articulis veri Christianismi*, in which he maintained that the Apostles' Creed, the Decalogue, and the Lord's Prayer furnished a sufficient statement of the fundamentals of Christian faith, obedience, and hope on which all Christians should agree.[80] In the same work he suggested that the ecumenical creeds ought to be received so far as they were clear; and that Lewis Bayly's *Practice of Pietie* and John Arndt's *True Christianity* should be received by all as valuable aids to the advancement of practical piety.

These suggestions only served to arouse the wrath of the members of the strict Lutheran party. They now refused to deal with Dury in public or private negotiations, but the Wittenberg theologian, John Meisner, attempted to answer Dury in a lengthy work entitled *Irenicum Duraeanum de Articulis Fidei Fundamentalibus, et Consensu ac Dissensu inter Lutheranos ac Reformatos, in Academia Wittebergensi Explicatum a Johanne Meisnero* (Wittenberg, 1675). In this work Meisner presented a critical review of Dury's union activities and irenic proposals. Petty charges against Dury were listed, such as the following: he had been disloyal to the faith of his parents; he had been partly responsible for the execution of Charles I; he had served under the regicides who controlled the Commonwealth and the Protectorate; and he had deserted his Rotterdam congregation to take up union activity before he was properly authorized to take such action.[81] He severely criticized Dury because of his unwillingness to take part in scholastic disputations.[82] He also charged him with misrepresentation as to the attitude of the English authorities toward his union activities.

Following a detailed criticism of Dury's *Brevis disquisitio*,[83] Meisner presented a lengthy discussion of the points in dispute between the Calvinists and the Lutherans.[84] He cited the impediments in the way of union and attempted to maintain the thesis that Dury's proposals would not remedy the evils of a divided Protestantism and to prove that the only remedy that could be effective and satisfactory

---

[80] *Christian Intelligencer*, XXIX, 28. John Meisner, in his *Irenicum Duraeanum de Articulis Fidei Fundamentalibus*, p. 23, presents a summary of the contents of Dury's *Brevis disquisitio*.

[81] Pp. 57, 58, 67, 376.   [83] *Ibid.*, pp. 72 ff.

[82] *Ibid.*, pp. 366 ff.   [84] *Ibid.*, pp. 120–361.

would be for the Reformed Churches to reject their errors and come over to the Lutheran position en masse.[85] Until they were willing to take this step the Lutheran theologians were under obligation to refuse all participation in reunion negotiations. This aggressive attack by an exponent of the Wittenberg school of Lutheran thought practically closed the way to all further negotiations with the Lutherans.

Increasing infirmities of age compelled Dury to limit his travels after 1674. Making his home in Cassel,[86] he attempted to continue his reunion activity by preparing a number of books and pamphlets. His later writings indicate that he was giving much thought to the possibility of the reunion of Protestants and Roman Catholics.[87] In 1674 he published a work entitled *Touchant l'intelligence de l'Apocalypse par l'Apocalypse même, comme toute l'Ecriture sainte doit être entendue raisonnablement.* This is one of the most unique of Dury's many publications. In the dedication of the work, which was addressed to the Landgravine Hedwig Sophia, he reveals the fact that his buoyant optimism had been displaced at last by a keen sense of disappointment over the failure of his efforts. But he was unwilling to give up his reunion activity in despair. On the contrary, he announced his intention of devoting the remainder of his life to an enterprise of greater scope than the work of uniting the Protestant groups. He would henceforth labor in the interest of the union of Protestants and Roman Catholics.

This time he approached the solution of the problem of the reunion of Christendom by suggesting new rules for the interpretation of Scripture. Both Protestants and Roman Catholics, he argued, claimed the Scriptures as the chief source of their teaching. If common rules of interpretation could be agreed upon by both parties, then a consensus could be reached through the direct method of Scripture exegesis.[88] Dury proposed seven rules for the interpretation of Scripture. Although it is evident that these rules did not provide measures for the reunion of the churches which were as effective as Dury claimed, it must be admitted that his suggestions present a

---

[85] *Ibid.*, pp. 361 ff., 402 ff.

[86] There are few references to Dury's family in his letters and publications. It is probable that his wife had died prior to his retirement at Cassel. His only child, Dorothea, had married Henry Oldenburg, the first secretary of the Royal Society.

[87] Leube, *op. cit.*, I, 234.   [88] See Bayle, *op. cit.*, II, 333, 334.

method of interpreting Scripture that was a decided improvement over the proof-text method, which was in vogue at the time.[89] Once more Dury was appealing to his contemporaries to shift their interest from the study of the confessions of faith and the dogmatic interpretations of the Christian religion to the study of Scripture. After announcing his new rules for the interpretation of Scripture, he attempted to illustrate the application of these rules by presenting an explanation of the Apocalypse. But his contemporaries, Spener included, were of the opinion that Dury's zeal for the discovery of arguments in favor of the reunion of the churches often prompted him to forget the rules which he had proposed.[90]

In his last years Dury once more renewed his interest in practical theology. In the year 1676 he published a work entitled *Le véritable Chrétien*. Here he repeated his proposals for a shift of emphasis in the theological schools from dogmatic to practical theology. This book made a favorable impression upon Spener, who, as the founder of the Pietist movement, was to be an able advocate of this change in theological discipline in German schools. Spener manifested an increasing interest in Dury's work during the closing years of his career. He often deplored the fact that the strict Lutheran party subjected Dury to a constant barrage of criticism until he died.[91] In 1677 William Penn visited Dury in his home at Cassel. The Quaker

[89] The rules for the interpretation of Scripture, as proposed by Dury in this work, are presented by Leube (*op. cit.*, I, 236, 237) as follows: "La première règle de la Méditation prophétique est de disposer son esprit comme je viens de dire présentement assavoir pieusement envers Dieu en soi-même humblement et envers tous ceux qui ont le don de Prophétie et d'intelligence modestement. 2. D'invoquer le nom de Dieu. 3. De n'admettre point aucune pensée ou conception qui ne soit evidemment proportionnée à la foi commune. 4. De n'arrêter rien conclusivement sur quelque grande apparente évidence sans l'avoir au préalable bien examiné et épluché pour observer les règles de la cohérence avec les autres matières qui sont dans le texte et par la collation avec les autres textes qui parlent ailleurs des mêmes matières pour voir la concordance. 5. De limiter toutes ses conceptions par les paroles expresses du texte et par conséquence d'éviter en méditant toute recherche des choses qui n'appartiennent point à la matière de laquelle il s'agit ou qui sont curieuses et n'ont point un exprès fondement à l'Ecriture St. pour l'usage d'édification en piété. 6. Qu'il faut toujours procéder par dégrès sans faire aucun faut, mais des choses claires et hors de doute il faut toujours inférer, ce qui est moins évident jusques on quelque proportion se trouve. 7. Qu'il faut prendre égard à la façon de parler prophétique pour ne pas entendre à la lettre ce qui doit être entendu spirituellement et au rebours n'entendre pas spirituellement ce qui doit être entendu littéralement, il faut donc distinguer les matières pour les entendre chacune en sa sphère et vers son but."

[90] Benzelius, *op. cit.*, pp. 69, 70.

[91] Spener, *op. cit.*, pp. 144 ff., 279 ff., 591 ff. Otto Ritschl, whose judgment of Dury is very critical, notes that the clergy of Cassel excommunicated Dury as a heretic in 1677 but gives no details or supporting evidence for this statement (see *op. cit.*, p. 267).

and the union advocate found that they had much in common in their interpretation of the essentials of the Christian religion.[92]

Dury died at Cassel in the year 1680. An account of his death was prepared by the pastor of the church in which he was accustomed to worship during the closing years of his life.[93] This brief notice indicates that Dury, despite the infirmities due to increasing weight of years, remained faithful unto death in the observation of the vow which he had taken in youth, when he consecrated the whole of his life to the advocacy of the cause of Christian reunion.

[92] Benzelius (*op. cit.*, pp. 75, 76) presents an account of Penn's visit to Dury and observes that the two had much in common: "Quackerus ille [Dury] fuit ante Quackeros." Mosheim (*Ecclesiastical History*, II, 382) says: "It is further to be observed with respect to Duraeus, that he showed a peculiar propensity towards the sentiments of the mystics and Quakers, on account of their tendency to favor his conciliatory and pacific project. Like them, he placed the essence of religion in the ascent of the soul to God, in calling forth the hidden word, in forming the divine spark in the recesses of the human mind, and in consequence of this system, was intimately persuaded that differences in theological opinions did not at all concern the essence of true piety."

[93] This account, prepared by M. Faucheur, the French pastor at Cassel, is quoted by J. C. Coler, *Auserlesene theologische Bibliothec* (1730), Part VI, p. 1076.

CHAPTER X
ESTIMATE

THE foregoing account of Dury's fifty-two years of union activity presents ample evidence of his position among the irenic leaders of the seventeenth century. No other advocate of peace and unity among the churches labored so long and in so wide a field. None manifested more ingenuity in shaping plans and developing programs of irenic effort. In his indefatigable zeal to make the Communion of the Saints a vital reality in his age, he established a record of reunion effort which in duration and extent has no parallel in the whole course of Christian history. Dury's efforts were for the most part unsuccessful. All his major union proposals were rejected. In the last analysis his failures were due chiefly to other men's failures in imagination and in sincerity. The trends toward division and denominationalism proved too strong for him to curb. In his letters and pamphlets he often speaks of himself as "rowing against the current of the times." The "contentious, dividing Age" in which he lived was unwilling to accept the peace proposals of this genial Scotsman.

For more than fifty years Dury was subjected to severe criticism by contemporaries who opposed his program. Their criticisms have been often repeated by later historians. There is marked uniformity in the charges presented against Dury. He is usually described by his critics as uninformed, impractical, unstable, and self-seeking. These accusations can be weighed in the light of his life-work as related above.

In the realm of technical theological scholarship, Dury was surpassed in training and ability by Calixtus and other contemporary irenic advocates. His writings frequently attest the fact that he had failed to master thoroughly many of the details of dogmatic theology which were being emphasized by the Protestant scholasticism of his day. Though Dury was conscious of his deficiencies in theological learning, he was quite undisturbed over his failure to qualify as an expert in the subtleties of theological debate. He repeatedly refused to engage in current disputes about doctrinal issues, because he regarded them as useless and harmful. He believed they served only to

create new obstacles to the recognition of the agreement on essentials
of faith which already existed among the Christian churches.

Masson states, as indicated above, that Laud regarded Dury's
schemes as "visionary nonsense." This opinion was shared by many
of Dury's contemporaries. His opponents were often correct in
charging that many of his union proposals were too vague, indefinite,
and impractical. Yet the major objectives defined by Dury and the
more important means and methods which he suggested for the
attainment of these objectives were approved by many of the most
practical-minded statesmen and ecclesiastics of his day. Gustavus
Adolphus and Oliver Cromwell regarded his union proposals as practical. These able rulers of the seventeenth century almost succeeded
in translating the supposedly impractical plans of Dury into reality.
The untimely deaths of these patrons of Dury did much to destroy
all chances for the immediate and successful realization of his plans
for the first steps toward the reunion of Protestantism.

Dury's critics have emphasized his frequent change of denominational and party affiliation. They have called attention to the fact
that he received ordination in a Reformed Church; then accepted
Anglican orders; and later closely associated himself with Presbyterian and Independent leaders. Such willingness to change denominational and party relationships naturally invited the charge of in-
stability. Yet any reader of Dury's letters and pamphlets can readily
understand his contention that his whole career was marked by consistent stability of purpose. He regarded denominational and party
lines with indifference. He was willing to remain *extra partes* or to
work with any denomination and any party in an effort to develop
peace and unity among the churches.

There is much less weight to the charge that Dury undertook and
continued his advocacy of Christian reunion as a means of gaining a
livelihood. The facts of his career definitely disprove this charge. He
relinquished a successful pastorate at Elbing in order to devote his
life to union activity. He often faced humiliating financial depend-
ence and actual want while he gave himself without reserve to the
cause to which he had pledged his life. He spent his own income, together with gifts from friends and allowances from supporting governments, in ceaseless propaganda work to advance this cause. Few
churchmen of all the ages have devoted themselves to Christian work
with a more zealous and sacrificial spirit.

Dury's extensive travels and varied contacts gave him unique opportunities to observe the condition of the churches. He was thus enabled to accumulate a wealth of information about religious conditions in England and on the Continent which is surprising in its comprehensiveness. It also seems evident that he manifested a wider acquaintance with the course of former reunion efforts than any of his contemporaries. He faithfully searched the records of the centuries for materials which might be used in establishing peace and unity among contending churches.

He made free use of the irenic methods, measures, and literature that had been created by his predecessors and contemporaries. He also developed and advocated new proposals which were designed to settle the peace of the churches. Many of the plans drafted and negotiations conducted by Dury distinctly foreshadowed types of irenic effort that are being used successfully in the present-day movement toward reunion. He was especially interested in efforts to consolidate the activities of contemporary irenic leaders and to apply the combined force of their efforts toward the solution of problems of doctrine, discipline, and worship then dividing the churches of Christendom. His appeals to all the churches uniformly sounded the call for Christians everywhere to make the Communion of the Saints a vital reality rather than a pious platitude professed in the creeds. Dury worked primarily to establish what he called "ecclesiastical pacification"—to restore peace between contending Christians, churches, and groups of churches. Wherever he found conflict among Christians, there he labored earnestly to persuade men to motivate themselves by love instead of hatred and to substitute the spirit of co-operation in place of the spirit of contention.

In the course of his negotiations he adapted his methods and program to meet the needs of the hour. With varying degrees of emphasis, he labored to settle the peace of the churches by the use of such methods as conference, co-operation, comprehension, and arbitration. He believed that the ultimate settlement of the peace of Christendom could be established by means of a gradated series of representative councils, which were to adjust differences in local, territorial, and national areas. This series of councils was to culminate finally in a universal conference on Christian faith, order, and duty. Although Dury devoted much of his time and energy to the settlement of local quarrels, it is clear that he always looked toward the objective of establishing peace between contending Christians and churches of each nation, with the ultimate hope that the Christians of each nation might be united in a single national church and that the national churches of Christendom might be combined in an organization embodying features of a federal union. Earlier advocates of conciliarism probably influenced Dury's ideas regarding the proper mode of government for a united church, but he apparently makes no acknowledgment of his indebtedness to them. He proposed that the churches of Christendom should be ruled by means of a gradated series of representative assemblies, with a general council, meeting at stated intervals, and with standing committees to promote Christian communion and co-operation in the intervals between the meetings of the general council.

The seventeenth-century irenic leaders produced a mass of literature on the problem of the reunion of the churches. Many of their books deserve a lasting place in the literature of Christian irenics. They furnish valuable suggestions as to methods of attaining cooperation, federation, and unity. Dury was the most prolific writer in this field during the century. As an author his style is equally tedious and repetitious in English, French, German, and Latin. Nearly all his works bear the marks of hasty composition. But his arguments are usually clear because they are frequently repeated. It was his habit to incorporate in his printed works all the opinions and judgments regarding his union proposals which he received in the course of his negotiations. Despite his tedious style, these writings are important because they furnish the most important available indexes of seventeenth-century opinion regarding the reunion of the churches.

Dury was convinced that the various branches of Protestantism were already in agreement on the essentials of the Christian faith. He deplored the denominational rivalries which were intensified by disputes about nonessential doctrines. For years he labored to secure the preparation of a common confession of faith that would combine and harmonize the basic teachings of the existing confessions. He believed that such a consensus, containing only matters of faith and practice that were essential to salvation, would furnish a satisfactory confessional standard for a united Christendom. This proposal sometimes provoked new controversies, such as the revival of the syncretistic debates in Germany. On the other hand, Dury's persistent advocacy of this procedure encouraged many men of irenic spirit to seek a confession of faith on which all could agree. The search for such a formula sometimes aided the development of an interest in comprehension. The incipient trend toward rationalism prompted some of Dury's contemporaries and successors to narrow the list of the essentials of the faith until they had developed a latitudinarian viewpoint which contributed to the rise of modern theological liberalism.

Throughout his career Dury deplored the divisive tendencies which arose out of the development of rigid types of Protestant scholasticism. He wished to shift the attention of theologians from debates over confessional differences to an interest in the development of "practical divinity" as a theological discipline of primary importance. In company with other precursors of German Pietism, he maintained the thesis that Christianity should be regarded as a way of life rather than as an attitude of intellectual assent to a given body of dogma. Impressed with the value of emphasis upon subjective religious experience, he was one of the chief agents in acquainting English theologians with the practical mysticism which had developed in Germany. Likewise, he helped to inform Spener and other Continental theologians regarding the merits of the best works of the Puritan writers in England. Dury argued that personal and social ethics should be given a definite place in the curriculum of each theological school. The insistence of Dury and like-minded contemporaries on the superiority of practical divinity over dogmatic theology, together with their laborious efforts to solve cases of conscience, helped to curb Protestant scholasticism and encouraged a new and significant emphasis on the ethical content of the Christian message.

Believing that contending Christian groups would forget their differences if they could be persuaded to work together in the conduct of constructive projects, Dury encouraged interchurch co-operation in missionary work and in publishing and educational enterprises. He was one of the most ardent early advocates of Protestant missionary activity. Although he held somewhat narrow views in regard to the principle of toleration, he was often the champion of oppressed minority groups, notably in the case of his attempt to secure the readmission of the Jews into England and also his successful effort to win Cromwell's intervention in behalf of the persecuted Waldenses of the Piedmont.

Comenius was the foremost seventeenth-century exponent of the idea that cultural unity would prepare the way for religious unity. Dury followed his leadership in promoting educational reform as an effective method of advancing the cause of Christian reunion. He made numerous and important attempts to persuade leaders of church and state in England to co-operate in the establishment of an improved, uniform, and universal system of popular education. He further aided the reform of English education by informing Englishmen regarding the significant progressive movements in educational and library work in the Continental countries. He also promoted cultural unity as a step toward religious unity by encouraging the international exchange of cultural ideas and by advocating the organization of scientific societies.

In conclusion, it should be said that Dury's unfailing enthusiasm for the cause of Christian reunion sometimes impaired his judgment of other values. In his impatient haste to hurry from the adjustment of one theological quarrel in order to make peace in another area of conflict, he occasionally failed to gain a thorough understanding of the issues which were dividing Christians into contending groups. Granting these and other valid criticisms of the man and his work, the fact yet remains that he was the most zealous, consistent, and successful advocate of the union of the churches in the seventeenth century. Dury has suffered at the hands of his biographers, who have uniformly stressed the fact that each of his major union efforts ultimately ended in failure. However, his labors served to soften some of the bitter hatreds of his age. Viewed in true perspective and with proper regard to environmental factors, his work should be regarded as successful, because he was able to preserve the concept of unity in an age when prevailing trends made further progress impossible. Dury, more than any of his contemporaries, transmitted to the modern church the reformers' ideas of the desirability of a united Protestantism and the ultimate possibility of a united Christendom. His ideas now enlist more support than they secured when they were first published to the world. His work is an important phase of the historical background of the present movement toward Christian reunion.

BIBLIOGRAPHY

ABBOTT, W. C. *The Writings and Speeches of Oliver Cromwell*, Vols. I and II. Cambridge, Mass., 1937, 1939.

ADAMSON, JOHN WILLIAM. *Pioneers of Modern Education, 1600–1700*. Cambridge, 1905.

AITON, JOHN. *The Life and Times of Alexander Henderson*. Edinburgh, 1836.

ALTHAUS, FRIEDRICH. "Samuel Hartlib, ein deutsch-englisches Charakterbild," *Historisches Taschenbuch* (6th ser.), III (Leipzig, 1884), 188–278.

ANGYAL, DAVID. *Geschichte der politischen Beziehungen Siebenbürgens zu England*. Budapest, 1905.

ARNOLD, G. H. *Historia Joannis Duraei*. Wittenberg, 1716.

ARNOLD, GOTTFRIED. *Unpartheiische Kirchen- und Ketzerhistorie*. Schaffhausen, 1740.

AUZIÈRE, LOUIS. *Essai historique sur les facultés de théologie de Saumur et Sédan*. Strassburg, 1836.

AYSCOUGH, SAMUEL. *Index to the Sloane Manuscripts in the British Museum*. Ed. J. L. SCOTT. London, 1904.

BAILEY, MARGARET LEWIS. *Milton and Jacob Boehme: A Study of German Mysticism in Seventeenth-Century England*. New York, 1914.

BAILLIE, ROBERT. *Letters and Journals*. Bannatyne Club ed. 3 vols. Edinburgh, 1842.

BAIRD, H. M. "Notes on Theological Education in the Reformed Churches of France and French Switzerland," *Presbyterian Review*, I (New York, 1880), 85 ff.

BARTLET, J. V., and CARLYLE, A. J. *Christianity in History*. London, 1917.

BASTIDE, CHARLES. *The Anglo-French Entente in the Seventeenth Century*. London, 1914.

BATTEN, J. M. "Life of Alexander Henderson," *Journal of the Presbyterian Historical Society*, IX (Philadelphia, 1917–18), 99 ff., 171 ff., 215 ff., 267 ff.

BAXTER, RICHARD. *Universal Concord*. London, 1660.

BAYLE, PIERRE. *Dictionnaire historique et critique*, Vols. I and II. Amsterdam, 1740.

BECKMANN, J. CHR. *Historie des Fürstenthums Anhalt*, Vol. VI. Zerbst, 1710.

BENZELIUS, C. J. *Dissertatio de Johanne Duraeo pacificatore celeberrimo maxime de actis eius Suecanis*. Helmstadt, 1744.

Biographia Britannica. 2d ed. 5 vols. London, 1778.

BIRCH, THOMAS. *The History of the Royal Society of London*. 4 vols. London, 1756.

BISCHOFFSHAUSEN, S. VON. *Die Politik des Protectors Oliver Cromwell in der Auffassung und Thätigkeit seines Ministers des Staatssecretärs John Thurloe*. Innsbruck, 1899.

BLOESCH, E. *Geschichte der schweizerisch-reformierten Kirchen*, Vols. I and II. Bern, 1898.

BÖHME, A. W. *Acht Bücher von der Reformation Kirche in England*. Altona, 1734.

Book of the Valuation of All the Ecclesiastical Preferments in England and Wales. Printed in the year 1680. n.p.

BOWMAN, JACOB N. *The Protestant Interest in Cromwell's Foreign Relations*. Heidelberg, 1900.

BOYLE, ROBERT. *Works*. 6 vols. London, 1772.

BRANDES, F. H. *Geschichte der evangelischen Union in Preussen*, Vol. I. Gotha, 1872.

———. "John Dury and His Work for Germany," *Catholic Presbyterian Review*, VIII (Edinburgh, 1882), 22–32, 91–102.

BRAUER, KARL. *Die Unionstätigkeit John Duries unter dem Protektorat Cromwells.* Marburg, 1907.

BRIGGS, CHARLES A. "The Work of John Durie in Behalf of Christian Union in the Seventeenth Century," *Presbyterian Review,* VIII (New York, 1887), 297–309.

———. *General Introduction to the Study of Holy Scripture.* New York, 1900.

———. *Church Unity: Studies of Its Most Important Problems.* New York, 1909.

———. "Symbolics and Irenics," *Church Quarterly Review,* LXXIV (London, 1912), 347–70.

———. *Theological Symbolics.* New York, 1914.

———. *History of the Study of Theology.* Ed. GRACE BRIGGS. 2 vols. New York, 1916.

BROOK, BENJAMIN. *The Lives of the Puritans: Containing a Biographical Account of Those Divines Who Distinguished Themselves in the Cause of Religious Liberty from the Reformation under Elizabeth to the Act of Uniformity in 1662.* 3 vols. London, 1813.

BROWN, P. HUME. *History of Scotland,* Vol. II. Cambridge, 1912.

BUNGER, C. *Matthias Bernegger.* Strassburg, 1893.

BURNET, GILBERT. *History of My Own Times.* 4 vols. London, 1766.

BURTON, THOMAS. *Diary of Thomas Burton, Esq., Member in the Parliaments of Oliver and Richard Cromwell from 1656 to 1659.* 4 vols. London, 1828.

CALDERWOOD, D. *History of the Kirk of Scotland.* Woodrow Society ed. 8 vols. Edinburgh, 1842–49.

Calendar of State Papers, Domestic Series. Charles I, 1627–1639. Ed. J. BRUCE and W. D. HAMILTON. London, 1858–71. *Charles I, 1639–1647.* Ed. W. D. HAMILTON. London, 1873–91. *Charles I, 1649–1661.* Ed. MRS. M. A. EVERETT GREEN. London, 1870–86.

CALIXTUS, F. U. *Via ad Pacem inter Protestantes Praeliminariter Restaurandam.* Helmstadt, 1700.

Cambridge Modern History, Vols. IV, V, and VI. New York, 1907, 1908, 1918.

CARLYLE, THOMAS. *Oliver Cromwell's Letters and Speeches.* London, 1850.

Catalogue of Printed Books in the British Museum. London, 1886———.

CATTERMOLE, RICHARD. *The Literature of the Church of England, Indicated in Selections from the Writings of Eminent Divines.* 2 vols. London, 1844.

CHAMBERS, ROBERT. *A Biographical Dictionary of Eminent Scotsmen,* Vol. I. London, 1870.

CHEETHAM, S. *A History of the Christian Church since the Reformation.* London, 1907.

CHEYNELL, FRANCIS. *The Divine Tri-unity of the Father, Son, and Holy Spirit.* London, 1650.

Clavis Apocalyptica: Or, A Prophetical Key: By which the Great Mysteries in the Revelation of St. John and the Prophet Daniel are opened; It being made apparent that the Propheticall Numbers com to an end with the Year of our Lord, 1655. Written by a German D. and now translated out of High Dutch. London, 1651.

COIT, CHARLES W. *The Life of Charles the First, The Royal Martyr.* Boston and New York, 1926.

COLER, J. C. *Auserlesene theologische Bibliothec,* Part VI. Leipzig, 1730.

Compendium historiae ecclesiasticae Gothanum. Gotha, 1723.

CORCORAN, T. *Studies in the History of Classical Teaching.* London, 1911.

COWAN, HENRY. *The Influence of the Scottish Church in Christendom.* London, 1896.

DAMOUR, CARL. *Die Epochen des Protestantismus.* Bern and Leipzig, 1935.

DAVENANT, JOHN. *Ad Fraternam communionem inter Evangelicos restaurandam Adhortatio.* Canterbury, 1640.

DEXTER, H. M. *Congregationalism of the Last Three Hundred Years as Seen in Its Literature.* New York, 1880.

Dictionary of National Biography. 63 vols. London, 1885–1911.

DIRCKS, H. *A Biographical Memoir of Samuel Hartlib.* London, 1865.

DOWDING, W. C. *German Theology during the Thirty Years' War: The Life and Correspondence of George Calixtus.* Oxford and London, 1863.

"Dury, Calixtus, and the Peacemakers," *Christian Intelligencer,* XXIX (London, 1855), 1–49.

DURY, JOHN. *See* "Trial List of the Printed Writings of John Dury" as given below, pp. 213–22.

EEKHOF, A. *De theologische Faculteit te Leiden in de 17de Eeuw.* Utrecht, 1921.

ELERT, WERNER. *Morphologie des Luthertums,* Vols. I and II. München, 1931.

FIRTH, G. H. *Oliver Cromwell and the Rule of the Puritans in England.* London, 1900.

FISCHER, T. A. *The Scots in Germany: Being a Contribution toward the History of the Scots Abroad.* Edinburgh, 1902.

———. *The Scots in Eastern and Western Prussia.* Edinburgh, 1903.

FORBES, JOHN. *Instructiones historico-theologicae de doctrina Christiana.* Amsterdam, 1645.

———. *The First Book of the Irenicum of John Forbes of Corse.* Ed. E. G. SELWYN. Cambridge, 1923.

FRIEDENSBURG, WALTER. "Kurfürst Friedrich Wilhelm von Brandenburg und die Wittenberger Theologen," in *Festgabe für Dr. Karl Müller* (Tübingen, 1922), pp. 228–43.

FRIEDRICH, HANS. *Georg Calixtus, der Unionsmann des 17. Jahrhunderts.* Anklam, 1891.

FULLER, MORRIS. *The Life, Letters, and Writings of John Davenant.* London, 1897.

GARDINER, S. R. *The Personal Government of Charles I.* 2 vols. London, 1877.

———. *History of the Commonwealth and Protectorate.* 4 vols. London, 1897.

———. *The Thirty Years' War.* London, 1912.

GASS, F. W. J. H. "Johann Heinrich Heidegger," *Allgemeine deutsche Biographie,* XI (Leipzig, 1880), 295, 296.

GASS, W. *Georg Calixt und der Synkretismus.* Breslau, 1846.

GEDDES, JAMES. *History of the Administration of John de Witt, Grand Pensionary of Holland.* New York, 1880.

GEE, HENRY, and HARDY, W. J. *Documents Illustrative of English Church History.* London, 1921.

GEISELER, JOHN C. L. *A Textbook of Church History.* Trans. H. B. SMITH. 5 vols. New York, 1862.

GEROULD, JAMES THAYER. *Sources of English History of the Seventeenth Century, 1603–1689, in the University of Minnesota Library.* Minneapolis, 1921.

GESSELIUS, TIMANNUS. *Veritas Pacifica: seu Articulorum Fidei Christianae delineatio, haustam de Verbo Dei veritatem salutiferam, solidae pacis coagulum, complexa.* Amsterdam, 1651.

GILLETT, CHARLES RIPLEY. *Catalogue of the McAlpin Collection of British History and Theology in the Union Theological Seminary.* 2 vols. New York, 1928.

GINDELY, A. *History of the Thirty Years' War.* Trans. A. T. BROOK. 2 vols. London, 1885.

GOEBEL, MAX. *Die religiöse Eigenthümlichkeit der Lutherischen und der reformierten Kirche.* Bonn, 1837.

GORDON, J. *History of Scots Affairs from 1637 to 1641.* Spalding Club ed. Aberdeen, 1850–51.

GRANNIS, RUTH (ed.). *John Dury's Reformed Librarie-Keeper.* Chicago, 1906.
GREEN, MRS. M. A. EVERETT. *Lives of the Princesses of England,* Vol. VI. London, 1855.
———. *Elizabeth, Electress Palatine and Queen of Bohemia.* Revised by S. C. LOMAS. London, 1909.
GROTIUS, HUGO. *Hugonis Grotii .... Epistolae quotquot reperiri potuerunt.* Amsterdam, 1687.
GRUB, GEORGE. *Ecclesiastical History of Scotland.* 4 vols. Edinburgh, 1861.
GUIZOT, F. *Histoire de la république d'Angleterre et de Cromwell.* 2 vols. Paris, 1854.
HAGENBACH, K. R. *Der evangelische Protestantismus in seiner geschichtlichen Entwickelung.* Leipzig, 1854.
HALL, JOSEPH. *The Works of Joseph Hall.* 12 vols. Oxford, 1837.
HALLER, WILLIAM. *Tracts on Liberty in the Puritan Revolution.* 3 vols. New York, 1934.
———. *The Rise of Puritanism.* New York, 1938.
HANBURY, B. *Historical Memoirs Relating to the Independents or Congregationalists.* 3 vols. London, 1839–44.
HARTLIB, SAMUEL. *The Necessity of some nearer Conjunction and Correspondency amongst Protestants, for the Advancement of the Nationall Cause and Bringing to passe the Effect of the Covenant.* London, 1644.
———. *Considerations Tending to the Happy Accomplishment of England's Reformation in Church and State.* London, 1647.
HASAEUS, THEODOR. *Bibliotheca Bremensis historico-philologica-theologica,* Vols. I and IV. Bremen, 1719, 1727.
HEATH, JAMES. *A Chronicle of the Late Intestine War in the Three Kingdoms of England, Scotland, and Ireland.* London, 1676.
HELD, FELIX EMIL. *Christianopolis: An Ideal State of the Seventeenth Century.* Translated from the Latin of JOHANN VALENTIN ANDREAE with a historical Introduction. New York, 1916.
HELLER, LUDWIG. *Nikolaus Hunnius: Sein Leben und Wirken.* Lübeck, 1843.
HELWEG, L. *Den Danske Kirkes Historie efter Reformationen.* 2 vols. Copenhagen, 1851.
HENDERSON, E. F. *A Short History of Germany.* 2 vols. in one. New York, 1923.
HENDERSON, G. D. *Religious Life in Seventeenth-Century Scotland.* Cambridge, 1937.
HENKE, E. L. T. *Georg Calixtus und seine Zeit.* 2 vols. Halle, 1856–60.
HENKE, H. P. K. *Allgemeine Geschichte der christlichen Kirche,* Part IX. Braunschweig, 1823.
HENSON, H. H. *Studies in English Religion in the Seventeenth Century.* London, 1903.
———. *The Relation of the Church of England to the Other Reformed Churches.* Edinburgh and London, 1911.
HERING, CARL WILHELM. *Geschichte der kirchlichen Unionsversuche seit der Reformation bis auf unsere Zeit.* 2 vols. Leipzig, 1836, 1838.
HETHERINGTON, W. M. *History of the Westminster Assembly of Divines.* 5th ed. New York, 1890.
HEUSSI, KARL. *Kompendium der Kirchengeschichte.* 5th ed. Tübingen, 1922.
HEYLYN, P. *Cyprianus Anglicanus, or the History of the Life of William Laud.* Dublin, 1668.
HISTORICAL MANUSCRIPTS COMMISSION. *Reports IV, V, VI, VIII.* London, 1869———.
HOPPUS, P. *Schism as Opposed to the Unity of the Church.* 2d ed. London, 1839.

HUBLER, S. "Unionsbestrebungen des John Durie," *Berner Beiträge zur Geschichte der schweizerischen Reformationskirchen*, ed. F. NIPPOLD (Bern, 1884), pp. 276–328.

HUDSON, W. S. "The Scottish Effort To Presbyterianize the Church of England," *Church History*, VIII (Berne, Ind., 1939), 255–82.

HURST, J. F., and OTHERS. *Church Unity*. New York, 1896.

HUTTON, W. H. *The English Church from the Accession of Charles I to the Death of Anne, 1625–1714*. London, 1913.

HYAMSON, A. M. "The Lost Tribes and the Return of the Jews to England," *Transactions of the Jewish Historical Society of England*, V (London, 1903), 114–47.

———. *A History of the Jews in England*. London, 1908.

JABLONSKI, DANIEL ERNEST. *Historia Consensus Sendomiriensis*. Berlin, 1731.

Jewish Encyclopedia, Vol. V. London, 1903.

"John Durie's Reformed Librarie-Keeper and Its Author's Career as a Librarian," *Library*, IV (London, 1892), 81–89.

JOHNSON, F. R. "Gresham College, Precursor of the Royal Society," *Journal of the History of Ideas*, I (New York and Lancaster, Pa., 1940), 413–38.

JORDAN, G. J. *The Reunion of the Churches: A Study of G. W. Leibnitz and His Great Attempt*. London, 1927.

JORDAN, W. K. *The Development of Religious Toleration in England*. 4 vols. Cambridge, 1932, 1936, 1938, 1940.

———. *Men of Substance*. Chicago, 1942.

JOSS, GOTTLIEB. *Die Vereinigung der christlichen Kirchen*. Leyden, 1877.

KELLER, LUDWIG. "Comenius und die Akademien der Naturphilosophen des 17. Jahrhunderts," *Monatshefte der Comenius Gesellschaft*, IV (Berlin and Münster, 1895), 133–84.

KLAHR, THEODOR. "Johannes Duraeus: sein Leben und seine Schriften über Erziehungslehre," *Monatshefte der Comenius Gesellschaft*, VI (Berlin and Münster, 1897), 65–76, 191–203.

KNUTTEL, W. P. C. *Acta der particuliere Synoden van Zuid-Holland, 1621–1700*. 5 vols. The Hague, 1908–16.

KURTZ, J. H. *Church History*, Vols. II and III. Trans. JOHN MACPHERSON. New York, 1890.

KVAČALA, J. *Korrespondence Jana Amosa Komenského*. Prague, 1902.

———. *J. A. Comenius*. Berlin, 1914.

LANDWEHR, HUGO. "Johannes Duraeus' Unionsverhandlung mit Kurbrandenburg," *Zeitschrift für Kirchengeschichte*, X (Gotha, 1889), 463–89.

———. *Die Kirchenpolitik Friedrich Wilhelms des grossen Kurfürsten*. Berlin, 1894.

LAUD, WILLIAM. *The Works of the Most Reverend Father in God, William Laud*. 7 vols. Oxford, 1860.

LAURIE, S. S. *John Amos Comenius, Bishop of the Moravians: His Life and Educational Works*. Boston, n.d.

LEUBE, HANS. *Kalvinismus und Luthertum im Zeitalter der Orthodoxie*, Vol. I. Leipzig, 1928.

LEVY, S. "John Dury and the English Jewry," *Transactions of the Jewish Historical Society of England*, IV (London, 1902), 76–82.

LINDEBOOM, J. "Johannes Duraeus en zijne werkzaamheid in dienst van Cromwell's politiek," *Nederlandsch Archief voor Kerkgeschiedenis*, XVI (new ser.; The Hague, 1921), 241–68.

LINDSAY, T. M. *A History of the Reformation in Lands beyond Germany*. New York, 1914.

LOBSTEIN, P. "Zum evangelischen Lebensideal in seiner Lutherischen und reformierten Ausprägung," in *Theologischen Abhandlungen und Festgabe für Julius Holtz-mann* (Tübingen, 1902), pp. 159–81.

LUPTON, J. H. *Archbishop Wake and the Project of Union, 1717–1720.* London, 1878.

McCRIE, THOMAS. *Life of Andrew Melville.* 2 vols. Edinburgh, 1819.

——. *Annals of English Presbytery from the Earliest Period to the Present Time.* London, 1872.

MACFARLAND, C. S. *Christian Unity in Practice and Prophecy.* New York, 1933.

McGIFFERT, A. C. *Protestant Thought before Kant.* New York, 1922.

MACKENZIE, K. D. *The Confusion of the Churches—a Survey of the Problem of Re-union.* London, 1925.

MACMILLAN, D. *The Aberdeen Doctors.* London, 1909.

MACMILLAN, KERR D. *Protestantism in Germany.* Princeton, 1917.

McNEILL, JOHN T. "Calvin's Efforts toward the Consolidation of Protestantism," *Journal of Religion,* VIII (Chicago, 1928), 411–33.

——. "Catholic Protestantism," *Canadian Journal of Religious Thought,* V (Toronto, 1928), 449–62.

——. "Cranmer's Project for a Reformed Consensus," *Journal of Religion,* VIII (Chicago, 1928), 539–65.

——. *Unitive Protestantism.* New York, 1930.

——. "Casuistry in the Puritan Age," *Religion in Life,* XII (New York, 1942), 76–89.

MASON, A. J. *The Church of England and Episcopacy.* Cambridge, 1914.

MASSON, DAVID. *The Life of John Milton Narrated in Connection with the Political, Ecclesiastical and Literary History of His Time.* 7 vols. London, 1859–94.

MATHER, COTTON. *Magnalia Christi Americana or the Ecclesiastical History of New England from Its First Planting in the Year 1620.* Hartford, 1855.

MATHIESON, W. L. *Politics and Religion: A Study in Scottish History from the Reformation to the Revolution.* Glasgow, 1902.

MATTHIAE, JOHN. "Ramus Olivae Septentrionalis." Reprinted by Dury in his *Irenicorum Tractatuum Prodromus,* pp. 332–78. Amsterdam, 1662.

MEDE, JOSEPH. *Works.* 2 vols. London, 1664.

MEISNER, JOHN. *Irenicum Duraeanum de Articulis Fidei Fundamentalibus, et Consensu ac Dissensu inter Lutheranos ac Reformatos, in Academia Wittebergensi Explicatum a Johanne Meisnero.* Wittenberg, 1675.

MENTZ, GEORG. *Deutsche Geschichte im Zeitalter der Reformation, der Gegenreformation und des Dreissigjährigen Krieges, 1493–1648.* Tübingen, 1913.

MEUSEL, CARL. *Kirchliches Handlexikon,* Vol. II. Leipzig, 1889.

MILTON, JOHN. *The Prose Works of John Milton.* Ed. R. W. GRISWOLD. Philadelphia, 1850.

MITCHELL, ALEXANDER F. *The Westminster Assembly: Its History and Standards.* Philadelphia, 1897.

MITCHELL, ALEXANDER F., and STRUTHERS, JOHN. *Minutes of the Sessions of the Westminster Assembly of Divines, Nov. 1644 to March, 1649.* Edinburgh and London, 1874.

MITSUKURI, G. *Englisch-niederländische Unionsbestrebungen im Zeitalter Cromwells.* Tübingen, 1891.

MONTAGUE, F. C. *The History of England from the Accession of James I to the Restoration.* London, 1907.

MORLAND, SAMUEL. *History of the Evangelical Churches of the Valleys of the Piedmont.* London, 1658.

MORRIS, EDWARD D. *Theology of the Westminster Symbols.* Columbus, Ohio, 1900.

MOSHEIM, J. L. *Ecclesiastical History*. Trans. A. MACLAINE. 2 vols. London, 1842.
MUNROE, PAUL. *Cyclopedia of Education*, Vol. II. New York, 1911.
MUNROE, W. S. *Comenius and the Beginnings of Educational Reform*. New York, 1900.
MÜLLER, KARL. *Kirchengeschichte*, Vol. II, Part II. Tübingen, 1923.
"Narrative of the Late Proceedings at Whitehall concerning the Jews (London, 1656)." Reprinted in the *Harleian Miscellany*, VI (London, 1812), 445–52.
NEAL, DANIEL. *History of the Puritans*. Ed. J. O. CHOULES. 2 vols. New York, 1844.
NEUDECKER, C. G. *Die Hauptversuche zur Pacification der evangelisch-protestantischen Kirche Deutschlands von der Reformation bis auf unsere Tag*. Leipzig, 1846.
New Schaff-Herzog Encyclopedia of Religious Knowledge. 13 vols. New York, 1910.
NOBBS, DOUGLAS. *Theocracy and Toleration*. Cambridge, 1938.
ORME, WILLIAM. *Life and Times of Richard Baxter*. 2 vols. Edinburgh, 1830.
Pack of Old Puritans, A: Maintaining the Unlawfulness and inexpediency of subscribing the new Engagement, Professing the dissatisfaction of their judgements and the unresolvedness of their Consciences with Mr. John Dury's Considerations and just Reproposals concerning it. London, 1650.
PATERA, A. (ed.). *Jana Amosa Komenského Korrespondence*. Prague, 1892.
PAUCK, W. *Das Reich Gottes auf Erden, Utopie und Wirklichkeit*. Tübingen, 1928.
PFAFF, C. M. *Introductio in historiam theologiae literariam*. Tübingen, 1724.
PROBST, J. A. *Die Wiedervereinigung der Lutheraner und Reformierten*. Allentown, Pa., 1826.
PRYNNE, WILLIAM. *Canterburies Doome*. London, 1646.
———. *The Time Serving Proteus and Ambidexter Divine Uncased to the World*. London, 1650.
QUICK, ROBERT H. *Essays on Educational Reformers*. New York and London, 1912.
RANKE, LEOPOLD VON. *History of England Principally in the Seventeenth Century*. 6 vols. Oxford, 1876.
Realencyklopädie für protestantische Theologie und Kirche. 3d ed. 24 vols. Leipzig, 1896.
REID, JAMES. *Memoirs of the Lives and Writings of Those Eminent Divines who Convened in the Famous Assembly at Westminster in the Seventeenth Century*, Vol. I. Paisley, 1811.
RICHARDSON, CAROLINE F. *English Preachers and Preaching, 1640–1670*. New York, 1928.
RITSCHL, OTTO. "Literarhistorische Beobachtungen über die Nomenklatur der theologischen Disziplinen im 17. Jahrhundert," in *Studien zur systematischen Theologie* (Tübingen, 1918), pp. 76–85.
———. *Dogmengeschichte des Protestantismus*, Vol. IV: *Orthodoxie und Synkretismus in der altprotestantischen Theologie*. Göttingen, 1927.
ROE, THOMAS. "Sir Thomas Roe's Mission to Gustavus Adolphus, 1629–1630," *Camden Miscellany*, Vol. VII (London, 1875).
RUTHERFORD, SAMUEL. *Letters*. Aberdeen, 1857.
SACK, KARL H. *Die evangelische Kirche und die Union*. Bremen, 1861.
ST. JOHN, WALLACE. *The Contest for Liberty of Conscience in England*. Chicago, 1900.
SANDER, F. "Comenius, Duraeus, Figulus nach Stammbüchern der Familie Figulus-Jablonski," *Monatshefte der Comenius Gesellschaft*, III (Leipzig, 1894), 306–26.
SCHAFF, DAVID S. *Our Fathers' Faith and Ours: A Comparison between Protestantism and Romanism*. New York, 1928.

SCHAFF, PHILIP. *The Harmony of the Reformed Confessions as Related to the Present State of Evangelical Theology.* New York, 1877.

————. *The Creeds of Christendom.* 3 vols. New York, 1877.

SCHENKEL, D. *Der Unionsberuf des evangelischen Protestantismus.* Heidelberg, 1855.

SCHMID, HEINRICH. *Geschichte der synkretistischen Streitigkeiten in der Zeit des Georg Calixt.* Erlangen, 1846.

SCOTT, HEW. *Fasti Ecclesiae Scoticanae.* 6 vols. Edinburgh, 1915.

SCOUGAL, HARRY J. *Die pädagogischen Schriften John Durys: ein Beitrag zur Geschichte der englischen Pädagogik.* Jena, 1905.

SEPP, C. *Polemische en irenische Theologie.* Leyden, 1881.

SHAW, WILLIAM A. *A History of the English Church during the Civil Wars and under the Commonwealth, 1640–1660.* 2 vols. London, 1900.

SHUCKBURGH, E. S. (ed.). *Two Biographies of William Bedell.* Cambridge, 1902.

SIEBENGARTNER, M. *Schriften und Einrichtungen zur Bildung der Geistlichen.* Freiburg, 1902.

SLOSSER, G. J. *Christian Unity—Its History and Challenge in All Communions and in All Lands.* New York, 1929.

SMYTH, NEWMAN. "John Dury: A Peacemaker among the Churches," *Constructive Quarterly,* IV (London, 1916), 406–23.

————. *Christian Ethics.* New York, 1923.

SMYTH, NEWMAN, and WALKER, WILLISTON. *Approaches to Church Unity.* New Haven, 1919.

SPEER, ROBERT E., and OTHERS. *Christian Unity: Its Principles and Possibilities.* New York, 1921.

SPENER, PHILIP JACOB. *Consilia et judicia theologica Latina.* Frankfort a M., 1709.

SPINKA, MATTHEW. "The Irenic Program and Activity of John Amos Comenius." Unpublished Ph.D. dissertation, University of Chicago, 1923.

————. "John Dury, the Peacemaker," *Christian Union Quarterly,* XIII (Baltimore, 1924), 372–85.

————. *John Amos Comenius, That Incomparable Moravian.* Chicago, 1943.

SPOTTISWOODE, J. *History of the Church of Scotland.* Spottiswoode Society ed. Edinburgh, 1847–51.

STERN, ALFRED. "Oliver Cromwell und die evangelischen Kantone der Schweiz," *Historische Zeitschrift,* XL (München, 1878), 52–99.

————. "Menasseh ben Israel et Cromwell," *Revue des études juives,* VI (Paris, 1882), 96–111.

STEVEN, WILLIAM. *The History of the Scottish Church at Rotterdam, to Which Are Subjoined, Notices of the Other British Churches in the Netherlands.* Edinburgh, 1833.

STILLINGFLEET, EDWARD. *Irenicum: A Weapon Salve for the Churches Wounds or the Divine Right of Church Government.* London, 1661.

STOUGHTON, JOHN. *History of Religion in England from the Opening of the Long Parliament to the End of the 18th Century,* Vol. II. New York, 1882.

STOWELL, W. H., and WILSON, D. *A History of the Puritans and the Pilgrim Fathers.* New York, 1888.

TABARAUD, M. *De la réunion des communions chrétiennes ou histoire des negociations, conférences, correspondances, qui ont été formés à ce sujet, depuis la naissance du Protestantisme jusqu'à présent.* Paris, 1808.

THOLUCK, A. *Das akademische Leben des 17. Jahrhunderts.* Halle, 1852.

————. *Vorgeschichte des Rationalismus,* Vol. II: *Das kirchliche Leben des 17. Jahrhunderts.* Berlin, 1861.

THOMASON, GEORGE. *Catalogue of the Pamphlets, Books, Newspapers, and Manuscripts Relating to the Civil War, the Commonwealth, and Restoration, Collected by George Thomason, 1640–1661.* 2 vols. London, 1908.

THURLOE, JOHN. *A Collection of the State Papers of John Thurloe.* Ed. THOMAS BIRCH. 7 vols. London, 1742.

TOLLIN, H. G. N. "Johann Duraeus," *Geschichts-Blätter für Stadt und Land Magdeburg* (Magdeburg, 1897–98), XXXII, 227–85; XXXIII, 27–81.

Transcript of the Registers of the Company of Stationers of London, 1554–1640, A. Ed. E. ARBER. 5 vols. London, 1875–77.

Transcript of the Registers of the Worshipful Company of Stationers, 1640–1708, A. 3 vols. London, 1913.

TREVELYAN, G. M. *England under the Stuarts.* London, 1905.

TURNBULL, GEORGE H. *Samuel Hartlib, With Special Regard to His Relations with J. A. Comenius.* London, 1919.

USSHER, JAMES. *The Reduction of Episcopacie unto the Form of Synodical Government Received in the Ancient Church.* Written in 1641. Published at London, 1656.

———. *Works.* Ed. C. R. ELLINGTON and J. H. TODD. 17 vols. Dublin, 1847–64.

VAUGHAN, ROBERT. *The Protectorate of Oliver Cromwell and the State of Europe during the Early Part of the Reign of Louis XIV.* 2 vols. London, 1839.

WÄTJEN, HERMANN. *Die erste englische Revolution und die öffentliche Meinung in Deutschland.* Heidelberg, 1901.

WAKEMAN, H. O. *The Church and the Puritans.* London, 1897.

WALL, MOSES (ed.). *The Hope of Israel.* London, 1651.

WATERHOUSE, GILBERT. *The Literary Relations of England and Germany in the Seventeenth Century.* London, 1914.

WATSON, FOSTER. "The State and Education during the Commonwealth," *English Historical Review,* XV (London, 1900), 58–72.

———. *The English Grammar Schools to 1660: Their Curriculum and Practice.* Cambridge, 1908.

———. *The Beginnings of the Teaching of Modern Subjects in England.* London, 1909.

——— (ed.). *The Encyclopedia and Dictionary of Education,* Vols. I and II. New York, 1921.

WEINGARTEN, HERMANN. *Die Revolutionskirchen Englands.* Leipzig, 1868.

WESTIN, GUNNAR. *Negotiations about Church Unity, 1628–1634.* Uppsala, 1932.

WHITELOCKE, BULSTRODE. *Memorials of English Affairs.* 4 vols. Oxford, 1853.

———. *A Journal of the Swedish Embassy in the Years 1653 and 1654.* London, 1855.

WINTHROP, R. C. (ed.). "The Winthrop Papers," *Collections of the Massachusetts Historical Society* (4th ser.), Vol. VII. Boston, 1878.

WOBBERMIN, GEORG. "Der gemeinsame Glaubenbesitz der christlichen Kirchen," in *Studien zur systematischen Theologie* (Tübingen, 1918), pp. 238–61.

WOLF, LUCIEN (ed.). *Menasseh ben Israel's Mission to Oliver Cromwell—Being a Reprint of the Pamphlets Published by Menasseh ben Israel To Promote the Readmission of the Jews to England, 1649–1656.* London, 1901.

WOLFE, D. M. *Milton in the Puritan Revolution.* New York, 1941.

WOOD, ANTHONY À. *Athenae Oxonienses.* Ed. P. BLISS. 4 vols. London, 1813–20.

WORDSWORTH, JOHN. *The National Church of Sweden.* London, 1910.

WORTHINGTON, JOHN. *The Diary and Correspondence of Dr. John Worthington.* Ed. JAMES CROSSLEY and RICHARD COPLEY CHRISTIE. 2 vols. "Chetham Society Publications." London, 1847–86.

WÜNSCH, GEORG. *Evangelische Ethik des Politischen.* Tübingen, 1936.

YOUNG, ROBERT F. *Comenius in England.* London, 1932.

A TRIAL LIST OF THE PRINTED WRITINGS
OF JOHN DURY

1. The Copy of A Petition, As it was tendered by Mr. Dury, to Gustavus, the Late King of Sweden, of glorious memory, when He was at Elbing in Prussia, in the yeer 1628. Translated out of French. London, Printed for Andrew Crook, and are to be sold in Pauls Church-Yard, at the signe of the Green-Dragon, 1641.

 Written in 1628; printed in 1641; and also reprinted by Dury in his *Briefe Relation* (1642), pp. 37–49.

2. Problemata de pacis ecclesiasticae consiliis capesscendis inter ecclesias evangelicas: Proposita pie doctis; ut conscientiae quibusdam casibus decisis, concordiae formandae firmandaeque ratio pacificis innotescat.

 In print as early as February, 2, 1630; see Historical Manuscripts Commission, *Report IV*, Part I, p. 159.

3. The purpose and Platform of My Journey into Germany.

 Written at London in 1630. Printed for the first time by J. Kvačala, *Korrespondence Jana A. Komenského*, pp. 6 ff.

4. De modo procedendi.

 Probably written in the year 1632. Printed in the *Unschuldige Nachrichten von alten und neuen theologischen Sachen* (1716), pp. 780–803; see C. W. Hering, *Geschichte der kirchlichen Unionsversuche seit der Reformation bis auf unsere Zeit*, I, 94 ff.

5. Generalis mediorum quaerendae ecclesiasticae pacis delineatio Jo. Duraei.

 Probably written in the year 1632. Printed in the *Unschuldige Nachrichten von alten und neuen theologischen Sachen*, pp. 803–17; see Hering, *loc. cit.*

6. Anonymi Theoria De Consiliis Ecclesiasticae Pacis inter Ecclesias Christianas capessendis. Cum Paraenesi ad Lectorem. Anno 1634. Pp. 49.

7. Quaestiones Parasceuasticae ad deliberandum propositae iis, qui in negotio Pacis ecclesiasticae promovendo receperunt aut recipient, se pium cum aliis commercium inire et fovere velle.

 Written in 1634; see H. Leube, *Kalvinismus und Luthertum*, I, 241.

8. A Summarie Relation of that which John Durie hath Prosecuted in the Worke of Ecclesiasticall Pacification in Germanie since Ye Latter End of Julie 1631 till 26 September 1633.

 The manuscript was discovered by Dr. Charles A. Briggs and printed for the first time in the *Presbyterian Review*, VIII (1887), 301–9. This manuscript is now in the McAlpin Collection, Union Theological Seminary, New York City. A slightly variant manuscript was discovered by Westin and published in his *Negotiations about Church Unity, 1628–1634*, pp. 264–76.

9. De Pacis Ecclesiasticae Rationibus inter Evangelicos usurpandis, Et de Theologorum fundamentali consensu in Colloquio Lipsiensi inito, Trium in Ecclesia Anglicana venerabilium Episcoporum, Dn. Johannis Davenantii, Episcopi Sarisburiensis, Dn. Thomae Mortoni, Episcopi Dunelmensis, Dn. Josephi Halli, Episcopi Exoniensis, Sententiae Johanni Duraeo ab ipsis ad Ecclesiarum Evangelicarum aedificationem et reconciliationem promovendam traditae. Anno MDCXXXIV. Pp. 43.

10. Concordiae inter Evangelicos quaerendae Consilia quae ab Ecclesiae in Transylvania Evangelicae Pastoribus . . . . approbata fuerunt. Anno 1634.

See *Calendar of State Papers, Domestic Series, 1654,* p. 431.

11. De pace ecclesiast. inter evangel. Ecc. decretum Comitis Gnesnensis, quo Augustanae Confessionis civibus Gnesnae Polonorum publ. c. religionis suae conceditur exercitium. Cum judicio ea de re theologorum Viteberg, Colon. 1635/1636.

See Tollin, *Geschichts-Blätter für Stadt und Land Magdeburg,*, XXXIII, 78.

12. Hypomnemata de studio pacis ecclesiasticae a Duraeo suscepto ab anno 1628 ad annum 1635.

Published at Amsterdam in the year 1636; see P. Bayle, *Dictionnaire historique et critique,* II, 333.

13. Declaratio Joh. Duraei, de legitimatione sua in Consiliis Ecclesiasticae Pacis, via Theologica inter Evangelicos tractandis.

Published in 1637; see Tollin, *loc. cit.*

14. Summa Capita Rerum in Studio Concordiae Evangelicae persequendo hactenus tractatarum.

Probably published in Stockholm, 1638; see Westin, *op. cit.,* p. 14.

15. An Information concerning the meanes of peace ecclesiasticall.

1639. A pamphlet addressed to Laud, probably written by Dury; see W. K. Jordan, *Development of Religious Toleration in England,* II, 255.

16. Informatio de iis, quae in studio ecclesiasticae concordiae, inter Evangelicos prosequendo agitare instituit Johannes Duraeus erga Ecclesiarum Danicarum Theologos.

Probably published at Bremen, 1639; see Westin, *op. cit.,* p. 15.

17. A Summary Discourse concerning the work of Peace Ecclesiasticall, How it may concurre with the aim of a civill Confederation amongst Protestants: Presented to the consideration of my Lord Ambassadour Sr. Thomas Row, at Hamburg in the yeare MDCXXXIX. By Mr. John Dury, A faithful and indefatigable Solicitour of the Gospel of Peace amongst Protestants. Now put to the Presse for the information of such as are able to countenance, and willing to help forward the Negotiation to some issue. Cambridge: Printed by Roger Daniel, Printer to the Universitie. Ann. Dom. 1641. Pp. vi+50.

18. De omnipraesentia corporali manducatione.

See *Calendar of State Papers, Domestic Series, 1640,* pp. 568, 569.

19. Informatio Ecclesiis Reformatis Oblata, De Consiliis, quae agitata fuerunt in Pace Religiosa Cum ecclesiis Augustanis quaerenda, à Johanne Duraeo ecclesiaste Britanno. Bremae, Typis Bertholdi Villeriani scholae typogr. Anno MDCXL. Pp. 11.

20. Consultatio Theologica super negotio Pacis Ecclesiasticae promovendo, exhibita submissaque judicio Reverendae Facultatis Theologicae in Academia Regia Upsaliensi. A Johanne Duraeo ecclesiaste Scoto-Britanno. Londini, Exeudebat G. M. pro Andrea Crooke, ad insigne viridis Draconis in Caemiterio D. Pauli. MDCXLI. Pp. iii+31.

21. John Dury His Petition to the Honourable House of Commons in England, now Assembled in Parliament. London, Printed in the yeere MDCXLI. Pp. iv.

22. Motives To Induce the Protestant Princes to Mind the worke of Peace Ecclesiasticall amongst themselves. London, Printed for William Hope, and are to be sold at the Unicorne in Cornehill, 1641. Pp. ii+10.

23. Consultatio theologica de via, qua pacis ecclesiasticae studia atque deliberationes inter ecclesias Evangelicas ad optatum perduci queant eventum.

Published at London, 1641; see Tollin, *loc. cit.*

24. The Several Forms of Government received in the Reformed Churches Beyond the Seas.

> First printed as a Preface to Francis Mason's *Validity of the Ordination of the Ministers of the Reformed Churches Beyond the Seas, maintained against the Romanists.* Mason's work, with the Preface by Dury, was included in a collection of pamphlets, entitled *Certain Briefe Treatises,* which was printed by Leonard Lichfield, printer to the University of Oxford, at Oxford in 1641.

25. Summa Capita de pace religiosa et concordia inter Evangelicos instituenda Stockholm 1637.

> Printed at Bremen, 1641; reprinted at London, 1657; see Tollin, *loc. cit.*

26. A Memoriall Concerning Peace Ecclesiasticall Amongst Protestants. By John Dury. London, Printed for W. Hope at the signe of the Unicorne in Cornehill, anno 1641. Pp. iv+12.

27. Epistolica Dissertatio Quam Johannes Dureus, Evangelicae concordiae Procurandae Ergodioctes misit authoribus Calvinismi (ut vocatur) Irreconciliabilis. D. D. Johanni Hulsemanno, Theol: D. et P. P. in Acad: Wittebergensi: Nec non D. Petro Rhebindero, Theol. Lic. et Superintendenti Lunaeburgensi, ut illos de reatu Schismatis continuandi inter Protestantes, evitando, fraternè, moneret. Anno 1641. Pp. ii+14.

28. A Petition to the House of Commons for the Preservation of the True Religion.

> Published at London, 1642; attributed to Dury by Chambers, *A Biographical Dictionary of Eminent Scotsmen,* I, 523.

29. A (second) Petition to the House of Commons; whereunto are added certaine considerations, shewing the necessity of a correspondence in spirituall matters betwixt all Protestant Churches.

> Probably printed at London in 1642; see H. M. Dexter, *Congregationalism of the Last Three Hundred Years as Seen in Its Literature,* Bibliographical Appen., p. 47.

30. A Briefe Relation of That which hath been lately attempted to procure Ecclesiastical Peace amongst Protestants. Published by Samuel Hartlib. London, Printed by I. R. for Andrew Crooke, and are to be sold at his shop in Pauls Church-Yard, at the signe of the Green-Dragon, 1642. Pp. ii+35.

> Written by Dury, but published by Hartlib; see above, p. 89.

31. A Motion Tending to the Publick Good of This Age, and of Posteritie. Or, The Coppies of certain Letters written by Mr. John Dury, to a worthy Knight at his earnest desire. Shewing briefly, What a Publik good is, and how by the best means of Reformation in Learning and Religion it may be advanced to some perfection. Published by Samuel Hartlib. For the better Information of all those who are willing of themselves, or instructed by others to set forward Pious and Learned Works. London, Printed by P. L. for Michael Sparke, Senior, in Green-Arbour in the little Old Baily, 1642. Pp. i+50.

32. Certaine Considerations, Shewing the Necessity of a Correspondencie in Spirituall Matters betwixt all Protestant Churches.

> Published at London, 1642; see Westin, *op. cit.,* p. 16.

33. A Copy of Mr. John Duries Letter Presented in Sweden to the truly Noble and Religious Lord Forbes: Briefly Intimating, The Necessity of a Common, Fundamentall Confession of Faith amongst those Christians that receive the holy Scripture as the only Rule of Faith and Practice, and in the Scriptures, have the same apprehension of the Tenour of Gods Evangelicall Covenant in Christ. The Possibility of framing such a Confession of Faith, which infallibly shall be approved (by Gods grace) by all that agree in these two fore-named Principles. The Manner of introducing this Confession amongst them. Published by Sam-

uel Hartlib. For the better improvement of Great Britain's solemne Covenant, and the advancement of Truth, Holiness and Peace amongst all Protestant Churches. London, Printed by G. M. for Thomas Underhill, 1643. Pp. 8.
Probably written in 1637, but published in 1643.

34. The Vow which J. D. hath made, and the covenant which he doth enter into with God, in reference to the national covenant of the kingdoms. Sent to London from the Hague, the 21st of December, 1643.
Reprinted in the *Harleian Miscellany*, VI, 208–12.

35. The Copy of a Letter Written to Mr. Alexander Hinderson. Printed in the Yeare, 1643. Pp. ii+14.

36. An Epistolary Discourse Wherein (amongst other particulars) these following Questions are briefly resolved. I. Whether or no the state should tolerate the Independent Government? II. If they should tolerate it, How farre, and with what Limitations? III. If they should not tolerate it, what course should be taken to bring them to a conformity with the Presbyterialls? Written by Mr. John Dury. To—Mr. Tho. Goodwyn, Mr. Philip Nye, Mr. Samuel Hartlib. Published by a friend, for more common use. Julii 27, 1644. Imprimatur, Ja. Cranford. London, Printed for Charles Greene, and are to be sold at his shop in Ivie Lane, 1644. Pp. i+44.

37. Letters dated 4 Dec., 1644, to May 1645. Probably addressed to Lady Ranelagh by J. Dury, concerning his marriage.
Printed at London, 1645; see George Thomason, *Catalogue of Pamphlets, Books, etc.*, I, 351.

38. A Description of a Transmarine School.
Probably written in 1645; the full text is quoted by T. Corcoran, *Studies in the History of Classical Teaching*, pp. 236–47.

39. Some Few Considerations Propounded.
Published at London, 1646; see Westin, *op. cit.*, p. 17 n. However, Westin's ascription of authorship to Dury is probably incorrect, though the pamphlet contains some Dury letters. Henry Robinson was responsible for this pamphlet (see W. K. Jordan, *Men of Substance*, p. 92).

40. Of Presbytery and Independency.
Published in 1646; attributed to Dury by Chambers, *loc. cit.*

41. Israel's Call to March out of Babylon unto Jerusalem: Opened in a Sermon before The Honourable House of Commons assembled in Parliament, Novemb. 26, 1645, being the day of Publique Humiliation. By John Durye, a Member of the Assembly of Divines. Published by Order of Commons. London, Printed by G. M. for Tho. Underhill, at the signe of the Bible in Wood-street. 1646. Pp. vi+49.

42. A Model of Church Government: Or, The Grounds of the Spirituall Frame and Government of the House of God. Shewing, What the holy Scriptures have therin delivered; What the best Reformed Churches do practise; What Tender Consciences may rest in. For the better Satisfaction of such as scruple at the Work of Reformation, declared and appointed by Severall Ordinances of Parliament. By John Dury, one of the Assembly of Divines; Who hath travelled heretofore in the work of Peace among the Churches. London, Printed by T. R. and E. M. for John Bellamy, and are to be sold at his shop at the three golden Lyons neer the Royall Exchange, 1647. Pp. xxxii+56.

43. A Peacemaker Without Partiality and Hypocrisy. Or, The Gospel-way to make up the present breaches of Brotherhood, and heale the divisions, whereby some of the reforming Professors and Ministers of this Kingdome at this time, sadly dishonour their profession, mainely obstruct our Reformation, utterly destroy

the safe Constitution of Church and State. Wherein are handled—1. How the means of Christian peace, as well Civill as Ecclesiasticall, may be found and ought to bee followed, both by Pastors and People. 2. What are the speciall lets of Ecclesiasticall Reconciliation, and what the causes of divisions are and how to be remedied. 3. What are the Grounds, Termes and Motives of Brotherly Unitie and Forbearance, which the Ministers and Members of the Churches of England ought to professe and practice one towards another, for the Gospels sake. All written upon severall occasions and severall times by Mr. John Dury, one of the Assembly of Divines, etc. and now published by Samuel Hartlib, to whom they were sent. London, Printed by R. Cotes for John Bellamy, at the three Golden Lions in Cornhill neer the Royall Exchange, 1648. Pp. 115.

44. Discourse concerning the ground, termes, and motives of brotherly unitie and forbearance.

London, 1648; see Jordan, *The Development of Religious Toleration in England*, II, 368. This pamphlet was reprinted in Dury's *Peacemaker Without Partiality*, pp. 26–114.

45. A Seasonable Discourse, written by Mr. John Dury upon the earnest requests of many, briefly shewing these particulars: (1) What the Grounds and Method of our Reformation ought to be in Religion and Learning; (2) How even in these times of distraction the work may be advanced, By a knowledge of Orientall Tongues and Jewish mysteries, By an Agency for Advancement of Universall Learning. Published by Samuel Hartlib. April, 24 1649. Imprimatur Joseph Caryll. Printed for R. Woodnothe at the Starre under Peter's Church in Cornehill, 1649.

See H. J. Scougal, *Die pädagogischen Schriften John Durys*, pp. 29–31.

46. A Case of Conscience Resolved: Concerning ministers meddling with State Matters in their Sermons: and how far they are obliged by the Covenant to interpose in the Affairs of Civil Government. By J. D. minister of the Gospel. March 15, Imprimatur, Joseph Caryl. London, Printed by R. L. for R. W., 1649. Pp. 30.

Reprinted in the *Harleian Miscellany*, VI, 196–212.

47. An Epistolicall Discourse of Mr. John Dury to Mr. Thorowgood Concerning his conjecture that the Americans are descended from the Israelites. With the History of a Portugall Jew, Antoine Montezinios, attested by Menasseh Ben Israel to the same effect. St. James, 27 Jan. 1649/1650.

Printed as a Preface (pp. 13–20) of Thomas Thorowgood's *Jewes in America, or Probabilities That the Americans are of that Race* (London, 1650).

48. Considerations Concerning the present Engagement, Whether It may lawfully be entered into; Yea or No? Written at the desire of a friend, by J. D. November 27, 1649, Imprimatur, Joseph Caryl. London, Printed by John Clowes for Richard Wodenoth, at the Starre under St. Peters Church in Cornhill. Pp. i+ 30.

49. The Reformed School, by John Dury. London, Printed by R. D. for Richard Woodnothe at the Star under St. Peters Church in Cornehill.

Probably printed in 1650. *A Supplement to the Reformed School* was issued by Dury in 1651; see J. W. Adamson, *Pioneers of Modern Education*, pp. 138–55; and Scougal, *op. cit.*, pp. 33–41.

50. The Unchanged, Constant and Single-hearted Peacemaker drawn forth into the World. Or, A Vindication of Mr. John Dury from the aspersions cast upon him in a nameless Pamphlet called, The Timeserving Proteus and Ambidexter Divine uncased to the world, Wherein The Two Letters written seventeen years ago, the one to Joseph Hall, then Bishop of Exeter, the other to William Laud, then

Archbishop of Canterbury, are cleared from the most false and injurious Interpretations put upon them. Entered according to the late Act concerning Printing. London, Printed by J. Clowes, for Richard Wodenothe at the Starre under St. Peters Church in Cornhill, 1650. Pp. vi+18.

51. Objections Against the taking of the Engagement Answered. Or, Some scruples of Conscience, which a godly Minister in Lancashire did entertain against the taking of the Engagement. Resolved by J. D. Wherein the Chief Mistakes of weak Consciences, about the matter of the Engagement, are in a friendly way discovered, and rectified by Scripture-grounds and right reason; and published for the satisfaction of others, who may be scrupled in the same kind. London, Printed by John Clowes, for Richard Woodnothe, at the Star under St. Peters Church in Cornhill, 1650. Pp. iv+24.

52. Considerations Concerning the Present Engagement, Whether It may lawfully be taken, Yea or No? Written at the desire of a Friend in London, by John Dury. The third Edition enlarged, with an Answer to a further scruple offered by a Letter out of the Country. Nov. 27, 1649, Imprimatur, Joseph Caryl. London, Printed by J. C. for Richard Wodenothe, at the Starre under St. Peters Church in Cornhill, 1650. Pp. i+26.

53. Two Treatises Concerning the matter of the Engagement. The first of an unknown Author, excepting against Mr. Dureus Considerations for the taking of the Engagement, to shew the unsatisfactoriness thereof. The second of Mr. Dureus, maintaining the satisfactoriness of his Considerations against the unknown Authors exceptions. London, Printed by J. Clowes for Richard Wodenothe at the Star under St. Peters Church in Cornhil, 1650. Pp. ii+61.

54. The Reformed Librarie-Keeper or Two Copies of Letters Concerning the Place and Office of a Librarie-Keeper. London, 1650.
    A new edition of this work, edited by Ruth S. Grannis, was published at Chicago in 1906.

55. A Second Parcel of Objections Against the taking of the Engagement Answered. Or, the doubts which som godlie Ministers in som neighbor Counties entertained upon that Subject; as they were proposed in several Letters to, and resolved by J. D. Whereunto is occasionably annexed a discoverie of the Weakness of the Plea of the Cheshire and Lancashire Ministers for non-subscribing. London, Printed by Will Du-Gard, 1650. Pp. i+106.

56. A Disingaged Survey of the Engagement. In relation to publike Obligations— 1. Precedent. 2. Present, In the Oaths of Allegiance and Supremacy, the Protestation, and the Covenant, and under the present juncture of Affaires. London, Printed for John Wright at Kings Head in the Old-Bayley, 1650. Pp. ii+22.

57. A Case of Conscience Concerning Ministers medling with state matters in or out of their Sermons resolved more satisfactorily then heretofore. Wherein Amongst other Particulars, these matters are insisted upon, and cleared. 1. How all Controversies and Debates among Christians ought to be handled Regularly and Conscionably to edification by those that meddle therewith. 2. What the proper employments are of Christian magistrates, and Gospel ministers, as their works are distinct, and should be concurrent for the publick good at all times. 3. What the way of Christianity is, whereby at this time our present Distractions, and publick Breaches may be healed: if Magistrates and Ministers neglect not the main duties of their respective callings. Where a ground is layed to satisfie the scruple of the Demurrer, and Grand Case of Conscience. Written by John Dury, minister of the Gospel, to give a Friend satisfaction: And published at the desire of many. Oct. 3, Imprimatur, Joseph Caryl.

London, Printed by Francis Neile for Richard Wodenothe at the Signe of the Star under Peters Church in Cornhill, 1650. Pp. i+195.

58. Just Re-Proposals to Humble Proposals. Or, An impartiall Consideration of, and Answer unto, the Humble Proposals, which are printed in the name of sundry learned and pious Divines, concerning the Engagement which the Parliament hath ordered to be taken. Shewing—How far these Proposals are agreeable to Reason, to Christianity, and to Policie. How far the proposers thereof may receive satisfaction therein, in all these respects. Hereunto are added, The Humble Proposals themselves; because they are not currantly to be found. Written by John Dury. Jan. 7, 1650, Imprimatur, Joseph Caryl. London, Printed by R. L. for Richard Wodenothe, at the Starre under St. Peters Church in Cornhill, 1650. Pp. i+30.

59. An Epistolical Discours, from Mr. John Durie to Mr. Sam. Hartlib, Concerning this Exposition of the Revelation by Waie of Preface thereunto.

Printed as a Preface (pp. 1–79) of the *Clavis Apocalyptica* (London, 1651).

60. Conscience Eased: Or, The Main Scruple which hath hitherto stuck most with conscionable Men, against the taking of the Engagement removed. Where amongst other things is shewed, First, How farre the Oath of Allegiance, and the Nationall League and Covenant are Obligations; either in their legal interests unalterable or at this time no more binding and alterable. Secondly, How farre in a free People the Subordinate Officers of the State, have a right to judge of the Proceedings of a King in that State. Thirdly, How Zedekia's Case in breaking his Oath to the King of Babylon, and our case in making use of our freedome from the Oath of Allegiance, and Supremacie to the King of England doe differ. The Author, John Dury. London, Printed for T. H. in Russell-Street, neere the Piazza of the Convent-Garden, 1651. Pp. ii+38.

61. The Reformed Spirituall Husbandman: With An Humble Memorandum concerning Chelsy Colledge, and a Correspondencie with Forreigne Protestants. London, Printed for Richard Wodenothe, and are to be sold at his Shop in Leaden Hall Street, next the signe of the golden Hart, 1652. Pp. vi+40.

Dury and Hartlib collaborated in the preparation of this pamphlet (see above, p. 144).

62. Harmonia Confessionum Protestantium.

Printed at Geneva in 1654; see Tollin, *op. cit.*, XXXIII, 78.

63. Irenicum: In quo Casus Conscientiae Praecipui, de Viis quaerendae et constituendae inter Ecclesias Evangelicas Pacis, breviter proponuntur et deciduntur, Ad exploranda super iis pie Doctorum Judicia, Vel ad Obtinendum super eorum decisione eorundem consensum. Londini, Impensis Richardi Wodenothe, in vico vulgo vocato Leaden Hall Street, 1654. Pp. 24.

64. An Earnest Plea for Gospel Communion in the Way of Godliness, Which is sued for by the Protestant Churches of Germanie, unto the Churches of Great Brittaine and Ireland: In a Letter written by them to these, which was sent hither to that effect, By the Hand of John Dury, Minister of the Gospell. London, Printed for Richard Wodenothe in Leaden-Hall-Market, next door to the Golden Hart, 1654. Pp. xviii+89.

There is some evidence that the first edition of this work may have been issued in 1652 and that the issue of 1654, as listed above, is the second edition.

65. A Summarie Platform of the heads of a Body of Practicall Divinity, Which the Ministers of the Protestant Churches abroad have sued for, and which is further enlarged in a Treatise, intituled, An Earnest Plea. Pp. iv+8.

Probably published in 1654; see C. A. Briggs, *General Introduction to the Study of Holy Scripture*, p. 573.

66. A Demonstration of the Necessity of Settling some Gospel-Government Amongst the Churches of Christ in this Nation; Held forth in an Answer to a Querie, whereby Mr. Saltmarsh did once endeavor to hinder the Settlement of all Church-Government in the Nation. Written in the year 1646, by Mr. John Dury, Minister of the Gospel. And now Published for the Present Use of these Times, wherein it may be seasonable to be taken into Consideration for the preventing of further Confusion and Disorder amongst the Professors of the Gospell. London, Printed for Richard Wodnothe in Leaden-Hall-Market, next door to the Golden Hart, 1654. Pp. viii+64.

Written in 1646, but published in 1654.

67. Bewegliche Ursachen, Welche die Fürnembsten Häupter der Republick, die Diener des Worts und Professores der Hohen-Schulen in England bewegt haben, Ein Religions-Correspondentz mit den Protestierenden ausserhalb gros Britannien zu suchen.

Published anonymously in 1655; Later issued in French and Dutch; see Westin, *op. cit.*, p. 18.

68. Syllabus Documentorum, quae ab Ecclesiis et Magistratibus per Helvetium et Germaniam Evangelicis, ad concordiae Ecclesiasticae Studium inter sese et apud exteros suis suffragiis excitandum et promovendum tradita sunt in Authographiis Johanni Duraeo, qui hactenus hanc causam apud Ecclesias solicitavit. 1656? Pp. xii.

69. A Case of Conscience, Whether it be lawful to admit Jews into a Christian Commonwealth? Resolved by Mr. John Dury. Written to Samuel Hartlib, esq. London, Printed for Richard Wodenothe, in Leadenhall Street, next to the Golden Heart, 1656. Pp. 12.

Reprinted in the *Harleian Miscellany*, VI, 438–44.

70. The Effect of Master Dury's Negotiations for Uniting of Protestants in a Gospel Interest.

Probably printed at London, 1657 or 1658; see Dexter, *op. cit.*, Bibliographical Appen., p. 83.

71. Ex apposito extracto harmonico cum addita obtestatione et monito; intelligetis meae solicitationis studium ad finem vergere.

Probably printed in 1657; see *Catalogue of Printed Books in the British Museum*, Vol. "Dru–Dyz," p. 191.

72. A Summarie Account of Mr. John Dury's Former and Latter Negotiation For the procuring of true Gospel Peace, with Christian Moderation and Charitable Unity amongst the Protestant Churches, and Academies. London, Printed for the Author, in the year 1657. Pp. 46.

73. The Earnest Breathings of Forreign Protestants, Divines & Others: to the Ministers and other able Christians of these three Nations for a Compleat Body of Practicall Divinity, and Cases, wherein the Grace of God hath more eminently appeared amongst us in these Islands, then in the rest of the World besides.

Printed at London, 1658; see *Catalogue of Printed Books in the British Museum*, Vol. "Dru–Dyz," p. 191; and Westin, *op. cit.*, p. 18.

74. Epistola ad Petr. Molinaeum de statu ecclesiae Anglicae, Scotiae et Hibernae sub Cromwello.

See Pierre Bayle, *Dictionnaire historique et critique*, II, 1044.

75. The Humble Petition of John Durie, minister, to the right honorable the knights, citizens, and burgesses, in parliament assembled .... Concerning the Parliament's Consulting about Matters of Religion. April, 1659.

The complete text of this petition is cited by John Thurloe, *A Collection of the State Papers of John Thurloe*, VII, 648–51.

76. The Plain Way of Peace and Unity in Matters of Religion. Shewed By some Maxims supposed to be undeniable, which John Durie hath made use of in Negotiating with all the Churches. And By some Expedients supposed to be effectual, which he hath endeavored to make practicable among the Churches, for the preserving and promoting of the Protestant Religion abroad. And now are offered For the preventing of further Breaches, and the Settlement of Unity amongst ourselves at home. London, Printed for F. Tyton at the three Daggers in Fleet Street, 1660. Pp. ii+14.

77. A Declaration of John Durie a Minister of Jesus Christ to witness the Gospell of Peace: Wherein he doth make known the Truth of his way and comportment in all these times of trouble; and how he hath endeavoured to follow Peace and Righteousness therein innocently towards all: That the offences taken against him, through the mis-construction of some of his actions may be removed; and the work of Peace and Unity amongst the Protestant Churches at home and abroad advanced in due time. London, Printed in the Year, 1660. Pp. 28.

78. Brevis Informatio de vero Scopo et Mediis propriis quibus Concordiam Evangelicam apud Ecclesias Protestantes prosequitur Johannes Duraeus.
  Reprinted by Dury in his *Consultationum Irenicarum Prodiorthosis*, pp. 7–14.

79. A discourse representing the liberty of conscience, that is practised in forreign parts.
  Printed at London, 1661. Appended to P. Pett, *A discourse concerning liberty of conscience* (London, 1661).

80. Johannis Duraei Irenicorum Tractatuum Prodromus. In quo Praeliminares Continentur Tractatus de—I. Pacis Ecclesiasticae Remoris è Medio Tollendis. II. Concordiae Evangelicae fundamentis sufficienter jactis. III. Reconciliationis Religiosae procurandae Argumentis et Mediis. IV. Methodo Investigatoria ad Controversias omnes, sine contradicendi studio et praejudicio pacifice decidendas. Quae praemittuntur Collectorum inter Protestantes Consiliorum Pacificorum Harmoniae, prope diem Deo permittente adornandae et in lucem edendae. Praefatio Tractatuum edendorum rationes explicabit. Amstelodami, Ex Officina Johannis Henrici Boom, anno 1662. Pp. xxxviii+548.

81. Concordia pia Jo. Melleti inter Protestantes procuranda.
  Printed at Frankfort a M., 1664; see C. M. Pfaff, *Introductio in historiam theologiae literariam*, Part III, p. 182.

82. Joh. Duraei et Joh. Melleti propemticum irenicum, continens brevem Informationem de vero scopo et mediis irenicis.
  See Tollin, *loc. cit.*

83. Consultatio de mediis concordiae Ecclesiasticae procurandae inter Dannhawerum, Bebelium et Duraeum.
  Printed at Amsterdam, 1664; see Pfaff, *loc. cit.*

84. Consultationum Irenicarum Prodiorthosis: Sive Acta Tractatuum de Mediis Concordiae Evangelicae procurandis, inter S. Theolog. Professores Argentinenses duos D. D. Joh. Conrad Dannhawerum, D. D. Balthasarum Boebelium, ab una parte, et Johannem Duraeum ab altera; Quae publici Juris fiunt ut aliorum Academicorum, et omnium piè doctorum Judicio aequo et sedato submittantur. Sub finem additur ad pleniorem informationem; Apographum Epistolae ad Imperii quendam Principem missae; Quae in Belgio ex Gallico in Latinum Sermonem fuit translata. Amstelodami, Ex officina Joannis Henrici Boom, An. 1664. Pp. 133.

85. Exercitatio de Conatu suo Irenico.
  Published in 1665. See Tollin, *op. cit.*, XXXIII, 79.

86. Johannis Duraei Appellatio ad Tribunal Supremi Judicis Jesu Christi Domini

Nostri, Adversus Accusationes et Condemnationes Nuncii emissi in vulgus à Johanne Conrado Danhawero, Doctore et Professore Theologo in Academiæ Argentinensi. Amsterodami. Ex officina Christophori Conradi, An. 1665. Pp. 96.

87. Brevis Relatio De Progressu Negotiationis agitate à J. D. Pro Reconciliatione Ecclesiarum Protestantium. Inde ab anno 1660 ad annum 1665.

> Published in 1665; see Westin, *op. cit.*, p. 19.

88. Apologeticum Duraei pro suo tractatu de concordia Evangelica cum duobus Academiae Argentinensis Doctoribus.

> Printed at Amsterdam in 1667; see Tollin, *op. cit.*, XXXIII, 79.

89. Axiomata communia quae procurandae et conservandae paci inter Evangelicos judicata sunt observatu necessaria.

> Printed at Cassel, 1670; see Tollin, *op. cit.*, XXXIII, 79.

90. Une Information touchant le jugement qu'on doit faire de l'harmonie des Confessions et comment on s'en peut servir, pour moyenner la paix des églises protestantes.

> Printed at Cassel, 1670; see Pfaff, *op. cit.*, Part III, p. 183.

91. Extractus ex Harmonia Confessionum, oblatum ecclesiis Reformatis, ut examinetur antequam opus ipsum Lutheranis offeratur.

> Printed in 1671; see Tollin, *op. cit.*, XXXIII, 80.

92. Acta collationis amicae antehac privatim per literas institutae inter Hier. Sievertum et Jo. Duraeum de concordia inter Protestantes procuranda.

> Printed at Cassel, 1672; see Pfaff, *op. cit.*, Part III, p. 182.

93. Brevis disquisitio de articulis veri Christianismi fundamentalibus.

> Printed at Cassel, 1672; see Tollin, *op. cit.*, XXXIII, 80.

94. Dissertatio brevis de mediis necessariis, quibus difficultates in opere irenico superari possunt, si adhibeantur.

> See Pfaff, *op. cit.*, Part III, p. 182.

95. Celeusma ad pacis evangelicae ministros.

> Printed in 1674; see Tollin, *op. cit.*, XXXIII, 80.

96. Touchant l'intelligence de l'Apocalypse par l'Apocalypse même, comme toute l'Ecriture sainte doit être entendue raisonnablement.

> Printed in 1674; see Bayle, *op. cit.*, II, 333.

97. On Christian Union.

> Printed in 1676; see "John Durie," *Dictionary of National Biography*.

98. Le véritable Chrétien.

> Printed in 1676; see Tollin, *op. cit.*, XXXIII, 77.

References to numerous secondary works which contain citations from Dury's letters, memorials, and papers have been presented in the foregoing account of his irenic activities.

INDEX